Charles Johnson's Fiction

Charles Johnson's Fiction

William R. Nash

UNIVERSITY OF ILLINOIS PRESS
URBANA AND CHICAGO

Manufactured in the United States of America
C 5 4 3 2 1

∞ This book is printed on acid-free paper.

Library of Congress Cataloging-in-Publication Data
Nash, William R., 1964–
Charles Johnson's fiction / William R. Nash.
p. cm.
Includes bibliographical references and index.
ISBN 0-252-02773-6 (cloth : alk. paper)
1. Johnson, Charles Richard, 1948– —Criticism and interpretation.
2. African Americans in literature.
I. Title.
PS3560.O3735Z78 2003
813'.54—dc21 2002005308

For Deb

CONTENTS

ACKNOWLEDGMENTS

In the process of such an endeavor, one incurs many debts. I have more than my share. First, I must thank Charles Johnson for his cooperation, generosity, and patience; in the time that I was working on this study, he never let one of my questions go unanswered, regardless of what other demands on his time he was juggling. The same is true of Professor Trudier Harris-Lopez, who guided me through the early stages of this project, when I planted its seeds in my doctoral dissertation. Throughout my graduate career and since, Professor Harris-Lopez has been an invaluable resource and an unceasing inspiration. I can honestly say that without her support this work would not exist.

I am also grateful for the commentary and support of Professors James W. Coleman, Margaret O'Connor, John McGowan, and Joseph M. Flora, who provided insightful comments on the dissertation version of the study. Professor J. Lee Greene deserves special mention, as he was the first to introduce me to Johnson's fiction. All of these faculty members from the University of North Carolina at Chapel Hill were helpful as I began this project. My graduate colleagues, especially Keith Clark, A. A. Markley IV, and David Grant Moss, provided support and commentary as my work progressed.

Every one of my colleagues in American Literature and Civilization at Middlebury College has been consistently interested in and supportive of my work on Johnson. I especially appreciate the assistance and insights that Brett Millier, John McWilliams, and Tim Spears gave by commenting on an early draft of the book manuscript. I also owe a debt of gratitude to the growing community of Johnson scholars who have welcomed me into their ranks. Jonathan Little, Marc Conner, William Gleason, Richard Hart, Robert Bunch, Michael Boylan, John Whalen-Bridge, Vernon Miles, and F. T. Griffiths all deserve special mention; I thank them one and all for their freely shared insights and commentary.

Both the University of North Carolina and Middlebury College have been generous with financial support for this work. The Department of African and African-American Studies at UNC funded my first trip to meet Johnson; Middlebury College gave me a leave to finish writing the book and also, through its Twilight Scholars program, subsidized Johnson's 1997 appearance in Middlebury, which gave us a valuable opportunity to discuss his work face-to-face.

I must also acknowledge my debt to Willis G. Regier, Theresa L. Sears, and all of the staff at the University of Illinois Press. Bill has been wonderful to work with, the kind of editor who is both supportive and challenging; I have benefited greatly from his encouragement and his suggestions throughout this process.

Finally, and most importantly, I thank my family, especially Deb and Hadley. Hadley, who arrived late in the process, has been an inspiration to get the work done and a welcome relief from its pressures. Deborah Evans has been, and is, a friend, colleague, and spouse—my best auditor and editor and the one who unceasingly encourages me toward clarity and comprehensiveness. The dedication of this volume is but a small payment on a vast and wonderful debt.

• • •

Dreamer (New York: Scribner, 1998). © 1998 by Charles Johnson.

English-language rights for the United Kingdom and Commonwealth (excluding Canada) for excerpts from *Middle Passage,* © 1990 by Charles Johnson, were granted by Macmillan Publishers, London, England.

Charles Johnson's Fiction

INTRODUCTION

Since the mid-1960s, the quest to define African American identity has inspired new modes of literary expression that balance the sometimes conflicting demands of race and aesthetics. From the separatist militancy of the Black Arts Movement to the inclusiveness of multiculturalist rhetoric—the two poles of a rich and complex continuum—this densely populated, wildly varying landscape forms the backdrop of Charles Johnson's creative development. In the course of his career Johnson's artistic values have shifted from fascination with the Black Aesthetic, through public disavowal of politics, to, at the end of the 1990s, a position that balances his social and creative concerns. At every stage, Johnson has aspired to create "art that interrogates experience" and that enables authors and readers to "work through the particulars of Black life from within and discover there . . . significant new perceptions" about racial and personal identity (Johnson, "Philosophy" 57).

In their purest form, these new perceptions would probably eschew politics; certainly Johnson aims at such social neutrality in *Oxherding Tale,* which he sees as the "foundation" for the rest of his aesthetic. And yet even in that context the author reminds his audience of the horrible injustices perpetrated by whites on African Americans since the seventeenth century. In each of his other novels the tension between ideal and application is even clearer. Despite the apparent paradox inherent in these creative choices, this recitation of racial injustice is in fact a crucial piece of Johnson's artistic program, one of the most effective means available for addressing "the particulars of Black life from within." His exploration of the burdens and benefits of black being in America yields "significant new perceptions" into universal questions about what we know and how that knowledge shapes what we see.

"To See Darkness Differently"

By his own account, when Charles Johnson left Evanston, Illinois, in 1966 to matriculate at Southern Illinois University, he moved from a family and community dominated by an integrationist ethos into an world increasingly marked by the Black Power and Black Arts movements. Chapter 1 of this study demonstrates the impact of these movements on Johnson's development as an artist. In that politically charged environment, he published two books of drawings and began his apprenticeship as an author. This early work shows some influence from Black Aestheticians like Larry Neal, Amiri Baraka (who came to SIU in 1969), and Hoyt Fuller. Each of these architects of the Black Arts revolution charged their audiences to make art for and about their racial community without regard for "the sphere of traditional Western forms, limitations, and presumptions" (Fuller 346).

The Black Arts approach necessarily generates a standard of racially defined authenticity against which all work must be judged. Although useful as a foundation for political action, such a "prescriptive" position has a "repressive impact . . . on cultural production" (hooks 111). Perhaps innate resistance to such limits made Johnson play with the rules of black cultural nationalism even as he explored its potential positive impact. As Jonathan Little has noted, such ambivalence is a hallmark of Johnson's collections of comic art, *Black Humor* (1970) and *Half-Past Nation Time* (1972). One also sees residual elements of this orientation in his first novel, *Faith and the Good Thing* (1974). Whatever the reason, Johnson's early recognition of the difficulties inherent in effectively melding politics and art establishes a pattern that resonates throughout his work.

This is not to say that the Black Aesthetic was or is not a valuable contribution to African American letters. Its heyday marks a watershed moment in black literary life, a declaration of independence from white cultural domination that enabled black artists to achieve new artistic heights. Some of that creativity is of the movement; much more came in response to it. From New Breed authors like Ishmael Reed and Al Young to advocates of the "New Black Aesthetic" like Trey Ellis, a broad range of African American writers resist the notion that art or artists can be "black enough." These writers have realized that there must be as many available forms of African American expression as there are modes of black being. As Ellis notes in "The New Black Aesthetic" (1989), "the culturally mulatto *Cosby* girls are equally as black as a teenage welfare mother" (235).

In many ways, Johnson stands at the forefront of those promoting this inclusive view of blackness. And yet, in noting that, I must qualify it, because

Johnson's stated motivation for portraying African American life this way varies somewhat from that of his peers. For all the diversity in perceptions I have briefly outlined, each depends on a fixed sense of black identity, a position that many writers see as affirming for the community. To Johnson, expanding the range of definitions associated with black life leads ideally not to racial solidarity, which he sees as divisive, but to the weakening and perhaps even the destruction of race as a category of definition. He repeatedly claims that he views race as a blinding limiter that impedes any meaningful interrogation of human experience.

That interpretation of blackness as fluid and illusory in many ways arises from his other primary creative emphasis, philosophy. As he pursues his notions about epistemology and ontology, race becomes a primary focus of his exploration. "What does it mean to be black?" his novels ask the reader, and "how does being black shape what we do or can know?" Chapter 2 outlines the author's philosophical program with particular attention to *Being and Race* (his critical book) and considers what possible answers his fiction offers to these questions.

"The Men and Women Who . . . Reflect on Experience"

This strain of epistemological and ontological exploration of race marks Johnson's most overt intellectual break with the Black Aesthetic. Perhaps not surprisingly, given his creative program, the beginning of his dissatisfaction with black cultural nationalism coincided with his study of aesthetics at SIU. That work, which challenged the limitations of a rigidly defined creative program, led him to what he describes as the two main philosophical systems that inform his work: phenomenology and Buddhism.

Modern phenomenology, as articulated by Edmund Husserl, privileges direct experience and attempts to strip away externally imposed preconceptions that impede full access to any object. One of Husserl's successors (whose work especially influenced Johnson), Maurice Merleau-Ponty, notes in *The Primacy of Perception* (1964) that Husserl developed his phenomenology in response to the then-popular belief that all opinion arose in response to combined external psychological, social, and historical conditions. In contrast, Husserl's epistemology relies on an intuition of essences that clarifies one's perception of any object or event. The difficulty in this approach, as Husserl notes, is that preconceptions about objects or events cloud one's ability to truly perceive these essences. The goal of phenomenology is to "bracket," or set aside, those preconceptions so that one can access the underlying essence that makes the thing or event what it truly "is." With its emphasis on the perceiver's attempts to get at the essence of things, phenomenology is, as Johnson notes, something you do rather than only an abstraction.

Even as phenomenology is something one can do, Husserl's idealistic version falls beyond the realm of common experience that constrains each individual's perceptive abilities. In response, Merleau-Ponty suggests that the proper goal of phenomenology is to see objects and experiences differently within the limitations of what he calls "the life-world." This application of ideas proves useful to Johnson. He recognizes that one can find revolutionary answers to questions about racial and personal identity within the life-world if one is willing to see differently. The quest for this new vision has become the most important recurrent theme in his fiction. Throughout his corpus, he presents protagonists who undergo a sort of organic phenomenological transformation. In demonstrating how they can come to see their blackness differently, he also offers readers a lesson in how to overcome, or at least attempt to set aside, the limitations of racialist thought in favor of a more expansive understanding of personal and group identity.

These efforts to overcome racialism also reflect the fundamental tenets of Johnson's Buddhism, most importantly the notion of transcending dualism. He sees this as vital, particularly with regard to racial matters, where conflict between blacks and whites and within the African American community generates suffering on virtually every experiential level. In accordance with Buddhist practice, Johnson views race, as he does all divisive influences that impede the aspirant's quest for enlightenment, as *maya,* or illusion. As such, it need not define an individual's search for liberation so long as one can recognize the disconnection between surface and essence that characterizes all objects or experiences. He demonstrates this notion in *Oxherding Tale,* where Andrew Hawkins becomes "the first protagonist in black American fiction to achieve classically defined *moksha* (enlightenment)" by reconciling the conflicting elements of his racially mixed ancestry and freeing himself from the bondage of narrowly defined identity (Johnson, Introduction xvi).

These apparent connections illustrate why Johnson finds both philosophical systems useful: they challenge basic premises of identity formation and lead inevitably to significant new perceptions of the self. By factoring a specific discussion of race into this process, he also points the way toward a sweeping revision of ideas about blackness that makes the category so loose as to be almost useless.

The qualifier is essential, as race is so firmly established in the national mind that one cannot easily dismantle it. One can hardly discuss any subject in American life without touching on or directly addressing issues of race. In phenomenological terms, one might identify it as an especially significant component of Johnson's experiential realm. In a world in which this issue is so important, one is at risk of missing new experiences because of the preconceptions that impede the perceiver's consciousness. Only in shedding that burden, an action that is harmonious with the promises inherent in phenomenology and Buddhism, can one find new approaches to being in the world through a racialized body.

These notions form a key component of Johnson's aesthetic; they also create a tension that consistently operates in his work, which I trace through the readings of the fiction presented in chapters 3 through 7. This transcendent approach to racial questions allows the individual to overcome mental limitations, but that alone cannot change the social, economic, and political realities that shape thought and action about race in American society. Throughout his work, Johnson increasingly returns to a litany of abuses perpetrated against African Americans as he struggles to respond effectively to American racialism. The particulars of black experience that he cites range from the horrors of slavery to the outrage of civil rights violations; he evokes them to remind his readers what African Americans have overcome on their way to new understandings of themselves. This serves his stated purpose by demonstrating how far the community has come and what is to be gained from cultivating new visions of itself. At the same time, the dialectical nature of his approach creates a dilemma for the reader. By using these examples of racist injustice to reinforce the need for understanding race as illusion, he strengthens the barriers that separate individuals from the very hope he attempts to foster. In the face of the Middle Passage or the suffering one finds on Chicago's South Side, how can one comfortably embrace his ideal vision?

Johnson's quest to resolve this difficulty shapes his evolution as an artist and ultimately yields a practical result. Though he might not achieve the apolitical ideal that he aspires to in his work, Johnson does provide his reader with new ways to engage in the struggle against an oppressive social order. That leads in turn to another sort of freedom from the confines of narrow, racialist preconceptions. This is especially true in *Dreamer* (1998), where he models this way of living for his audience and offers them a new way of thinking about Martin Luther King Jr.'s example and of applying his values in their daily living.

"A Heap of Signifyin'"

Throughout the readings of Johnson's fiction, I also trace his interracial signifying on literary predecessors to demonstrate how he applies his intersubjective model of racial identity to the act of writing. At the heart of Johnson's creative quest lies his belief that "the history of literary practice creates objective aesthetic possibilities, artistic works demanded historically by the foul-ups and partial breakthroughs . . . created by the oversights and omissions of those writers (white and black) who preceded us" (Johnson, "Whole Sight" 2). In his view, the serious writer's responsibility is to build on the past to create a new literary vision. Johnson approaches this by experimenting with form. As he explains in *Being and Race,* one develops as an author by studying other writers' work intensively, copying certain forms in an attempt to perfect the craft and then adding the unique touches that make the form distinctive to each successful practitioner. This also becomes an opportunity to create new perceptions about fiction by breaking down generic barriers. Such is the case in *Middle Passage,* which is part sea story, part love story, part naturalist novel, and part slave narrative. In making this argument, he encourages black writers to reach "back to an earlier age of master artists" or to generate "entirely new techniques" for revising received preconceptions about blackness and black experience (*Being* 57).

In addition to dismantling generic boundaries, Johnson also challenges racially imposed canonical distinctions. Throughout his corpus, he signifies on a range of literary predecessors, including Zora Neale Hurston, Theodore Dreiser, Frederick Douglass, Herman Melville, Ralph Waldo Emerson, Ralph (Waldo) Ellison, Saul Bellow, John A. Williams, Richard Wright, and James Baldwin. Although he does not necessarily turn to each writer for specific commentary on race, he draws on their epistemological and ontological commentaries as he forges his own statements about black being. By breaking down racial lines in that process, he also comments on the falseness of such rigidly defined dichotomies as they commonly exist in our thought about literature.

The most telling illustration of this in his work is Johnson's dual debt to "the Ralph Waldos," Emerson and Ellison. From the former, he takes the query in "Fate": "How shall I live?" (330). This statement defines Emerson's growing awareness of and discomfort with man's imperfectability. From the latter, he incorporates *Invisible Man*'s famous reminder of mutuality: "Who knows but that, on the lower frequencies, I speak for you?" (581). By interweaving their influences throughout his fiction, Johnson reminds readers of the problem of and the best response to intellectual racial divisiveness, of why and how authors need to think about challenging structures that emphasize division over harmony.

Taken together, these statements also reconcile the social and artistic tension in his corpus, as they represent the ideal standard to which he holds himself and the reality that he achieves. His art reminds readers of the complex web of intersubjectivity that holds us all together; at the same time, it also demonstrates the difficulty of applying such an ideal in a broken world. Fortunately, although the challenge has proven difficult, Johnson has throughout his career continued to struggle with it, achieving new heights of creativity in African American fiction and providing in the process a fascinating record of the evolution of that literary tradition.

• • •

The organization of this volume reflects my twofold purpose: first, to briefly consider the influences and experiences that led Johnson to take up these questions; and second, to trace the evolution of the responses to them that he presents in his fiction. Chapter 1 frames the major questions of the study and demonstrates the relationship between Johnson's biography and the evolution of his ideas. Chapter 2 outlines Johnson's aesthetic aims and explains the philosophical underpinnings that support them, paying particular attention to his critical writings. With chapter 3, I begin a chronological assessment of Johnson's published fiction.

In his first published novel, *Faith and the Good Thing,* Johnson uses African American folklore and Western philosophy to raise questions about black personal and literary identity. As he recounts the story of Faith Cross's suffering and her eventual recognition that the greatest good lies not in a particular thing but in the process of the quest, Johnson argues the value of transcending racialism and recites a litany of social and economic abuses that plague contemporary African American society. This establishes a pattern of tension that recurs throughout his corpus: even as he presents an ideal of thought and behavior that exists outside the dualistic boundaries of regular experience, he reminds the reader of the difficulty of meaningfully and enduringly applying that standard in a society beset by racialism. Much of the growth in Johnson's fiction comes as a result of his efforts to reconcile this dichotomy.

Chapter 4 treats the stories that *The Sorcerer's Apprentice* (1986) comprises. Although the collection appeared after *Oxherding Tale* (1982), Johnson wrote the individual pieces in the years when he was composing his second novel. I read the individual stories, particularly "The Education of Mingo," the title story, "Exchange Value," "Alethia," and "China" as evidence of Johnson's struggles to balance social and artistic concerns as he prepared for what would become his "platform novel" (Johnson, Introduction xvii). With "Exchange Value" and "Alethia," he returns to the South Side Chicago environment of *Faith and the Good Thing* and shows readers radically different pictures (one negative, one qualifiedly positive) of what life in that community can be for African Americans. The frame stories, "Mingo" and the title tale, provide the first published glimpses of the Allmuseri, the fictional African tribe of wizards who will become the central symbol of Johnson's aesthetic. They also give accounts of Johnson's efforts to redefine his relationships with his literary ancestors and especially with his mentor, John Gardner. The story that unites these divergent strands is "China." In this tale of an African American postman's liberating encounter with Eastern martial arts, Johnson demonstrates what his growing interest in Buddhism means to his own creative development.

That fusion of Eastern and Western ideas is the hallmark of *Oxherding Tale,* which I treat in chapter 5. In this neo–slave narrative that draws inspiration from the Buddhist visual arts, Johnson most strongly makes the case for his idealistic vision. His biracial narrator, Andrew Hawkins, gains liberation only by embracing both his blackness and his whiteness, by eschewing dualism in favor of a unifying model of selfhood that he learns from his Allmuseri guide, Reb. With his portrait of this detached coffin-maker, Johnson brings the symbol of his ideal to its most pure articulation. Furthermore, he takes the inspiration of Andrew's social experiment and translates it into commentary on literary identity politics as well. With this novel and its immediate successor, *Middle Passage,* Johnson masters his signifying readings of the American canon, black and white alike.

As I demonstrate in chapter 6, though, the integrationist literary impulse that he sustains does not have an exact social counterpart. Working again with the Allmuseri tribe, Johnson raises the earlier tension between ideal and application that he diminishes somewhat in *Oxherding Tale.* The horrors of the Middle Passage challenge the tribe's ability to sustain their idealism and suggest to the reader that perhaps the dream of intersubjectivity is too elusive; how, the novel asks us, can one overcome the heritage of suffering associated with the transatlantic slave trade and go on to live a positive, affirming existence? Although the narrator, Rutherford Calhoun, accomplishes this on an individual level, the disappearance of almost all the Allmuseri suggest how difficult such an endeavor is. The aesthetic goals still work on a literary level, as Johnson's signifying on Herman Melville demonstrates, but the social questions appear to be increasingly pressing.

Johnson addresses them more fully in *Dreamer,* which is the subject of chapter 7. With this tale of Martin Luther King Jr.'s final two years and his impact on a spiritually broken physical twin, Johnson finds a means of reconciling the tensions that characterize most of the earlier work. One of his literary models for this transformation is Ralph Waldo Emerson, whose essay "Fate" marks an important transition from the idealism of the early major essays to a more qualified, applied vision. Admitting the presence of uncontrollable forces marshaled against humanity, Emerson raises a telling question: "How shall I live?" ("Fate" 330). This balance becomes the hallmark of Johnson's vision in this stage of his career. As he tells the story of the minister's end and the transformation that King wrought both in Chaym Smith, the body double, and in Matthew Bishop, the narrator, Johnson suggests the need to struggle against oppressive racialist forces and the best motivation for such conflict: the creation of what King called "the beloved community." This balance, which informs Johnson's subsequent fiction and essays, enables him to write works that are simultaneously politically engaged and aesthetically satisfying, to find a means of applying his creative ideal for the greater social good.

• • •

One final note concerns the issue of terminology. Readers will see that I use "black" and "African American" interchangeably throughout the text. This apparent inconsistency is deliberate and was done for two reasons. First, my subject uses these terms interchangeably, which often means that in quoting him I must necessarily adopt the practice. I suspect that his reasons for this choice arise from his unwillingness to rest with one model of black identity. Given that each of the terms that Americans have adopted as racial signifiers have different political connotations, one makes a statement by restricting oneself to a single term. In contrast, the equal employment of various terms implicitly challenges essentialism. This is my primary motivation in making this choice, as it seems the most consistent with the aims of this study.

1 Origins and Influences

Against separatist African American critics who predict inescapable conflict between blacks and whites, Charles Johnson presents a generally hopeful vision that challenges essentialist racial characterizations. Rather than accept received assumptions about African American identity, he argues that no single definition encompasses what it means to be black in America. He weaves that vision of racial identity into his novels, using Western philosophy and Eastern religion to lift his characters from suffering to enlightenment. In his novel *Dreamer,* he adds yet another dimension to his work as he blends an account of Martin Luther King Jr.'s first northern campaign with the story of a disillusioned artist who embraces the civil rights leader's philosophy. Appearing at the end of Johnson's third decade as a professional artist and author, the novel presents a reflection on his creative efforts and a celebration of King, who so successfully formulated a new vision of black being.

Dreamer alternates chapters describing King's struggle for racial justice with a version of Johnson's recurrent quest story. The seeker is the embittered, world-weary Chaym Smith, whose striking physical resemblance to Dr. King wins him a position as a body double. In preparing to "be" King in public, Smith must "become" him intellectually and spiritually. As he studies King's mannerisms and sermons, he loses his cynicism and hostility and becomes the civil rights leader's philosophical twin.

In addition to absorbing King's message, Smith also reflects some of Johnson's own values. Like the author, he is a Buddhist, and he uses the meditation skills he has learned as he reflects on the minister's life and work. He also makes use of his creative skills; in another deeply personal move, Johnson makes Smith an artist whose evolving technique demonstrates his progress toward racial and religious enlightenment. These elements coalesce in the presentation of Smith's Buddhist art, which the narrator, Bishop, encounters when paging through Smith's sketchbook.

He finds that Smith has drawn "a series of eight charcoal illustrations of a herdsman searching for his lost ox. Finding it. And leading it home, where—in the final panel—both hunter and hunted vanished in an empty circle" (93). These drawings reference the *Ten Oxherding Pictures,* fifteenth-century Japanese drawings illustrating a symbolic quest for the self. The *Oxherding Pictures* are a key source for *Oxherding Tale,* Johnson's neo–slave narrative account of Andrew Hawkins' quest for racial and personal freedom. Smith's series of *eight* drawings, an incomplete rendering of the narrative the images tell, suggests that his quest for wholeness is unfinished. By modifying this important symbol from the work that he views as the "foundation" of his aesthetic project (Nash 51), Johnson emphasizes King's role in Smith's development. He also reflects on his own efforts to teach, through his fiction, his readers Ways (in the Buddhist sense) to overcome narrow, restricted visions of self.

As William Gleason notes in "The Liberation of Perception," Andrew Hawkins experiences all the stages of awareness that the drawings describe. In losing the ox (frames 1–2), the oxherd symbolically manifests his alienation from his surroundings. Pursuing and catching the ox (frames 3–6), he can then forget his individuality (frames 7–8). This self-forgetfulness leads to a complete fusion with the universe (frame 9), which enables the newly enlightened oxherd, now a Buddha, to return to the village and share his enlightenment with others (frame 10). As Andrew struggles to define his personal and racial identity, he becomes "the first protagonist in black American fiction to achieve classically defined *moksha* (enlightenment)" (Johnson, Introduction xvi).

By contrast, Smith's version of the drawings in *Dreamer* stops with an empty circle, the traditional eighth frame of the sequence. Symbolically, he remains abstracted, aware of his connections to his environment but removed from the hope a return to society brings. Only his encounter with King can move him through the last two stages of the process. In this formulation, Johnson equates what King gives Smith with the message he presents in *Oxherding Tale.* Andrew's life, in all its absurdity, illustrates how anyone can achieve enlightenment. By drawing this parallel, Johnson positions himself as a contributor to the cause, a promoter of the universalist worldview that King embodied and sacrificed himself for.

Smith's sketchbook also illuminates another important chapter in Johnson's own aesthetic development. Late in the novel, after Smith has disappeared with two FBI agents plotting against King, Bishop turns again to the drawings. As he notes, Smith had "descended into hell in his earlier work . . . facing . . . the . . . most paralyzing features of color and caste and inequality." By contrast, "His new sketches were simplicity itself. . . . Smith had decided that if the world our absent fathers made was hideous, unfair, and unacceptable, a realm where we were condemned, then all right: he would reinvent it from scratch, if need be, in his art and actions" (209–10).

Smith's drawings demonstrate that making art allows him to transcend the limitations of his negative, isolated worldview. The idea that Chaym, who earlier claims that violent struggle is inherent in the human condition, can come to this level of hopefulness further demonstrates Johnson's belief in the transformative power of art. It also marks a step in Chaym's movement back toward the village to share his enlightenment.

Unfortunately, external forces conspire to keep Smith from being the Buddha he has trained to become, just as the assassin's bullet keeps Dr. King from fully achieving the beloved community. And this points to a significant tension in *Dreamer* between hope for liberation and a strong sense of the difficulty of ever achieving true unification. Although Chaym reinvents the world in his drawings, once he moves out of seclusion he cannot sustain this vision in the face of a society founded on racial separation.

Johnson wrestles with this idea throughout his fiction. He repeatedly reinvents the world in his novels as part of his artistic quest. In each novel, the protagonist achieves enlightenment, overcoming the sense of victimization that has plagued him or her up to this point. And yet, in every case the world remains, as Johnson includes a chronicle of the oppression and injustice that African Americans face. In the process of offering hope for individual transcendence, he reminds the reader of the greater social pressures still effectively blocking any collective change. This complicates his assertion that race is an illusion, as the reiteration of how racialism materially shapes interaction through American history somewhat diminishes the power of that notion.

Johnson's struggle to simultaneously overcome racialism and to assert its negative effect on the black community places him in a tradition of African American writers concerned with the conflict between denying and reifying the power of race in our society. In *Color and Culture: Black Writers and the Making of the Modern Intellectual* (1998), Ross Posnock coins the term "*antirace race man or woman*" to describe adherents to this position (5).[1] His list of authors fitting this description comprises the early novelists Pauline Hopkins, Charles W. Chesnutt, and W. E. B. Du Bois; the Harlem Renaissance luminaries Alain Locke, Jessie Fauset, Wallace Thurman, Nella Larsen, Jean Toomer, and Zora Neale Hurston; and the later writers Richard Wright, Ralph Ellison, and James Baldwin. Many of these writers are important influences on Johnson, and one sees him signifying on their work in his novels.

Interestingly, part of what Johnson shares with these antirace race predecessors is a willingness to draw on literary sources outside the African American canon.[2] So, as he refers to these authors, he also follows their example of signifying on white literary antecedents, including, in his case, Herman Melville, Ralph Waldo Emerson, Theodore Dreiser, and Saul Bellow. This ability to cross literary boundaries speaks well for the notion that divisive influences can be overcome. Posnock notes, however, that the recitation of racial grievances, which reinforces separation, somewhat compromises that idea. The antirace race author eternally struggles (with varying degrees of success) to keep both ascendance and accountability in play at all times. In each of his novels, Johnson addresses this challenge; as he progresses toward *Dreamer,* the balance shifts toward the collective and the need for social change, although he still recognizes the power of the individual. Like his predecessors, he works to illuminate the universal through a close examination of the particulars of black life. Furthermore, as they did, Johnson sometimes finds that those particulars, which he treats systematically in his series of historical novels, may threaten to obscure or contradict those universal values.

As he shares their struggles, he also adds to their successes; for although this universalist position is difficult to maintain, it offers the reader valuable insights. The personal change Johnson describes in his advocacy of "whole sight" makes an important contribution to any significant societal reformation. Perhaps the path to group enlightenment is a simultaneous celebration of the individual and an indictment of society. Certainly that notion resonates in the work of Ralph Waldo Emerson, to whom Johnson reasonably compares himself. In the transcendentalist's best-known works, including *Nature* and "Self-Reliance," he repeatedly suggests that the individual's mandate to be true to him- or herself supercedes any adherence to the established social order. Furthermore, Emerson argues that the best society will automatically arise from the voluntary association of enlightened individuals.

Prior to *Dreamer,* Johnson seems to occupy this position, too. But, like his predecessor, he experiences a sea change. As Emerson's example shows, such an idealistic attitude wavers in the face of life's real tragedies or society's nefarious proclivities. On the verge of profound disillusionment, Emerson changes his orientation, admitting humanity's limitations and asking how one might best respond to such restrictions. The result, as one sees in essays like "Fate" and "Experience," is a useful, if more sobering, program of behavior. And in *Dream-*

er, one finds Johnson backing away from his idealism to confront racialism and its realistic impact on African American identity.

• • •

Johnson's artistic project has grown from deep personal roots. Reared in Evanston, Illinois, a suburb of Chicago, in the 1950s and early 1960s, he experienced a political awakening in college when he encountered and briefly embraced the ideology of the Black Arts Movement. He backed away from that position soon after, largely because of his education in philosophy, and embraced the Buddhism that has become the spiritual underpinning of his work. That action brought him back to an expansive view of race and identity; and yet, even as his artistic vision developed, he never fully lost sight of the social pressures operating on black Americans. He recounts them frequently, with particular vividness in *Dreamer;* in that novel, he also gives readers a view of his Evanston ancestors, whose methods of overcoming this oppression have influenced his worldview. In a sense, *Dreamer* completes for Johnson a circular aesthetic development that mirrors his personal growth.

Born on April 23, 1948, Charles Richard Johnson is the only child of Ruby Elizabeth (née Jackson) and Benny Lee Johnson, who came north to Evanston as part of the Great Migration (Grossman 3). Johnson describes the city as "very attractive" (Nash 49) and says that he and his friends, both black and white, grew up believing that "bigotry, as we understood it then, was simply 'uncool'" (Boccia 613). Certainly, some elements of Evanston's history suggest such harmony. Evanston has one of the oldest African American communities in the Midwest; blacks were settled there prior to the Civil War. The strong African American presence manifests itself in many ways. Evanston Township High School, for instance, has never been segregated. Furthermore, Evanston's city government has been integrated since 1932, when Edwin Jourdain was elected Alderman (Dorsey 92). Despite all of that, the situation was more complex than Johnson's memoir suggests.

Jourdain's election points to the complexities of Evanston race relations. He represented an all-black ward on the city's West Side, where most African Americans live. Real estate codes controlled African Americans' housing options until the 1960s, and the effects of those codes remain today. Similarly, for years Evanston had segregated hospitals and swimming beaches. Northwestern University offered no housing for black students until the mid-1950s. Despite some efforts at racial progress, Evanston was "probably as racist as any place around" when Johnson was growing up there (Quinn).

That the author could have such positive recollections of a hostile environment speaks to his convictions about how the individual must respond to oppression. He credits his ancestors and their peers for this attitude, calling them "a breed of black men and women . . . so toughened by prejudice, by the rule of having to do twice as much to get half as far, that they regarded no problem as insurmountable" (*Dreamer* 127). Such refusal to accept limiting racialized characterizations of identity inspired Johnson. Although he has never forgotten the conditions that demanded such an attitude, he focuses primarily on this refusal to submit as the best response. As his literature shows, he has continued to apply that same standard throughout his creative career. Spending his formative years in Evanston also prepared Johnson to be an artist in practical terms. Evanston Township High School was considered one of the best high schools in the nation, and it offered courses in art, photography, and creative writing. Johnson took them all, laying the groundwork for his future career. He published his first drawings and stories in the school and city newspapers.

His pursuit of writing and drawing in high school grew from early artistic aspirations that his parents nurtured. Ruby Elizabeth and Benny Lee Johnson each contributed vital elements to Johnson's worldview and to his art. Johnson describes his father as "a quiet, deeply conservative, pro-black man with a fifth-grade education, who until the 1960s voted Republican" and his mother as "emotional, moody, a high school graduate who believed in integration, belonged to three book clubs, and always voted for Democrats." He also notes that, for all their differences, they "actually complimented [*sic*] and completed each other" ("Charles" 224). The tensions between their worldviews provided Johnson with personal and artistic difficulties and the means of resolving them.

Johnson's father taught his son a strong code of values and emphasized the importance of a well-developed work ethic. The latter concern grew naturally from his struggles to provide for his family, which required him at some points to hold three jobs. It also gave rise to a crucial episode in Johnson's life. Consumed by his passion for drawing, Johnson told his father that he wanted to become a professional artist. Benny Lee replied, "'They don't let black people do that. You should think about something else'" ("Charles" 228). Initially frustrated, Johnson wrote to the white artist Lawrence Lariar, who would become his drawing teacher. Lariar's reply convinced his father that his narrow view was wrong. When he came around, Benny Lee even paid for the lessons. Johnson's frequent retelling of this story indicates its importance to his creative development. Benny Lee's negative linkage of race and art challenged the integrationist values that Johnson says dominated his adolescence;

his ability to overcome this view, and to reach his father in the process, must have affirmed that vision.

Johnson also weaves this story into his fiction. His protagonists struggle with their fathers over whether or not their blackness defines them. In every case, the fathers are both fiercely proud of their race and convinced that it limits their possibilities. By contrast, the children demonstrate a more fluid sense of personal and racial identity. Significantly, all of these children are artists of some sort, using the creative process to help them overcome or escape their fathers' attitudes. This clearly reflects Johnson's position. Notably, however, in every case the fathers' views grow from crushing experiences with a racially hostile society. I read a tribute to Johnson's father in this, as well as a recognition of the realities of race in American life. Even though these individuals gain enlightenment, Johnson does not let the reader forget the pressures and conditions that have held African Americans back throughout the nation's history.

If Johnson's father inspired what the author has called his "life's first real crisis" ("Charles" 228), his mother provided an important counterexample by encouraging him to browse among her book shelves, which "reflected her eclectic tastes in yoga, dieting, Christian mysticism, Victorian poetry, interior decorating, costume design, and flower arrangement" (226). The variety of her library enabled him to juxtapose works such as Richard Wright's *Black Boy,* Johann David Wyss's *The Swiss Family Robinson,* and the poems of Rainier Maria Rilke (226). Such eclecticism marks his own writing, as he blends materials from divergent traditions to create literature that challenges conventional generic and canonical limitations. Furthermore, as he absorbed this diverse information, he realized that the only limits to his fusion of ideas were externally imposed. In his fiction, this grounds his response to his father's statement about blacks and art. Having learned by his father's example what he would have to resist in order to have an artistic career, Johnson found in his mother's approach an intellectual tool that has served him well in his struggles with essentialism.

Johnson experienced a profound challenge to his parents' way of seeing the world when he enrolled at Southern Illinois University in Carbondale. He arrived in Carbondale in 1966, part of "a wave of Illinois black kids . . . most of them . . . from the Chicago area" (230). These students found the university relatively friendly territory, though Carbondale and the surrounding environs were "tightly segregated" (Harper, *University* 132). The town's attitude is not surprising. Southern Illinois is in many ways attitudinally more sympathetic with its neighbors, southern Missouri and western Kentucky, than with northern Illinois. More unusual is the university's history. At the behest of its president, Delyte Morris, SIU had integrated in the early 1950s, well before schools in many southern states. The African American comedian and activist Dick Gregory, who was a student at SIU in that era, had even made initial efforts to integrate the town movie theater by refusing to sit in the balcony (Koplowitz 54).

Between 1962 and 1965, SIU's Student Non-Violent Freedom Committee investigated racism in southern Illinois. This push toward greater activism threatened the relative harmony that existed on campus in the late 1950s (Koplowitz 12–14). Morris's egalitarian educational vision made him amenable to integration; simultaneously, his paternalistic, proprietary attitude made him resist others' suggestions. When the students of Johnson's generation wanted more than the president's initiatives on racial equality, he fought every concession to their demands (Harper, *University* 215–17). As a result, racial tensions as well as increasing student unrest over Vietnam made SIU a political hotbed during Johnson's career there.

These racial and political tensions did not affect Johnson immediately. Although protest over racial conditions occurred at SIU in 1966, he seems to have stayed away at first from that conflict. Instead, he pursued his drawing career, worked for the campus and town newspapers, and threw himself into his classes. Majoring in journalism required him to take a philosophy course; he found in the material another pursuit equal in significance to his artwork. Even more importantly, he entered a sustained discussion of aesthetic issues dating back thousands of years, which provided grist for his artistic mill. As an aspiring professional artist now seeking to articulate his own personal aesthetic theory, Johnson was prepared for the two encounters that would profoundly shape his creative evolution.

The first of these came in 1969, when Amiri Baraka visited SIU. His presence on campus, which culminated a year of strife, indicates an important moment in the student struggle for racial awareness. Efforts to bring Stokely Carmichael, the former head of the Student Nonviolent Coordinating Committee and the coiner of the phrase "Black Power," to Carbondale had failed in May 1968. Frightened by extreme unrest in the wake of Martin Luther King Jr.'s assassination, university officials cancelled his appearance (Koplowitz 16). A group of between two and four hundred black students occupied President Morris's office to protest the decision. Eight leaders of the group were arrested and summarily expelled (Mitchell 167, 169–71). Hostilities quickly escalated. General student dissatisfaction took a violent turn with the burning of Old Main, the university's oldest building, in June (Harper, *University* 259). Although tensions abated somewhat over the summer, the 1968–69 school year brought still more conflict. In addition to the racial strife, SIU increasingly felt the impact of student antiwar demonstrations. Protesters targeted the university's Center for Vietnamese Studies and Programs, newly created in March 1969. Students saw the federally funded center as a front for covert operations intended to extend and intensify the war. They took to the streets, on campus and in Carbondale, and the National Guard had to intervene (285).

Given the community climate during his visit, one might be surprised that Baraka was allowed to speak on campus. Baraka's reading was remarkably significant for a black artist awakening to the political and racial tensions informing his environment. At the time Johnson heard him, Baraka was delivering the message of the Black Arts Movement that he helped found in 1965, when he started the Black Arts Repertory Theatre/School in Harlem with a group of peers, including Larry Neal. Neal defines the movement's fundamental premise in his seminal essay, "The Black Arts Movement," which "advocates a cultural revolution in art and ideas" and charges black artists "to speak to the spiritual and cultural needs of Black people" (798). In many ways the descendent of Langston Hughes's ideas in "The Negro Artist and the Racial Mountain" (1926), the movement rejects the limitations of white-defined creative standards. Like the drive to expand conceptions of African Americans' role in the national history, the impulse to redefine black art reclaims and revises established perceptions of black being and black accomplishment. Without this reclamation and revision, Black Aestheticians argue, progress is impossible.

As the Black Arts Movement artists sounded their call for revolution, they also articulated a new critical standard for black art. Claiming that white criticism caused "cultural strangulation" by controlling the "terms in which the Black Artist will deal with his own experience," the architects of the movement advocated the development of a Black Aesthetic generated and controlled by the black literary community (Gayle, "Cultural" 44). Wedded as it was to the Black Power movement, the Black Arts Movement saw art's "real function" as making "revolution, using its own medium" (Karenga 33). This idea resonates with Addison Gayle's claim that "the serious black artist of today is at war with the American society" (Introduction xvii).

This was the challenge Baraka brought to Carbondale in 1969, only months after he and Neal published *Black Fire,* the movement's definitive anthology (Salaam 73). Flanked by imposing security guards and refusing to take questions from white members of the audience, Baraka charged his listeners to "take [their] talent back to the black community." Inspired, Johnson dropped everything else to draw cartoons "exploring the history and culture of black America" (Johnson, "Charles" 235–36). Working steadily and obsessively for a week, he produced what would be the first of his two published collections of comic art, *Black Humor.*

Knowing where Johnson's aesthetic journey led him, one might wonder what he found compelling in Baraka's message. Perhaps idealism moved him toward Baraka and his cohorts. Certain premises in the Black Arts approach are, in their purest sense, harmonious with Johnson's approach. Addison Gayle claims, for instance, that the idea of the Black Aesthetic is to help "men in becoming better than they are" and to move from a standard of beauty in the work, a value propagated from Aristotle to the New Critics, to valuing "the transformation from ugliness to beauty that the work of art demands from its audience" (Introduction xxii). At face value, this sentiment enriches the sense of the good that art can do, an idea that might well have appealed to a young artist wrestling to define his aesthetic position. The Black Aestheticians' sense of how their art opens up definitions of black being may also have been pertinent. As Hoyt Fuller puts it, authors of "the new black literature are deeply concerned with image and myth. They are about the business of destroying those images and myths that have crippled and degraded black people, and the institution of new images and myths that will liberate them" (327). Johnson takes up precisely this task in *Faith and the Good Thing,* where he remakes the African American folk tradition in ways that promise liberation for both reader and character.

Whatever drew Johnson to the movement initially, he has subsequently become conflicted about its place in his development. In "Where Philosophy and Fiction Meet" (1988), he notes that "cultural nationalism . . . makes me uncomfortable, precisely because I was once one of its converts. Indeed, my first publication would never have come about if it had not been for the black arts movement" (36). By contrast, in a 1996 interview with Michael Boccia, he claims, "a part of me sympathizes with black nationalist concerns, such as economic self-sufficiency. . . . But I just never bought into black cultural nationalism. It always struck me as naive" (Boccia 614). Certainly one's understanding of one's past changes over time. The fundamental difference between these comments, however, suggests something more powerful, a manifestation of the tension between ideal and application that marks Johnson's aesthetic. Given his subsequent turn toward intersubjectivity, a fascination with racial separatism does not fit with Johnson's creative and personal vision. Nevertheless, in his reminders about the realities of racial division in America one can see why black cultural nationalism's emphasis on redressing racial grievances might have appealed to him. I believe that this ideology *was* important to Johnson's development and that he embraced its premises early on. The evidence suggests, however, that even at the point of his greatest interest in the movement, Johnson was not entirely comfortable with it.

As Jonathan Little notes, *Black Humor* is "a collection of eighty-nine cartoons that deal with a wide range of topics [and] extensively examines North American racial politics during the sixties" ("Comic" 582). Manifesting early signs of Johnson's ambivalence about Baraka's message, the collection alternately celebrates and undercuts radical black politics. It also comments on stereotypes through the misadventures of a racially mixed couple, points toward important developments in Johnson's aesthetic as he moves toward fiction writing, and displays his perception of central twentieth-century African American literary texts. Throughout, Johnson references himself in ways that illuminate his artistic evolution.

In one of the more striking drawings, he revises his encounter with Baraka. The image is a two-page representation of a revolutionary figure, who appears throughout the book, preparing to give a street-corner speech and declaring, "I won't speak till all the honkys leave!" (figure 1). In the next frame, the adult audience has dispersed, leaving the dejected revolutionary facing one small black boy. This image both mocks Baraka's refusal to communicate with whites at SIU and represents Johnson's sense of his own innocence in adhering to the poet's position. In poking fun at himself, Johnson suggests that although Baraka's challenge is inspirational, the message he wants to take

Figure 1. Reprinted from *Black Humor,* © 1970 by Charles Johnson.

back to the community in his cartoons encompasses more than the ideology of the Black Aesthetic.

Another cartoon from *Black Humor* expresses even more clearly the tension that Johnson conveys throughout his body of work. The frame shows a young African American couple with two small children living in extreme poverty. While the man, who strongly resembles a young Charles Johnson, looks out the open window, a book under his arm, the woman demands, "How *dare* you be an idealist?" (figure 2). This very personal image affirms Johnson's hope for the individual even in the face of a particularly grim reality. The bitterness of the caption tinges the humor here, and the drawing is as ironic as it is funny; in a sense, the joke is the conflict between ideal and application. One wonders how

How dare you be an idealist?

Figure 2. Reprinted from *Black Humor,* © 1970 by Charles Johnson.

a book and a dream could assuage the horror of the squalid apartment, especially given the extra pressure of the two suffering children. Even as the image undermines the association of economic determinism with attitudes about race, it provides a window into an environment where such pressures operate. This man's struggle with his surroundings resurfaces throughout Johnson's canon, especially in *Faith and the Good Thing,* "Exchange Value," "Alethia," and *Dreamer.*

After *Black Humor,* Johnson, who by this point was planning to pursue a graduate degree in philosophy, became increasingly interested in transcending essentialism. He also grew less tolerant of the Black Arts and Black Power movements. His second book of cartoons, *Half-Past Nation Time,* even more pointedly rejects political approaches to questions of racial being and mocks the foibles of the Black Panther party. In the preface, he defines his role in challenging separatist ideology: *"The hour is late in American history—racism, the Vietnam war, poverty, militarism, and stale lives have caught up with us."* He counters the impact of this potential horror by claiming, *"it is not too late for the dangling ends of black, white, female, and ethnic union to be brought together. Our artists can help, can give us interpretations of ourselves in their mediums to illuminate where we are, where we are going"* (2). He places himself in that vanguard, affirming the hope that he hints at in the grim apartment in *Black Humor.* Change comes, he suggests, when people recognize what joins rather than what separates them.

To that end, he mocks the Black Panthers, repeatedly showing the inconsistency of their ideas. He melds that with his critique of Black Arts ideology in an image of three Black Panthers mocking two policemen who have been turned to swine (figure 3). His representation of the police as "pigs" provides an amusing counter to the portrayal in *The Black Panther Coloring Book,* which represents the police as brutal, sharp-tusked animals in tight uniforms, armed with big pistols. Here the animals' dazed expressions and ridiculous appearance belie any sense of menace. Furthermore, in an implicit rejection of the separatist ideology driving the Panthers and the Black Aestheticians, Johnson draws on classical literature for the cartoon's caption: "I don't know where this sister named Circe came from but she's got a great sense of humor." His evocation of Homer's *Odyssey* clearly undercuts the idea that black art is necessarily separate from white. It furthermore suggests that the Black Panthers and their adherents have an incomplete understanding of the relationship of their culture to the Western literary tradition. The Panthers appreciate Circe even though they don't know where she came from. Ironically, if they were to know her origin, they would be ideologically bound to reject her despite her use to them. Johnson's mockery of this attitude demonstrates his resistance to political demands on his personal aesthetic vision. Like other antirace race artists, he recognizes the need to improve conditions for African Americans, an aim that they share with revolutionaries like the Black Panthers. Despite this similarity of goals, though, he refuses to restrict the creative arm of the struggle to the realm of black texts.

As his interest in philosophy, particularly phenomenology and Buddhism, intensified, Johnson's creative impulse expanded beyond visual expression.

"I don't know where this sister named Circe came from but she's got a great sense of humor."

Figure 3. Reprinted from *Half-Past Nation Time,* © 1972 by Charles Johnson.

Once *Half-Past Nation Time* was accepted for publication, Johnson turned to writing novels, producing six apprentice novels, as yet unpublished, in the span of two years. Writing a novel each quarter of his master's program in philosophy at SIU, Johnson produced a martial arts story, "a novel told as a slave ship's log, all about the middle passage, but . . . told from the white captain's viewpoint; a semi-autobiographical novel about being a black college student juggling school and family dilemmas; and a trilogy, covering the childhood, adulthood, and middle-age of a black musician." Each allowed Johnson to hone a different element of his craft, but ultimately he found the fiction too formulaic, because he was working in a mode that evoked writers he was reading at the time. As he says of his apprenticeship, "what was problematic for me in the first 6 novels was that I was working with received ideas, interpretations of the black world and black 'experience' not my own . . . these were not, I realized in 1972, my experiences, or my voice. The early books rang false to me and I could never go back to read them after one was written" (e-mail 7 Nov. 1996).

Setting those texts aside, Johnson began *Faith and the Good Thing,* a story that addresses the philosophical and personal questions with which he had been wrestling. He also sought feedback from John Gardner, who was to be his mentor and his careful commentator on every draft of *Faith.* A gifted novelist, who in 1972 taught his fiction-writing course from his farm on Boskydell Road near Carbondale, Gardner influenced an entire generation of novelists. Johnson arranged a series of private meetings with him to discuss his work in progress. A much more personal relationship developed as the elder writer offered his protégé the benefits of his writing and teaching experience.

An experimental spirit and a broad aesthetic perspective mark Gardner's fiction; when Johnson met him, he had recently published *Grendel* (1971), a retelling of the Beowulf story from the perspective of the monster's mother. Seeing the depth of Johnson's commitment to his craft, Gardner offered commentary and insight that helped Johnson shape the text. At the same time, Johnson read all of Gardner's fiction and nonfiction, which helped him articulate his own aesthetic. He blended his growing interest in phenomenology with Gardner's belief that the writer had what Johnson calls "the philosophical (and moral) duty of presenting an aesthetic vision which, to the best of our ability, embodies as many perceptions as possible in a fiction" in pursuit of his artistic goal (Johnson, "Phenomenology" 152–53). He also took seriously Gardner's claim that moral art "ought to be a force bringing people together, breaking down barriers of prejudice and ignorance, and holding up ideals worth pursuing" (Gardner, *On Moral Fiction* 42). This notion effectively fulfills Johnson's promise in the preface to *Half-Past Nation Time.* Under Gardner's tutelage, Johnson began to find a way to bring his ideal of resisting racial limitations to bear in novels that expand understandings of black identity and black literature.

Gardner introduced Johnson to numerous other authors and helped him find a literary agent. He also assisted Johnson in securing a teaching position at the University of Washington in Seattle, where he remains today as Pollock Professor of English, holder of his department's first endowed chair in creative writing.

• • •

Johnson published *Faith and the Good Thing* in 1974. This first literary fruit of his evolving artistic vision resonated with the works of a small but active group of African American writers dissatisfied with the Black Aesthetic. Often referred to as the New Breed, these writers, including Ishmael Reed, Al Young, Cecil Brown, and Quincy Troupe Jr., "found the Black Aesthetic too prescriptive and narrowly political" and "felt the battleground was not the street but the mind. They wanted to dethrone the Western mind from the seat of intellectual power and prestige" (Harris, "Black Aesthetic" 69). Johnson applauds the New Breed authors in *Being and Race* for their literary innovations and their progressive vision of black community and artistic identity. He praises Reed in particular, noting his peer's courage and intelligence and celebrating his willingness to take on the Western mind.

Chief among the characteristics he values in Reed is his conviction that "each black writer is his own aesthetician," a position that opens the range of definition for black art (64). Reed's individualistic approach also incorporates a healthy irreverence for sacred texts from both the Euro- and African American canons. In *Flight to Canada* (1976), an important precursor to *Oxherding Tale,* he attacks the slave narrative and parodies *Uncle Tom's Cabin.* He critiques Eurocentric attitudes and demonstrates how limiting such a perspective is to blacks. Here and throughout his oeuvre, Reed's harshest satire focuses on black characters that militantly adhere to white aesthetic standards and thereby remain removed from the black community.

Although Johnson sees the value in Reed's method, he questions its strength as an aesthetic position. Reed, Johnson says, cannot simultaneously advocate the thoroughgoing rejection of Western hegemony and make good art. "A more systematic approach," he claims, "one using vivid characters, Aristotelian mimetic principles, and poetically charged language, would be for Reed . . . spoiled by Western philosophy's demand for a certain kind of coherence, completeness, and consistency in any expression" (*Being* 67). Although he and Reed share some motives, Johnson learned lessons from John Gardner that compel him to take a different approach. He hopes to challenge rigid conceptions about race, but he sees a way to do so within the boundaries of artistic expression that Reed rejects. This choice increases his conflict with the Black Aestheticians and even more firmly aligns him creatively with predecessors like Jean Toomer, Zora Neale Hurston, W. E. B. Du Bois, and Ralph Ellison.

Ellison's impact on Johnson is especially clear. As early as *Black Humor,* Johnson demonstrates admiration for Ellison's ideas. One particularly striking image shows a revolutionary standing over a throng of blackface dancing dolls; the caption reads, "He bought them all so he could set them free" (figure 4). The image clearly signifies on the Tod Clifton section of *Invisible Man,* in which a disillusioned former participant in the Brotherhood's struggle takes to selling such dolls on the street near Times Square. In other drawings, Johnson revises several of the party scenes from Ellison's novel as well as the image of the nude dancer from the battle royal episode. These humorous references to Ellison's text convey his ambivalence about black cultural nationalism. For many radicals of that era, Ellison simply was not "black enough." Addison Gayle claims that with his "remarkable grasp of the Afro-American's historical past," Ellison could have articulated the voice of race more clearly than any of his literary predecessors, but he condemns him for choosing assimilationism instead ("Function" 413). Some even suggested that Ellison was an Uncle Tom, effectively echoing John Oliver Killens's condemnation of *Invisible Man* as "a vicious distortion of Negro life" (7). I find this description of the novel and novelist who raised such significant challenges to established attitudes about racial and literary identity profoundly ironic. Apparently, even at this early point in his career, Johnson did, too. He does not completely affirm Ellison; Tod Clifton's dancing dolls have no hope of freedom, after all. Nevertheless, by drawing Ellison into *Black Humor,* he challenges the party line and suggests a different place for the master in this debate. That early spirit of respect for his predecessor carries throughout Johnson's career. He speaks positively of Ellison's legacy in *Being and Race.* When he won the National Book Award in 1990, he used the occasion to pay tribute to Ellison. One might say that Johnson is Ellison's spiritual heir and that the circularity of his aesthetic development and his literary career are of a piece with his return to his forebear's lessons.

Ellison and Johnson also arrive at similar answers to the dilemma Du Bois conveys in his classic formulation of double consciousness: "One ever feels his twoness,—an American, a Negro; two souls, two thoughts, two unreconciled strivings; two warring ideals in one dark body, whose dogged strength alone keeps it from being torn asunder" (*Souls* 9–10). Both see the transformation of perception as a means to at least live with that internal conflict. The com-

He bought them all so he could set them free.

Figure 4. Reprinted *Black Humor,* © 1970 by Charles Johnson.

mon element that each of Johnson's novels shares with *Invisible Man* is a protagonist on a quest for new ways of understanding his or, in *Faith and the Good Thing,* her black identity. When the protagonists find that new sense of self, they can overcome the suffering and victimization that characterizes their peers' experiences. This approach also reflects the values Johnson affirms in *Dreamer.* In his subsequent writing, Johnson returns more and more frequently to this approach. From his essay "The Second Front" to his *New York Times* article on "the Negro National Anthem," James Weldon Johnson's "Lift Ev'ry Voice and Sing," he offers this view of black identity as an antidote to contemporary manifestations of racism.

Johnson's response to double consciousness also involves the elements of his art that make him unique: his Buddhism and his particular amalgamation of philosophical influences. His religion provides the commitment to transcending dualism, thereby strengthening his response to Du Bois's binary model of identity. In conjunction with this, his interest in philosophy pushes him to explore fundamental epistemological and ontological questions. The confluence of these impulses is a new, rich approach to his task as an African American writer. He challenges essentialist, divisive formulations of racial identity by raising questions about how people come to understand and define race and being. These concerns give rise to the title of his one critical book, *Being and Race: Black Writing since 1970,* which explicates his artistic position at length. In the process of articulating and applying this aesthetic, Johnson fulfills the promise of generations of his literary forebears and counters what he sees as the negative impulses of many of his contemporaries.

And yet, even as he offers this answer to the dilemma of double consciousness, his novels suggest that some sense of separation remains. In the realm of his work, he never forgets the pressures of the context in which his characters strive for this ideal. As we trace the development of Johnson's new way of seeing, we will also note an increasing awareness of the difficulty of completely escaping this environment. Even as he offers new means of engaging in the struggle, Johnson reminds his readers that the conflicts are far from resolved. This conflict in his fiction further strengthens his affinities with Martin Luther King Jr. and adds another dimension to the notion of *Dreamer* as evaluation of the movement and of himself. By 1966, when the novel opens, the historical King had realized the need for privileging economic issues in his campaign to end oppression. Love remains important, but one must neither overlook nor cease to denounce the inequities of African American life. Johnson takes this position in the novel, thereby crystallizing a tension that has been building in his work since *Black Humor.* By bringing it above ground, he opens up lines of inquiry that affirm the richness of his work and its significance to African American letters.

2 The Aesthetic Articulated: *Being and Race*

Johnson's aesthetic is driven by efforts to enrich understanding of black identity and to expand the creative possibilities available to African American writers. These values appear in essays published throughout his career. He advocates applying philosophy to black life to raise consciousness about how racialism shapes experience. Strikingly, however, his sense of and response to the environment in which racial perceptions arise modulates. He begins with a politicized vision, shifts away from it somewhat in the 1980s, and arrives in the 1990s at a fusion of the two positions that tends toward social action. The foundation of Johnson's aesthetic is *Being and Race: Black Fiction since 1970* (1988), which comprises elements of earlier individual pieces. Variations on major themes in some of the essays reflect the complex relationship between art and activism that manifests itself in his novels and stories.

Being and Race affirms the importance of philosophy to the writer's craft, beginning with a prefatory explanation of phenomenology that also illuminates some of the basic principles of the earlier essays. He begins by referring to the work of the German mathematician Edmund Husserl.[1] In *The Primacy of Perception* (1964), Maurice Merleau-Ponty notes that Husserl's phenomenology responds to the notion that opinion develops as the result of combined external psychological, social, and historical conditions. Instead of relying on external constructions, Husserl's epistemology is neither deductive nor purely empirical, an intuition of essences he calls *Wesenschau.* In order to reach Wesenschau, one considers the universal aspects of lived experiences (Erlebnisse). In these terms one can use a single instance of racial oppression to quantify and better understand the abstraction "injustice." Similarly, even though a convivial gathering in the African American community, like a 1930s Harlem rent party, does not define black life, it illuminates the concept of "celebration." Husserl would say that this Wesenschau clarifies that toward which our consciousness is directed. In Johnson's terms, one sees black life more clearly by recognizing the link between particular African American experiences and the universal human attitudes and actions they represent.

Intentionality is Husserl's term for perception, which he sees as something that humans *do,* and are always doing, or *intending, toward another thing* (Detweiler 9). As the consciousness "apprehends" objects, they simultaneously reveal themselves; in that interplay is existence. The problem with this interpretation is that preconceptions about what things "should" be cloud one's perceptions when objects reveal themselves. For Johnson, this obstruction drives racialist conflict, as people's beliefs about the racial Other impede efforts to achieve new understandings of blackness and whiteness. Somewhat idealistically, though, Husserl offers a response to such a situation that promises transcendence of those limitations. He posits the existence of another level of perception, pure of all interfering preconceptions, which he calls the *pre-objective world.* This realm, the goal of Husserl's intellectual practice, is the world "as it is and of which we are before we reorganize it into common-sense, logical, or empirical categories" (Detweiler 9).

One accesses the pre-objective world through the *epoché,* a process in which perceptions of the natural world are "bracketed," not denied but only temporarily ignored. The resultant attitude promotes "descriptive neutrality" rather than interpretation. Not the empirical scientist's method of inductive observation intended to determine causality, this state allows the perceiver to access experience before the constructions that shape our communal and individual consciousness cloud it. It resembles the prelinguistic stage of child development, when the association of externally imposed names with objects does not yet circumscribe infants' experiences.

The epoché leads to the most controversial part of Husserl's phenomenological method: the two-part process called the *reductions.* First, one implements the *eidetic* reduction, which exposes an object's essence through systematic testing of what can be discarded from it without destroying its identity. What remains present to consciousness after excluding everything that contributes to an object's empirical constitution is its *eidos.* One can see this principle at work in *Faith and the Good Thing* when the Swamp Woman sheds her skin. The eidos that remains might be called her "werewitchness," that which signifies her nature to the perceiver even without her identifying external features. Having distilled the eidos, one then performs the *transcendental* or *phenomenological* reduction, bracketing, in our example, the identified residue of "werewitchness" and focusing on the pure stream of consciousness lying beneath it. The goal is to further transcend one's own existence at this particular moment, escape the fixed conception of what makes the Swamp Woman what she is, and encounter pure intentionality. Achieving that awareness allows the perceiver to realize his or her own contribution to the process of creating the object.

In the abstract, Husserl's process is fascinating. Unfortunately, because environment and interpersonal communications affect each perceiving subject, it falters when applied. Husserl recognized this limitation, and as he began to look beyond the isolate to the individual within a society, he came to believe that practicing the transcendental reduction leads to the recognition of the *transcendental ego,* which makes the individual ego and its universe possible. This concept, which speaks to the connectedness or "intersubjectivity" of all things, allowed subsequent philosophers like Merleau-Ponty to transform Husserl's idealistic philosophy into a more practical system.

Like Husserl, Merleau-Ponty attempts to clarify the nature and function of perception; also like Husserl, he hopes to strip away distractions that obscure its deeper significance. Merleau-Ponty diverges from Husserl, however, by arguing that the individual always acts within a world he or she cannot possibly transcend, the "life-world." Within that realm, Merleau-Ponty believes that temporal existence defines perception. In the translators' introduction to *Sense and Non-sense* (1948 French; 1964 English), Hubert L. Dreyfus and Patricia Allen Dreyfus note that "for Merleau-Ponty the body is just the capacity to experience perceptual solicitations and to make them more determinate by moving to reveal what is concealed. . . . Our body, then, is our way of being-at-the-world-from-within-it" (xii).

One sees Johnson applying this idea most clearly in his first major essay about philosophy and race, "*The Primevil Mitosis:* A Phenomenology of the Black Body" (1976), which began as the fulfillment of a requirement for the Ph.D. in philosophy at the State University of New York at Stony Brook. The piece addresses Eldridge Cleaver's argument about the irreconcilability of black and white experience, especially in regard to the division of mind and body. Johnson characterizes Cleaver as associating blacks with physicality and whites with a mentality that abstracts them from the body. Cleaver's position echoes long-established social mythology about racial difference. Articulated originally by whites to justify their oppression of blacks, it becomes in the black cultural nationalist tradition a way for African Americans to signify on the white Other and assert their own superiority. In response, Johnson cites Merleau-Ponty and posits that the mind-body duality is itself an illusion. Instead, he argues, the body becomes the medium for one's awareness of the world (50). This means that racialism necessarily shapes both an individual's and the group's understanding of his or her body; it follows that the link between race and experience is inescapable.

On one level, then, the question becomes how one *interprets* the reaction to the racialized body. In his later work, Johnson suggests that African Americans' refusal to accept conventional characterizations of themselves as racial Others promises liberation from oppression. At this early stage, though, he indicts the social forces that perpetuate the idea of Otherness. Aware of the phenomenological ideal, he nevertheless concerns himself mostly with the real-world conflict that impedes it. Salient examples in the essay include his description of being "seen" by white patrons in a Manhattan bar and by one of his graduate school professors. In each case, Johnson's interiority, his private sense of his own personality, is invisible; instead, the intentionality that the Other brings to the act of perception defines Johnson entirely on the basis of phenotypic characteristics. This "epidermalization" (54) process marks his consciousness with the same "stain" (53) of blackness that the whites see in each instance. He also describes an encounter with a friend who calls a prominent black athlete a "jungle cat," with no regard for the impact of such a description on Johnson. The outrage that Johnson feels tempts him to embrace other stereotypes associated with race: "('Yeah,' I scream of [*sic*] my white friend in the Village, 'we're naturally superior to you at sports. Uh huhn, and we satisfy our women better *too*!')" (57). In all instances, the white view of the author's blackness threatens the interiority that he has constructed.

Johnson offers three possible responses: tricksterism disguised as acceptance (an attitude one finds, for example, in Ralph Ellison's Rinehart); assertion of his interiority (Ellison's narrator); or a militant, cultural nationalist reversal of Otherness that privileges blackness over whiteness (Ellison's Ras the Destroyer, or Cleaver himself). Although he mocks it here, he will ultimately embrace the second option as a primary mode in his fiction. At this point, he notes only the "ambiguity yet to be resolved" with regard to the dilemma of how blacks experience and enact racial identity (57). Similarly, despite his recognition of its problems, Johnson does not reject the cultural nationalist response to this dilemma outright. Concerned by the notion of merely *inverting* the terms of the power dynamic rather than effecting positive change for both racial groups, Johnson nevertheless notes the benefits of such an awareness to blacks trying to escape the "stain" of race as a defining feature. Even as he applies philosophy in analyzing the race problem with the hope of rectifying the simplistic adherence to the split that Cleaver describes, he also reestablishes the conflict of double consciousness. How can one modify experiences of raciality when the body that gives one the world is externally determined by the white Other? One finds in this the roots of the conflict that evolves through Johnson's fiction between what he aspires to and what he believes that one can achieve.

In subsequent essays like "Philosophy and Black Fiction" (1980) and "Whole Sight: Notes on New Black Fiction" (1984), Johnson primarily devotes himself to black artists' responses to the racial identity question. Moving pointedly away from the stridency of the Black Arts correlation of art and politics, he begins articulating the more universalist elements of his creative program. Chief among them is the claim that writers must push beyond the particulars of their racial identity to access other groups' racial views and the larger intersubjective truths that all such perspectives contain.

In "Philosophy and Black Fiction," Johnson argues that African American life is so rigidly codified that white writers' descriptions of it pass for authentic. This assertion evokes an image from *Half-Past Nation Time:* a white writer in a book-lined study labors over his typewriter, producing a vividly drawn "Black Power" scene for a novel (figure 5). His ability to "write black" conveys all of the difficulties that Johnson sees in rigidly nationalist art. For him, such a conception of black being proves that black artists "have frozen [their] vision in figures that caricature, at best, the complexity of [their] lives and leave the real artistic chore of interpretation unfinished" ("Philosophy" 60).

To counter this narrow view, Johnson calls on his peers to make "art that interrogates experience." For him, this process involves applying the intellectual apparatus he describes in "*The Primevil Mitosis,*" albeit with different results. Phenomenological assessments of black culture, he says in "Philosophy and Black Fiction," allow artists to "work through the particulars of Black life from within and discover there not only phenomenon [*sic*] worthy of philosophical treatment in fiction, but also—and here I'll make my wildest claim today—significant new perceptions" (57).

The word "significant" indicates a move from indeterminacy to advocating philosophy as an antidote to the plague of raciality. No longer only an enduring dilemma, double consciousness has apparently become a surmountable obstacle. Now, Johnson suggests, the black writer can free him- or herself and the race from limitations like the ones that plagued him when he was "seen" in that Manhattan bar, and intersubjectivity clearly provides the ideal means to that end.

Johnson expands upon these points in "Whole Sight: Notes on New Black Fiction," explaining that one achieves "whole sight" by articulating a particular perspective in fiction, such as a "black" point of view, and then expanding the "expression and vision" of that viewpoint in an effort to access the universal. In terms of the hope advanced in "Philosophy and Black Fiction," this is

"... Rufus turned on the white racists who breathed hotly down his back: he turned defiantly upon them, snatching the noose away from the Ku Klux Klansman and raised his clenched fist, shouting 'Black power, Black power' . . ."

Figure 5. Reprinted from *Half-Past Nation Time,* © 1972 by Charles Johnson.

the most "significant" of the possible "new perceptions" he describes. Reiterating his demand for a fuller exploration of what blackness can mean, he also comments specifically on how contemporary African American writers should situate themselves with regard to their predecessors. As he says, "the history of literary practice creates objective aesthetic possibilities, artistic works demanded historically by the foul-ups and partial breakthroughs in past literary art, novels and stories and poems that fill in the blanks and potholes created by the oversights and omissions of those writers (white and black) who preceded us" (2). The philosophical writer's responsibility, in short, is to build on the literary past to create a new vision for American literature in general and African American literature specifically.

The process Johnson describes here resembles Henry Louis Gates Jr.'s theory of signifying, arguably one of the most prominent critical paradigms for African American literary study since 1980. Gates's vernacular theory describes a process of renaming and revising antecedent texts toward the end of articulating an authentic "black difference" that sets African American literature and literary criticism apart from the white Western tradition (xxii–xxiii). Chief among the techniques of the signifying author are tropological revision, the use of parody and pastiche, and emphasis on the indeterminacy of language. As we shall see, these are also among the rhetorical tools Johnson brings to the construction process he describes in "Whole Sight."

Despite these similarities of approach, some critics question this connection on the basis of each author's stated motives. Gates's claim to be developing a *black* theory of literature troubles scholars who see Johnson as wholly committed to his universalist project. Jonathan Little, for instance, argues that "Johnson's pervasive metaphor of polyconsciousness blurs the metaphoric dualisms and sense of 'signal difference' on which Gates's theory rests." Although Johnson concerns himself with a vision of perception that transcends strict adherence to the binary of double consciousness, Little overstates the differences between Gates's and Johnson's positions. His condemnation of "Gates's gatekeeping exclusion of Johnson in lists of significant contemporary African American writers" turns largely on the notion of Gates's "black exclusivity" principle regarding the texts that signifying authors reference and revise (*Charles Johnson's* 15). In fact, Gates does *not* restrict signifying to black texts; indeed, he does not even restrict the process to black authors. As he notes in his introduction to *The Signifying Monkey,* "the implicit premise of this study is that all texts Signify upon other texts" (xxiv). His primary concern is with how black writers respond to antecedent texts, but certainly one can say the same of Johnson, both in his criticism and in his fiction.

Perhaps even more compelling in considering Johnson's relationship to Gates is Sandra Adell's claim that Gates's theory is "fundamentally Hegelian" (135). She argues that his effort to assert a uniquely black theory of reading breaks down because it requires the existence of and reinscribes itself in the white Western tradition against which he defines signifying. In participating in a totalizing unity even as he tries to separate himself, Gates "makes numerous gestures towards deconstruction only to end up in a kind of reconstruction" (133). This flaw marks Gates's system as dialectical in Adell's eyes; dialectics are part of the foundation of Johnson's universalist impulse. The process of making new philosophical black fictions demands both revision and retention of literary antecedents, as does signifying. I use Gates's term, therefore, to describe Johnson's modification of the disparate sources he weaves into his fiction.

This notion of dialectics also suggests the difficulties Johnson faces in trying to apply this aesthetic. In the process of showing how his individual characters overcome racial oppression, he reasserts the power of the social forces marshaled against the black community. It seems that separation from the idea of race is, in the final analysis, scarcely more efficacious as a means of liberation than racial separatism. One could argue that what Johnson seeks is not liberation from race so much as variation in what the term means. But deconstructing the idea of race automatically demands its reconstruction as well. As Adell notes, "to summon a tradition by reconstructing it, is to search for an authority, that of the tradition itself. . . . This is what makes the role of the black critic or anyone else concerned with advancing certain emancipatory ideas particularly burdensome" (137). Adell's formulation describes the "double bind" that Du Bois and his adherents faced; it is, I believe, the essence of Posnock's "antirace race" difficulty. It also clearly applies to Johnson as well, although one must recognize how his interests shift from the transcendent to social engagement. One result of this is an increasing level of comfort with the reestablishment of a more conventional understanding of race and racialism in his work. In taking this position, Johnson also more fully recognizes and embraces the burden that Adell describes.

In 1988 Johnson published his most comprehensive aesthetic statement to date: *Being and Race,* a project that he originally proposed as the topic of his doctoral dissertation but that he did not actually complete until after publishing *Oxherding Tale.*[2] In the first chapter, "Being and Race," he calls again for a new philosophical black fiction and explains the difficulties he faced when first embarking on a creative career. From his particular experience he posits the universal dilemma of the black artist. He begins with the premise that the novelist does not represent "real world" experiences; instead, the author organizes a fictional life-world for his or her characters. He goes on to explain how black literature has traditionally circumscribed the range of experiences it creates by emphasizing the African American community's suffering, overlooking in the process a broader spectrum of meanings black fiction could encompass. In his opinion, this untapped potential is the foundation upon which innovative black writers must build. Noting that an artist "cannot begin *ex nihilo*" (5), Johnson first explains how one must break free from others' interpretations of particular experiences in order to make individualized, innovative art and then suggests the need for a thorough reassessment of black literature.

Johnson then traces the development of black fiction from its beginnings to 1970. The recurrent theme of his discussion is that black literature is "about" identity, specifically a "crisis of identity" that he traces to the struggle between nineteenth-century separatists and integrationists (8). In the twentieth century, that topos resonates in writers' attempts to address the problem of double consciousness. In Johnson's view, although many African American writers have taken up this subject, only a few (his predecessors in the universalist tradition) have addressed it in sufficiently expansive terms. The effort to develop a broader vision of racial identity becomes a fundamental, if sometimes elusive, premise of Johnson's aesthetic program. Here, in this ideal version of his vision, he provides some context for that decision.

He begins with what critics recognize as the first published novel by an African American, William Wells Brown's *Clotel; or, The President's Daughter* (1853), although he cites the title of the 1867 version, *Clotelle; or, The Colored Heroine.*[3] The difference between editions is significant, since the original version emphasizes Clotel's familial relationship to Thomas Jefferson and thereby advocates overcoming racial boundaries. By contrast, the 1867 edition downplays the presidential connection; as the subtitle indicates, Brown concerns himself primarily with his heroine's racial identity in this version. Noting the tragic, highly political tone of *Clotelle,* Johnson comments on the ideological nature of the black novel in the nineteenth century. For much of the time between 1853 and 1900, the form was important as a political tool, first to advocate equality between the races and second to protest specific injustices against blacks. Authors such as Brown, Harriet E. Adams Wilson (*Our Nig* [1859]), Frances E. W. Harper ("The Two Offers" [1859]; *Iola Leroy; or, Shadows Uplifted* [1892]), Pauline E. Hopkins (*Contending Forces* [1900]), and Charles W. Chesnutt (*The House behind the Cedars* [1900]; *The Marrow of Tradition* [1901]) protested a wide range of social abuses, beginning with slavery and extending to include the vicious repression that followed Reconstruction and the economic and social injustice of life in the late nineteenth-century South. In many cases, as Johnson notes, that agenda led writers to sacrifice consummate artistry in service of the greater good of social reform. This is not to say that these early works have no artistic merit. Nevertheless, although some writing of this period is aesthetically satisfactory, in his view the dual demands of artistry and ideology often required the artists to engage with a relatively narrow range of vision for black identity.

Essentially bypassing the novels of the pre–World War I "old guard" (Bell,

Afro-American 76), he focuses next on the Harlem Renaissance. Integrationist/separatist conflict over black identity undeniably exists in this period, as George Schuyler and Langston Hughes's exchange about what they call "Negro" art illustrates. Nevertheless, the marked success of Hughes and the other adherents to his position typically leads one to think of this as an era when African American artists asserted an effective, distinct vision of themselves and their community. Johnson has reservations about this viewpoint. With the exception of a few writers such as Jean Toomer and Zora Neale Hurston, he faults most Harlem Renaissance writers for overemphasizing the idea that blacks are best and most clearly seen in terms of their essential difference from whites. He also objects to such authors' conscious efforts to show only the good sides of black life when, as he puts it, "we find the black world *overflowing* with meaning, so rich and multisided that literally anything—and everything—can be found there, good and bad, and one of the first chores of the writer is to be immersed in this embarrassment of rich, contradictory material" (11). I would suggest that one *can* find portrayals of both the good and the bad of black life in Harlem Renaissance novels; indeed, much to the chagrin of Du Bois and his adherents who valued accentuating the positive, writers like Claude McKay portrayed Harlem life as brutal, passionate, and violent (Posnock 172). Furthermore, I see novelists like Rudolph Fisher balancing these conflicting, class-oriented visions and showing Harlem as "*overflowing* with meaning." In Johnson's view, though, the art of this era falls short of his ideal.

By contrast, Johnson warmly praises Richard Wright's *Native Son* (1940), the story of Bigger Thomas, whose racialized sense of self shapes his every encounter with the world. The novel strongly indicts the social system that creates black people like Thomas. It also, in Johnson's opinion, presented the reading public for the first time with a fully articulated black life-world; forced to see all events from Bigger's perspective, the reader must understand the world differently. This, in Johnson's view, is the change in perceptions that all great fiction should create. He also argues that *Native Son* illustrates how the mind manages and creates experience, exemplifying Merleau-Ponty's convictions about how objects arise in the consciousness. Bigger's fear and hatred of whites and his sense of alienation drive everything he does. In many ways, his preconceptions control him, just as established attitudes about him motivate the mobs calling for his death. In demonstrating how received opinions determine experience, Johnson says, Wright creates "a phenomenological description of black urban life" (13) and moves a step closer toward the new black fiction he hopes to see.

Still, even Johnson's praise of *Native Son* includes an important qualifier, as he distances himself from Wright's deterministic point of view. Despite his sympathy with his predecessor regarding the impact of economics on the African American community, at this point he rejects the notion that social forces dictate the parameters of black experiences. Here, at the most significant critical distance he achieves from the positions advanced in "*The Primevil Mitosis,*" he pointedly disavows any linkage to the social concerns of separatist artists. Instead, he focuses solely on the aesthetic of intersubjectivity, praising Ellison and his universalist peers for their ability to transcend the boundaries of politicized racial art.

With a critique of both Negritude and black cultural nationalism, Johnson returns to the subject of political art. His objection to these movements rests on his conviction that they are "doctrine, not analysis," an ideology rather than an aesthetic (19). He distinguishes ideology from philosophy by noting that "while philosophical inquiry is devoted to understanding, a process that may or may not lead to political change, ideology must ever be geared toward action, making the reader *do* something" (26). This position marks a great distance from his impassioned response to Baraka in 1969. And yet, despite this overt rejection of activism, Johnson incorporates elements of a social agenda into his most significant work of this era, *Oxherding Tale.* While he mocks George Hawkins's rabid nationalism, he endorses Andrew's recognition and enactment of his social duty. Late in the novel, reflecting on his marriage, Andrew notes that his "dharma, such as it was, was that of the householder" (147). As Little notes, in "the householder stage of life, in which one marries, works, has children, and pursues spiritual development, one must realize that one's duty, or *dharma,* is not only to oneself, but also to the wider community" (*Charles Johnson's* 87). Although not a revolutionary in the conventional sense, Andrew must nonetheless *do* something; and as Johnson's ideal protagonist, he sets an example for the reader as well. I see in this the stirrings of Johnson's initial values. Although he is perhaps more flexible than the black cultural nationalists, he promotes action with his writing. This impulse, and the conflict between it and his ideal creative goals, becomes even more apparent in the later work, culminating in *Dreamer,* where the social agenda is clearest.

In chapter 2, "Being and Fiction," he argues that universalist authors must restructure the fiction writing *process* as well as revise the end *product.* The first step in this reformation comes when black writers reexamine how they manage information. They must resist the "uncritical" accumulation of experience (31), which one might define as putting out to sea in an open boat to learn what Stephen Crane knew, as a means of broadening the range of material upon which to base their fiction. The problem with this sort of fieldwork, in Johnson's view, is that most often the people who do it have decided what they expect to find before they even look. Limited by preconceptions, these writers cannot take anything new from experiences; instead they use them to confirm what they already thought they knew before undertaking the journey.

Johnson counters that impulse by calling on writers to imagine, invent, and interpret fictional universes that transcend the intellectual limitations governing lived experience. Claiming that philosophy and fiction are essentially "sister disciplines" (32), he suggests that authors draw on the elements of phenomenology inherent in fiction that strip objects and texts of the external elements limiting perception. For example, he challenges black writers to imagine seeing the world from the perspective of a complicated, fully developed white character. This action requires African American writers to transcend the experience of the world that their racialized bodies give them and to create instead new fictional life-worlds that expand their own and their readers' perceptions. One sees an excellent application of this idea in Flo Hatfield, the hedonistic white slave master in *Oxherding Tale.* Johnson gains as a writer by imagining her way of being in the world. He inscribes that knowledge in the story; as Andrew learns to see the world through her eyes, he realizes that bondage to desire is not determined by race. His experience also connects the particular to the universal by opening a new discussion of the abstract idea of freedom.

Johnson also complains that too often black writers accept language without challenging the attached preconceptions. Instead, the writer must embrace the interplay between his or her "perceptions and experiences [and those of writers] who came before [him or her] and despoiled words" (39). Speakers of a language assign arbitrary labels to symbols based on collective experience. Those assignments "fix" language within boundaries that make innovation difficult. As Mikhail Bakhtin notes, "'language, for the individual consciousness, lies on the borderline between oneself and the other. The word in language is half someone else's. It becomes "one's own" only when the speaker populates it with his own intention, his own accent, when he appropriates the word, adapting it to his own semantic and expressive intention'" (qtd. in Gates xxix). To make new fictions, authors must "unfix" language by using it in new and unexpected ways. This notion proves even more compelling when one considers the element of race. The rejection of the master's tongue becomes an act of resistance that frees authors from limiting definitions of identity. One sees this idea of language applied in much of the poetry of the Black Arts Movement, in which unconventional orthography signals a rejection of social constructs of blackness. For Johnson, this move also liberates them from concomitant narrow understandings of what black art can be.

One performs these innovations by using the language inventively, the process Johnson calls "transform[ing] the expressive instrument" (63). In all of his writing, Johnson attempts to expand understandings of language; *Oxherding Tale* and *Middle Passage* illustrate his methods of generating linguistic ambiguity. In both novels, he creates an alternative grammar and subverts readers' linguistic expectations through his use of anachronism and shifts in register. These variations on standard English usage also prepare his audience for his ultimate proposal: a language that transcends the limitations of white Western languages. He assigns this language to the Allmuseri, a tribe of African wizards he creates as a central symbol of his aesthetic. The figure of the tribe's language, part of his primary phenomenological trope, opens the way to the alternate version of experiential philosophy Johnson advocates. It also represents the challenge inherent in any attempt to fully achieve that vision.

Before creating the Allmuseri tongue, however, he experimented with more familiar modes of speech. As a first step, he uses anachronism to break down the chronological barriers of the novels' settings. In both *Oxherding Tale* and *Middle Passage,* characters refer to events or objects that they should not know about, given the chronology of the text. In *Oxherding Tale,* the narrator, Andrew Hawkins, describes in 1843 his tutor's adherence to the educational principles articulated in John Stuart Mill's *Autobiography,* a text published in 1856 (Hayward 695). In *Middle Passage,* he has Jackson Calhoun encouraging Peleg Chandler to donate his estate to Oberlin College in 1830, three years before the school even existed.

He makes an even more striking use of this device in *Middle Passage* as the narrator, Rutherford Calhoun, in 1830, refers to the bulky enforcer, Santos, who is chasing him, as follows: "'You have seen, perhaps, sketches of Piltdown man? Cover him with coal dust, add deerskin leggings and a cut-away coat tight as wet leather, and you shall have Santos's younger, undernourished *sister*'" (11). The passage describes a phenomenon the nineteenth-century speaker could not have known; Piltdown man was not discovered until 1912 and was proved bogus in 1915, fully eighty years after the moment of Rutherford's reference.[4] One sees a similar use of anachronism in the works of Ishmael Reed, although the authors differ greatly in their motivations for using the technique. Reed uses anachronism to create a fragmented, postmodernist fictional landscape. For Johnson, anachronism becomes a tool for creating unity rather than separation. By blending nineteenth- and twentieth-century events and challenging our linear sense of history through the apparent misuse of language, Johnson achieves a "yoking which flows over all the artificial categories we impose upon experience" (interview, 23 Mar. 1991).

Johnson also employs other effects to challenge conventional perceptions about language. He occasionally shifts the register of a character's speech rather abruptly. For example, in the midst of a scholarly monologue on narrative movement in *The Narrative of the Life of Frederick Douglass,* the narrator of *Oxherding Tale* talks about the "narrative *oomph*" of the text; elsewhere in the passage he talks about fugitive slaves "haul[ing] hips North" (118). This disrupts the linguistic flow of the story. At the same time, it materially contributes to the narrative flow, once again serving Johnson's larger purpose of altering how we view the "knowledge" the text presents about characters and, in this case particularly, expanding understandings of what one can expect black literature to contain. He also uses dialect in interesting ways. The most significant example of this occurs in *Oxherding Tale.* Andrew Hawkins, like the narrators of *Incidents in the Life of a Slave Girl* and *The Narrative of the Life of Frederick Douglass,* speaks perfect standard English. In contrast, Horace Bannon, the white slave hunter, or Soulcatcher, speaks thickly accented, unlearned dialect. "The Soulcatcher's voice, I swear, was black. The kind of deep-fried Mississippi Delta twang that magically turned floor into *flow.* Door into *doe*" (67). Johnson explicitly racializes this use of dialect forms, thereby evoking traditional perceptions about black speech. By putting those sounds in the mouth of an apparently nonblack character, Johnson challenges cognitive restrictions and also comments on the limitations of the constructs one erects to define and explain blackness. In many ways, this description of racial characteristics by a narrator who supposedly "belongs to" that race echoes another Johnson: James Weldon, on whose *Autobiography of an Ex-Coloured Man* (1912) the author is clearly signifying in *Oxherding Tale* (Kutzinski). Here, as in that novel, the racially mixed narrator's ability to comment dispassionately on features of African American life subverts the notion that there is any such thing as "black speech." By extension, all such racialist categories are automatically suspect.

Even more intriguing than these approaches to the problem of language is his creation of a non-Western language system for the Allmuseri. The Allmuseri, whose name comes from the Arabic "al-museri," meaning "a spiritual gathering place or mosque," are noteworthy for their spiritual and philosophical advancement.[5] They also embody all of the fundamental principles of Johnson's aesthetic. When inventing this tribe, Johnson decided that he "wanted a written language, and a spoken language. Everything [he had] ever learned about a culture other than Western culture became funneled into the details that reinforce the overall spiritual vision" (interview, 23 Mar. 1991). The Allmuseri language develops in terms compatible with Johnson's phenomenological goals. Although there is no sustained representation of a character speaking in the Allmuseri tongue, both *Oxherding Tale* and *Middle Passage* comment on its linguistic structures. In each case, the details highlight the limitations of Western language.

In *Oxherding Tale,* Andrew Hawkins remarks, "the Allmuseri had no words for *I, you, mine, yours.* They had, consequently, no experience of these things, either, only proper names that were variations on the Absolute. You might say, in Allmuseri, all is *A*. One person was A_1, the next A_2. (These are Western analogues. Don't make too much of them)" (97).

The idea of using individual names as variations of an Absolute is foreign to most conventional Western language systems. Johnson reinforces this oddity by emphasizing that Western language cannot accurately present these concepts to the reader. With even this small detail, Johnson reconsiders both the limitations and the possibilities of language as a shaper of experience. Noting the presence of a linguistic system that English cannot explain, Andrew reinforces the idea of limitations in the language he shares with his implied reader. Similarly, as Johnson posits a language without modes of articulating either personal distinction or possession, he challenges his audience to consider how these structures in Western language shape their relationship to the environment.

This statement only hints at Johnson's innovations in *Middle Passage,* where he explains the sounds of the Allmuseri's spoken language and expands upon his earlier statements about their written language. He describes their speech as "a melic way of breathing deep from the diaphragm that dovetailed articles into nouns, nouns into verbs" (77). In this pattern of speech, one does not even find separation between the words themselves. Johnson then notes, "nouns or static substances hardly existed in their vocabulary at all"; in addition, "each verb was different depending upon the nature of the verb acted upon" (77). These details show that nothing can be named or "fixed" in Allmuseri speech; everything the tribe knows they describe in terms of its function in a given instance.

In the Allmuseri tongue, Johnson illustrates how language can expand, instead of restrict, meaning. One sees the roots of such a language in Yoruba culture, where the tribes' myths emphasize indeterminacy (Gates 26). Johnson takes this idea to an extreme, however, and creates a language that he cannot present directly to his audience. One wonders, then, how effective the metaphor is as a means of conveying his aesthetic. Is recognizing the unknowability of an idea sufficiently instructive? Perhaps this detail speaks to a larger concern with the Allmuseri, which I will address below: the issue of excessive detachment or abstraction. At any rate, it suggests the tension between ideal and application that shapes Johnson's artistic program.

He addresses another important point in chapter 3 of *Being and Race,* "Being and Form." The learning and performance of traditional Asian martial arts, which Johnson has studied since 1967, provides a vehicle for his considering the function of form in philosophical black fiction. Learning a martial art involves three significant phases. In the first, practitioners select an art (in Johnson's case Chinese *choy li fut kung fu*) and intensively study the movements that the *sifu,* or master, teaches. The purpose is to internalize how previous students have traditionally done things. In the second stage, the new practitioners try to exactly replicate the lessons seen in order to understand and participate in the tradition. A student who has learned the master's movements and can copy them successfully is, in Johnson's words, "honoring the form" (47). In the third and most important stage, practitioners adapt the moves to their particular strengths and needs. A student six inches taller than the sifu needs a somewhat different movement than the teacher does to shift an opponent's weight for a throw. In modifying the steps of the exercise to fit personal physical demands, the student individualizes the art. As the students merge thousands of years of practice with their experiences, they renew both their understanding of the form and the form itself.

Johnson translates this description of martial arts training directly to the stages of learning to write. In developing as an author, he says, one studies other writers' work intensively, copies certain forms in an attempt to perfect the craft, and then personalizes the forms by adding the unique touches that make the form distinctive to each successful practitioner. Invoking Northrop Frye's *The Educated Imagination* (1964), Johnson reminds the reader that writers create their own personal styles by imitating those works that they first experience as readers. He goes on to say that all plots in contemporary writing arise from a wealth of common experience, and he emphasizes looking backward to these earlier sources for inspiration. These older sources are more powerful, in his opinion, because "meaning *accumulates* in the form, infuses these fictions with dignity, affirmation, and a timeless sense of value" ("Phenomenology of *On Moral Fiction*" 147–49).

For Johnson, much twentieth-century black fiction does not sufficiently participate in the stages of this process. He criticizes African American writers for not studying the moves of older artists and for relying on a limited array of forms that emphasize the heritage of victimization that he sees as fatal to innovation. Instead, Johnson calls on black writers to challenge "current literary practice by reaching back to an earlier age of master artists or by forging entirely new techniques" for creating new fiction that revises preconceptions about blackness and black experience (*Being* 57).

Although the martial arts analogy and the idea of honoring the form appeal at first glance, it seems that Johnson reinstitutes a binary opposition even as he works to break down all such divisions. The notion that black writers must look to the past, with that term defined as being beyond the scope of forms African American writers do use (such as the slave narrative or the protest novel), affirms the standards of literary value that the Black Aestheticians rejected. Similarly, the notion of timelessness evokes the ongoing debate over canonicity and the definition of the so-called great books tradition. At bottom, both arguments turn on a hierarchical vision of literary merit that privileges "white" texts. One wonders to what extent an author can create "significant new perceptions" about blackness when operating from this model. To be fair, Johnson *does* achieve new perceptions in his own work. Accomplishing that, however, demands that he modify this most extreme version of his aesthetic. Although he claims this absolute standard, it is in fact his signifying amalgamation of traditions, the fusion of black and white texts, that opens up new views of black being and black art.

The other irony in this passage concerns his use of the martial arts as a metaphor for synthesizing traditions. His analogy works with regard to the individual practitioner, but the foundation concept contradicts his main point. Although now widely enjoyed and pursued by a broad spectrum of individuals, traditional martial arts practice was for centuries restricted on the basis of ethnicity, and telling the secrets of the art to an Other was expressly forbidden. At the heart of this tradition is an entrenched sense of racialized identity; even with the opening of *dojos* and *kwoons* to westerners in the past few decades, a hierarchy of culture persists. On some level, the choice of the martial arts as a metaphor for creating a transformative, intersubjective experience seems contradictory. Of course, one could argue that perfect consistency is too much to hope for. Nevertheless, these issues suggest how difficult transcending questions of racialism must be and point once again toward the impending shift in Johnson's values. By the time of *Middle Passage* and *Dreamer,* the issue of transcendence will be replaced by a growing desire to confront and undermine racialist ideology.

• • •

In the second part of *Being and Race,* Johnson applies the artistic principles in "First Philosophy" to recent African American literature, dividing the authors by gender. In a move that echoes Merleau-Ponty's "Metaphysics and the Novel," the chapter entitled "The Men" begins by asserting what makes writers great: "Our most interesting writers . . . consciously formulate . . . an esthetic, a project, or ensemble of artistic and cultural problems common to us all that they hope to address, then provisionally to answer in their work." Johnson goes on to note that "such a project requires, in some cases, that they transform or personalize the expressive instrument—language—to suit their purposes, and sometimes completely re-envision the enterprise of fiction by breaking with convention, challenging current literary practice by reaching back to an earlier age of master artists or by forging entirely new techniques" (57). Significantly, this definition (which embodies all the principles he articulates in "First Philosophy") describes Johnson's own approach to his craft. By establishing his own enterprise as the standard of evaluation, Johnson complicates assessment here; for what are we to make of the tension between this call for a broad perspective, a literature that contains a sweeping richness of meaning, and the assertion of the author's view as most valid? Perhaps this points to a certain creative ideology on Johnson's part, an effort to get the reader to embrace intersubjectivity or universalism over separatism. Whether or not his plan is so overt, Johnson's self-professed discomfort with separatist fiction affects his ability to critique his peers, as do his reservations about accentuating the negative in portrayals of black life.

This latter point is, in fact, the principal objection he offers to each of the authors he addresses. He praises his male peers for innovations in form and content, citing David Bradley's reimagining of history, Samuel Delany's play with language, and Clarence Major's and Ishmael Reed's experiments with form as examples of what is right in contemporary black letters. In every case, though, he returns to the same fundamental objection: all of this literature is too much grounded in a shared sense of oppression, too fixed on the victimization blacks have experienced at whites' hands. Such a vision, he says, automatically limits the possibilities for any completely realized portrayal of black life. In his view, even the writers who try to overcome this separatist perspective fail to escape its boundaries. He emphasizes this point with a strong critique of black cultural nationalism, a thorough assessment of John A. Williams, and a reference to James Baldwin. With these particular examples, he distances himself from the influences of his apprentice period, apparently preparing the way for his own ascension to the heights his description of "interesting writers" promises.

And yet, even in this self-assertive act, one finds elements of what holds him to the position he has just disavowed. In his praise of Williams as "a hero to apprentice writers desperately searching for strong models of black manhood," Johnson remarks, "it is not easy to be black *and* a man *and* a writer in a culture that emasculates black men and places before its authors of color so many restrictions." This statement synthesizes Johnson's past and present, voicing both what Williams meant to his early development and his outrage over the obstacles he faces as an author working in a "racial world [that] is still a Divided Landscape" (85). Such a claim aligns him with the view of black suffering that he has so pointedly rejected in his peers' work. Although this is a significant issue, in all fairness I must note that this is not merely Johnson's challenge. Rather, it is the foundation of the antirace race man or woman dilemma that Posnock describes. Like his predecessors in that tradition, Johnson wants a broader definition of black being *and* an improvement of actual conditions. Here the specific focus of the melioristic impulse is opportunities for black artists. That concern also informs his analysis of the women writers, although with somewhat different results that illuminate further complications of Johnson's ideas.

As in his reading of the men, Johnson castigates black women writers for their inability to transcend a black cultural nationalist view of racial identity. He once again praises individual writers for their successes, citing Gloria Naylor's amalgamation of genres and effective evocation of a fictional landscape in *The Women of Brewster Place* (1982), Toni Morrison's "technical prose mastery" (101), and Alice Walker's experimentation with form in *The Color Purple* (1982). All of these compliments come, however, in the context of complaints about an overall narrowness in these authors' works. As he pointedly puts it, black women's literature is "more at the stage of criticism of social crimes than of presenting a coherent, consistent, complete 'identity' for black women, one that distinguishes its essential elements from Cultural Nationalism or Negritude." He further argues that the introduction of gender into the creative equation "*triples* the number of philosophical and political dilemmas to be resolved in pursuit of selfhood" (117). In his view, one of the worst consequences of this increased pressure is a failure by black women writers to portray African American males as anything other than bestial.

His asserting this point aligns him with a group of writers and critics whose attitudes are perhaps best represented by Stanley Crouch. In a column entitled "Aunt Jemima Don't Like Uncle Ben," Crouch decries "black female writers who pay lip service to the women's movement while supplying us with new stereotypes of black men and women." Positing that white publishers are exacting vengeance for the "anti-white, anti-Semitic and violent tendencies of black nationalism," he claims that the "celebrations of the militant mediocrity and self-pity of Ntozake Shange and the horror stories of Gayle [*sic*] Jones, in which maddened black women bite off the penises of their black brutalizers, are part of that backlash" (29). Johnson's critique of these same authors is subtler, but backhandedness pervades the praise he offers in this section. For instance, in the guise of defending the intellectual weight of black women's writing, he suggests that critics must not use a double standard of evaluation that is tougher on white male writers than on minority authors. Such a move, he says, undermines the integrity of both the art and the assessment.

This comment raises a fairly explicit objection to the praise that black women writers have gotten at the expense of black male authors. Johnson bears this attitude out in the introduction to the 1995 Plume edition of *Oxherding Tale,* where he comments that "the 1980s began as a decade when the work of black male writers was systematically downplayed. . . . For example, *Oxherding Tale* appeared the same year as Alice Walker's *The Color Purple.* I leave it to readers to decide which book inhabits most confidently the space where fiction and philosophy meet" (Introduction xviii). For the record, I share Johnson's reservations about the artistic merits of Walker's third novel. The difficulty with his critique, though, is that it privileges engagement with philosophy as the standard for evaluating contemporary African American literature. At no point does Walker suggest that this is her objective in *The Color Purple;* how reasonable is it to condemn her work for failing to meet that standard? And the specific problem with Johnson's reading of Walker is one of the difficulties with his entire assessment of the black women's tradition. Another complication concerns his reestablishment of another binary opposition; *Being and Race* effectively equates artistic ambition and accomplishment with gender, which counters the basic claims of Johnson's aesthetic.

Of course, one cannot assign accountability for this complication solely to Johnson. Gender conflict within the African American authorial community is pervasive, and it would be unrealistic to expect him entirely to escape or overcome the struggle. The position of black women writers between race and gender camps in the identity wars of recent decades undeniably generates extra pressures on them that neither black men nor white women can fully grasp. And, certainly, there is a strain of black women's fiction, especially in the 1970s and early 1980s, that portrays black men's brutality toward black women. But these circumstances do not change the fact that Johnson's critique of this school of writing complicates his own aesthetic position. Full achievement of a rounded image of black life demands the inclusion of Walker's vision, regardless of the discomfort it causes African American males. To do anything else would be to stop short of the ideal that Johnson promotes.

Being and Race concludes with a reassertion of the limits of black cultural nationalism and a lament over the state of African American writing in the post–Black Arts Movement era. Even as Johnson decries the movement for its failure to produce good art, he recounts the social evils perpetrated against the black community that gave rise to it. In the final assessment, he says, "the primary thrust of Cultural Nationalism is the reaffirmation of the hope of black men and women . . . that they can lead lives of deeper creativity and spirituality" (120). The tension between aspiration and actuality here is the source of both his fascination and his discomfort with the movement. After all, deeper creativity and spirituality are among his own goals. But at this juncture in his career, he privileges artistry over activism, which moves him firmly away, for the moment at least, from the idea of racial art. Instead, he holds out hope for "a fiction by Americans who happen to be black, feel at ease both in their ethnicity and their Yankeeness, and find it the most natural thing, as Merleau-Ponty was fond of saying, to go about 'singing the world'" (123). This statement, which directly denies the power of the double-consciousness model of existence, is of the sort that fuels questions about whether or not Johnson is "black enough" to participate in the ongoing struggle over racial identity.

Significantly, though, this is not the endpoint of his aesthetic development. In 1993, he revised and republished "*The Primevil Mitosis,*" titling the new version simply "A Phenomenology of the Black Body." With only a few minor variations, which have to do mostly with the placement of certain paragraphs, he reproduces the original argument. Then, strikingly, he adds a section called "Postscript, 1993." Reflecting on the process of composing the original, he notes that black males in the 1990s face the same pressures that he described in the mid-1970s. Listing violations of black male selfhood that range from the portrayal of Willie Horton to the savage beating of Rodney King, from the public examination of Clarence Thomas's sexual behavior to the overtly hostile, nihilistic posturing of gangsta rap, he laments the difficulties black men face in defining themselves beyond the parameters of the beast-image. Then, using Spike Lee's cinematic portrayal as his evidence, he suggests how a full representation of the many facets of Malcolm X's experience offers black men (and the rest of the world) insight into who they *can* be. He closes with a litany of names of currently prominent black males, including Colin Powell, Seattle mayor Norm Rice, Arthur Ashe, and the astronaut Ron McNair. This list functions much as his collection of essays, *Black Men Speaking* (1997), will: it serves to "expand and qualify our experience of black men" (121). This is *not* the statement of a writer who "happens to be black"; rather, these are the words of an African American writer concerned with correcting the misconceptions about and the social injustices enacted upon his race. He shifts, in other words, from the studied neutrality of *Being and Race* to a position encompassing both art and activism. The call in the postscript is for a change in conditions, not only in perceptions, and his subsequent writing, especially *Dreamer,* reflects this dual desire.

I find the evolution of Johnson's aesthetic fascinating, as it reflects the conflicts and currents of twentieth-century African American intellectual life. Taken on its own, his writing about art provides insight into how and why black writers address the social and creative concerns that shape their experiences. As he is not primarily a critic, however, we must not rest with this level of assessment. What remains is to test these principles against the author's novels and stories, which offer the best illustrations of his developing artistry and most clearly illuminate the challenges he faces in pursuing his ideal.

3 Philosophy and Folklore in *Faith and the Good Thing*

Faith and the Good Thing (1974) recounts an individual's struggle to overcome a narrow, racialized vision of identity through her pursuit of a universal good. The specific medium for Johnson's exploration of these notions is African American folklore; he tells the story as a folktale and incorporates elements of the oral tradition into the narrative. This choice of form places him in a lineage of African American writers that includes Charles W. Chesnutt, Jean Toomer, Langston Hughes, Ralph Ellison, John Oliver Killens, and Toni Morrison. It also illustrates some of the complexities of his early position on questions of racialism and selfhood.

The folktale covers a broad range of functions, from entertainment to education, and provides etiologic explanations, applied illustrations of appropriate and inappropriate behavior for intra- and extra-group interactions, and a sense of history. For oppressed groups, the folktale also presents heroes who subvert the larger society's domination; one sees an example in the anthropomorphized animal stories of Br'er Rabbit and Br'er Fox made famous in the late nineteenth century by the white writer Joel Chandler Harris. In the African American stories Harris drew on, Br'er Rabbit, the physically weaker but smarter animal, uses his intelligence to conquer stronger adversaries such as Br'er Fox; he is a "trickster," using deception to gain ascendancy, who represents a culture transcending destructive forces. This tricksterism becomes a core in-group response to oppression, as Johnson notes in *"The Primevil Mitosis."* As Ralph Ellison notes in his essay "Change the Joke and Slip the Yoke" (1958), the trickster works from within the system, employing the dominant society's preconceptions about the trickster's minority group to subvert established power relationships and to redefine itself on its own terms. Still, as liberating as this model promises to be, it turns on and reasserts a certain type of bondage to ideas about otherness.

Although Johnson subsequently claims that folktales "are unquestionably universal. They are timeless. They are, one might say, our human inheritance," the fact remains that even when the intent is to universalize experience, considering a group's traditions emphasizes to some extent what makes that group unique, or Othered ("On the Nature" xiii). For instance, Zora Neale Hurston explains what makes black culture distinct from white culture in "High John de Conqueror," an essay describing a mythic figure who came with the blacks from Africa and supported them through their sufferings in America, teaching them a number of tricks to survive bondage. Even as she offers white America the chance to "share" High John de Conqueror, she explains what makes him uniquely and completely black, thereby ensuring all efforts at sharing him will fail.

In the mode of universalist predecessors like Du Bois, Toomer, Ellison, and Hurston, Johnson addresses this conflict by fusing folkloric elements with allusions to other texts. His range of signifying references comprises fiction by Du Bois, Hurston, and Theodore Dreiser as well as a specific philosophical reference point: Maurice Merleau-Ponty's essay "Faith and Good Faith," which explores the conflict between an individual's need for something to believe in and the value of resisting fixed, limiting definitions of identity. Within the framework of this diverse amalgamation, Johnson hopes to articulate a new vision of black literary and personal identity. The former effort proves successful, as he performs significant formal variations on the tradition. With regard to the latter question, his results are somewhat mixed. Although Faith Cross achieves individual liberation, the resolution to her personal search raises significant questions about the applicability of her response to the pressing social concerns that her story presents.

• • •

As the novel opens, Faith Cross's mother, Lavidia, is dying "her second death," a reference to the fact that her heart had stopped briefly once before (1). Faith's father, Big Todd, who populates her childhood with magical figures from the folk tradition, was lynched years before for resisting two white strangers bent on examining his genitalia. Therefore, Lavidia's passing on Faith's eighteenth birthday leaves her alone in the world. With her dying breath, Lavidia urges her daughter, "'girl, get yourself a good thing'" (4), advice the confused young woman discusses with Reverend Brown, her mother's preacher. Brown insists the good thing is her Christian salvation, which he ties to a false conversion experience Faith had shortly after Big Todd's death. Rejecting that assessment, Faith visits the Swamp Woman, Hatten County's revered hoodoo worker, a "werewitch" with mythic powers. Based on the Swamp Woman's story of Kujichagulia's and Imani's quest for the Good Thing and the signs the werewitch reads in a pile of hog intestines, Faith goes to Chicago seeking her ideal.

Arriving there, Faith encounters Richard Barrett, an apparently mad philosopher who robs her; her confusion drives her into the arms of a "rescuer," Arnold Tippis, a desperate, broken man who thinks that Faith is a prostitute. He rapes her and leaves twenty dollars on her pillow. Believing herself now branded a "whore," Faith sells her body and Big Todd's folk stories to survive. Her luck and her convictions begin to change when Barrett reappears and gives her back her money and the focus she has lost. Like Faith, Barrett seeks the Good Thing; he, however, has some insight that Faith lacks at this point. Spinning the tale of his life, he inspires her to resume the quest. Unfortunately, Faith stumbles onto another destructive path when she marries a journalist, Isaac Maxwell. An overbearing boor who spouts endless aphorisms about Will Power but who sees himself as a racial victim, Maxwell first smothers Faith and then emotionally abuses her. When he learns about her past, he forces her back into prostitution as a means of advancing his career. She remains in this nightmare until Alpha Omega Holmes, the childhood sweetheart she has idealized as the "perfect love," reappears.

When Faith first visits his squalid apartment, she sees his portrait of the Swamp Woman, which symbolizes everything she believes Holmes can give her. Reawakening her desire to live and impregnating her as well, Alpha reconnects Faith to her Hatten County roots. Unfortunately, Holmes's rigid conception of his artistry and his inability to make room for Faith and a child in his life destroys their relationship. He abandons Faith to Maxwell, who beats and rejects her when she tries to convince him that he is the child's father. With nowhere else to go, Faith returns to her old rooming house to have her baby. She bears her girl child on a cold, snowy day; the weather knocks the power out. Her landlady, who helps with the birth, inadvertently knocks over the candle by the bed, and the new baby perishes in the resulting blaze. Faith is badly burned and symbolically purified, a cleansing further figured in her rejection of Tippis and Maxwell, who both appear at the hospital and offer to help her. Instead, she returns to Hatten County and has one final interview with the Swamp Woman, who reveals that she is Imani. From the werewitch's story and from her speech about conjuring as one means of achieving her goal, Faith learns that the Good Thing is process rather than product, the quest itself instead of the object quested for. She and the Swamp Woman agree to try each other's path to get new experience; in the final scene they exchange skins and Faith/Swamp Woman awaits two young children coming through the bog to visit her.

Throughout Faith's journey, she assumes many roles and must resist many definitions, ultimately choosing to make her own way in the world. Her indomitable spirit and the value she finds in consciousness transformation are rooted in the particular philosophical substructure Johnson creates for the story, and her process of development in many ways mirrors the steps of phenomenological "being in the world." As Faith strips away the experiential limitations that keep her from the Good Thing, she learns to see the world more completely. Equipped with this new vision, she achieves a liberation that eludes her peers, each of whom seeks mental freedom but falls short of true enlightenment because of a particular obsession or fixation. Their collective blindness illustrates the novel's other major philosophical premise, which Johnson derives from Merleau-Ponty.

"Faith and Good Faith" plays off Søren Kierkegaard's ideal of faith as "an irrevocable commitment to someone or something which so defines the self that to deny this commitment is to destroy the self and the world" (xxvi). Merleau-Ponty agrees that faith involves commitment but rejects the idea that one can fix devotion on another person or thing; rather, he argues, one should eternally re-form oneself by incorporating the lessons one receives from personal experiences. This re-creation of the self necessitates a certain flexibility regarding perception of anything external; he calls this "good faith" and argues that "commitment . . . consists of a higher awareness which enables [a person] to determine the moment when it is reasonable to take things on trust and the moment when questioning is in order, to combine faith and good faith within himself" (179). Throughout her journey, Faith encounters individuals damaged by the objects or ideals that they use to define themselves: Reverend Brown adheres to conventional religious doctrine, Doctor Lynch to empirical science, Richard Barrett to abstract philosophy, and Alpha Omega Holmes to a romantic conception of art. Faith experiments unsuccessfully with each belief system. When the last bad-faith object fails her, she returns to the Swamp Woman, who combines elements of all these separate paths. This fusion of sources enables the werewitch, and Faith after her, to build a more flexible worldview that leads to the "higher awareness" of Merleau-Pontian "good faith."

Faith's existence between various identity systems begins in her childhood home. Her parents live in dire poverty as sharecroppers at the whim of their landlord, a state of affairs representative of many black families' lives in the rural South throughout much of the twentieth century. Playing out a pattern common in much contemporary African American literature, Lavidia blames

Todd for his inability to ease their suffering, and he resents her repeated reminders of his inadequacy, which only reinforce his personal sense of failure. Unfortunately, as an exacerbation of their difficulties, Big Todd and Lavidia adopt conflicting coping mechanisms that make their marriage a continuous act of bad faith. Big Todd lives by the folkways of his rural black community, which afford him the illusion of personal power; Lavidia chooses organized belief systems, religion and science, to make sense of the world she sees herself trapped in. Torn between Lavidia and Todd's worldviews and needing nurturance from both her parents, Faith must assemble her own hybrid belief system.

As a child, she finds her father's worldview most appealing. Big Todd is an entertaining storyteller and a dreamer who offers explanations of an entirely unreasonable world. He also modifies the tradition to make himself a place in the black folk pantheon, thereby giving himself and his daughter a sense of security. Whenever he recounts his own exploits for Faith, he represents himself as the unbeatable, irresistible "bad man" of the African American folk tradition. The bad man plays a prominent role in black folklore from the late nineteenth century onward and appears in modified form in contemporary culture, particularly in the aggressive posturing of the gangsta rap tradition. In Roger D. Abrahams's view, this figure "commits acts against taboos and mores in full knowledge of what he is doing. In fact he glories in this knowledge of revolt. . . . As a social entity he is rebelling against white men's laws. As a male he is revolting against woman's potential domination. As a poor man he is reacting against his perpetual poverty. He copes in a contentious world" (65–66).

The root of the bad man's self-conception is empowerment at the expense of whites. Like the trickster, he is symbolically important for African American culture. He focuses rebellion on a particular object and embodies the hope that one can successfully resist oppression overtly and covertly. One can see why such figures would appeal to Big Todd. Unfortunately, because he inhabits the novel's realm of the actual and not the fantastic, he cannot live as these mythic men do. Where they are sexual powerhouses, he kneels by his bed, "all naked and hairless like a salamander, pleading with Lavidia, who pretended, and rather poorly, to be asleep or sick" (43). Where they frighten whites into giving them whatever they want, Cross screams ineffectually against the white men who lynch him for refusing to drop his pants. Superior neither as lover or fighter, Big Todd only dreams of being a bad man himself, a futile wish in a world circumscribed by his deep sense of inadequacy.

The disconnect between Big Todd's ideal and actual behavior illustrates the challenge to any effort to escape racialism. While his illusions momentarily free him from pain, they cannot destroy the oppressive racism that is his reality. In phenomenological terms, his black body determines how the world of experience gives itself to him. Big Todd believes himself to be a victim, which causes him to retreat from the world into his fantasy realm of talking pots and pans and superhuman exploits. Significantly, though, he *is* a victim, as the economic and social conditions of his life amply prove. The awareness of that oppression, which comes crashing onto Faith along with the weight of Tippis's body, includes historically accurate scenes of her father's humiliation, reminders of an era when restrooms were segregated and African Americans had to buy clothes without trying them on. It also includes a graphic account of the horrors of the Middle Passage. The pain associated with this "history of the race" informs Johnson's conclusions, as he ultimately suggests that Faith must avoid that trap to escape isolation (195).

Big Todd's approach to this dilemma is hardly ideal; his sense of suffering makes not only his but also his family's existence utterly miserable. Nevertheless, the idea that avoiding the trap of history is a better response seems disingenuous in this context. In her position as solitary conjure woman at the novel's end, Faith *represents* a key positive piece of the race's history. The novel also stingingly revisits the negatives of black history. Not only does Johnson trace that history back to the slave trade, he also critiques the economic and social inequities of contemporary life in the picture of Faith's life on Chicago's South Side. The reminder of what African Americans must escape forms a pervasive undertone in the novel; as a result, this idea of seeing black life differently and thereby transcending isolation seems problematic. The tensions between these positions anticipate the argument Johnson will make more explicitly in *"The Primevil Mitosis."*

With her father dead, Faith must depend entirely on the mercy of her more practical mother, whose faith, although bad, is more complex than Todd's. Disgusted with her husband's ineffectual folkloristic responses to injustice, Lavidia accepts the corrupted religious teachings of Reverend Brown and the nihilistic empiricism of Dr. Leon Lynch. Still angry at her husband, she attacks Alpha Omega Holmes, Faith's boyfriend, who reminds them both of Big Todd. She casts her protection of Faith in terms of her conversion, telling Holmes that Faith is "married to God" and asking him, "'Are you God?'" (15). With these actions, Lavidia unwittingly cuts the connection between Faith and her own religious faith. She compounds her mistake by telling Faith that she had paid Holmes to court her because Faith is too ugly and worthless to ever get a man on her own.

Lavidia's spitefulness, which indicates a deep sense of inadequacy mirroring Big Todd's internal turmoil, grows from her own great need for her daughter's love. Afraid of how empty her life would be if Faith left her to marry, Lavidia deliberately destroys all chances of her daughter's happiness. One source of her bad behavior is Doctor Lynch's terrifying theory of existence. When Lavidia asks the pompous rationalist about her real condition, he identifies dying as the purpose of living and insists that the exchange of oxygen and carbon dioxide is the most important life process. Interpreting the doctor's theory as a dictation of a finite number of breaths allotted her, Lavidia gives up everything important and spends her remaining life frantically counting breaths left, dying the second time when she believes she has reached her allotted number.

Given the harm Lavidia does her daughter, her deathbed advice is all the more enigmatic. What can a woman counting her breaths toward death mean by "a good thing" (4)? Although one might argue that Lavidia's conception of a good thing involves Faith's catching a man who can offer her security and companionship, I believe that Lavidia's marital experiences exclude men from her definition. Furthermore, Faith's immediate transformation of her mother's "good thing" into "the Good Thing" indicates that she seeks not a male partner but rather the greatest good. Her change to Lavidia's charge is all the more striking in that she stumbles forward with it in Chicago through a series of bad relationships with four men, each of whom tries to inflict his bad faith on Faith. Johnson further emphasizes their shortcomings by showing the men in patterns of binary opposition, thereby demonstrating the "either/or" nature of bad-faith living and illustrating the inefficacy of such rigid worldviews.

These binaries also represent another of Johnson's fundamental concerns: dualism, which he sees as the heart of all conflict. So long as one inhabits the world of either/or, one cannot avoid the barriers that inhibit complete, effective seeing. In each of Johnson's novels, characters find individual relief from racial conflict by rejecting dualism for a unified vision that embraces both sides of every dichotomy. To achieve this transcendence, Faith must reconcile the various divisive forces that threaten her. She encounters the first pair of binarily opposed males, Brown and Lynch, before leaving Georgia.

Ironically, the minister's religion generates his bad faith. Johnson's expression of this tension aligns him with a group of twentieth-century African American writers, including Hurston, Morrison, and Reed, who object to the way that Christianity limits modes of black being, especially with regard to the tension between the church and hoodoo. Johnson recognizes this dilemma; one can also read some reservations about the church's impact on the black community in his noting that Faith imagines herself and her ancestors being "tossed into the belly of *The Trinity*" for the Middle Passage (66). Still, in the main he resists reducing the conflict to a simple binary, preferring instead to leave himself room for a more complex critique of religious institutions.

Brown relies on stock phrases of Christian ethics in every crisis. When Faith asks him what her mother meant, he reminds her that Jesus is the good thing she already has. He expects this will sufficiently comfort her, not recognizing that Faith has fallen away from her conversion experience at a tent revival led by the "great-spirit man," Alexander Magnus (8). In the spirit of Jonathan Edwards's "Sinners in the Hands of an Angry God," Magnus evoked the image of a spider dangling over a candle to illustrate the precariousness of the congregation's situation and painted a terrifying picture of hell's torments. His nightmarish vision strongly parallels Lynch's creation story, especially since Magnus argued also that physical life is a process of moving toward death. His bleak outlook and dire threats of divine retribution show the flaws in his perspective and affirm the rightness of Faith's repudiating such a forced conversion. That Brown cannot see this only emphasizes the narrowness of his vision. When he realizes that appealing to Faith's memory is ineffectual, he suggests that the question is not sin and salvation but having something to believe in that will order the chaos of the universe. For him, religion is the only sensible ordering principle. When Faith suggests alternatives, reaching again to the folklore she associates with her father and mentioning the Swamp Woman, Brown responds dogmatically. His hostility toward the werewitch, and the fact that she torments him from afar with a voodoo doll, further illustrates Johnson's reservations about Brown's position and his celebration of the possibilities inherent in the conjuration process.

The werewitch embodies many important concepts of Johnson's aesthetic. When Faith visits her, expecting a comprehensible answer to her question about the Good Thing, she finds a woman steeped in classical philosophy, who celebrates experience as the means of gaining enlightenment, who knows that things must not be taken at face value, and who understands learning and life as processes. This amalgamation of insights, coupled with her recognition that one must continually reinvent oneself, makes her the ultimate example of phenomenological good faith. Although she cannot explain all of this to Faith, because experience is the only way to understanding, she plants the seeds of Faith's eventual enlightenment.

The Swamp Woman acts out her good faith in performing her magic. She specializes in altering people's lives, responding to the specific requests of many Hatten County residents, all of whom have a narrow view of what they want from the werewitch. In every case she adds her own twists to their dreams as she grants their wishes. Old plantation masters seeking youth unexpectedly trade bodies with young slaves and suffer the consequences of prior cruelty; men seeking love potions receive powerful charms designed for women and must face pursuit by younger men. Delivering a technically accurate but spiritually skewed version of each request, the Swamp Woman reminds the supplicants that they must see the world more completely to guard against the kinds of suffering she visits on them.

When the werewitch realizes that Faith wants a deeper satisfaction, she restricts her torment to some mild teasing designed to push her visitor toward enlightenment. By way of explanation, she offers Faith a riddle about the Good Thing that reflects all the experiences to come in the course of her quest: "'it must be the right functioning of an organism . . . or gettin' in the right relationship with the Lord (or Lords, or y'self, dependin' upon your persuasion), or followin' the Hedonistic Calculus in all matters of equally appearing desires . . . or maybe avoidin' Bad Faith. . . . Take your pick, sweetheart'" (24). One can see each of the Swamp Woman's options figured somehow in at least one of the relationships Faith establishes with the novel's bad-faith people. Lynch emphasizes the right functioning of organisms, Brown talks about Faith's relationship to the Lord, and Arnold Tippis lives by the Hedonistic Calculus. The one thing Faith's other would-be teachers cannot do is avoid bad faith. That is the lesson the Swamp Woman knows Faith must learn, even as she knows the young woman is not yet ready for it.

The werewitch's good-faith conjure process starkly contrasts with Big Todd's bad-faith folk living. Although both are immersed in the African American oral tradition, she views it somewhat differently than he does. The collection of artifacts in her hut includes "a rotten ferryboat oar from the Styx," "Wood . . . from the cross at Calvary, [a] philosopher's stone . . . speckled philosopher's eggs [and] imaguncula—clay, wax, and wooden figures . . . used for divination" (26–27). In the mix of the Swamp Woman's media, one finds fragments of diverse philosophies and pursuits that admit many definitions of the Good Thing. Significantly, Big Todd's folklore also demonstrates a diverse range of influences. As the classicist Frederick T. Griffiths notes, "Big Todd cites the Aristophanes myth of anthropogony from the *Symposium*" in his tale of gender difference and what makes bad marriages (letter, 22 Jan. 1995). Big Todd, however, only wants to make sense of the frustrating realities of his life. Bound by the preconceptions of his racial victim position, he misses a crucial means of healing the divided consciousness that tortures him. In the end, Faith's ability to embrace the wholeness that the werewitch's model offers will save her from the forces that destroy her father.

The mix of traditions apparent in the Swamp Woman's hut also speaks to the issue of racial and cultural identity as defined in the moment of the novel's composition. As Johnson grows more engaged with the diverse philosophical and aesthetic traditions he explored as a part of his graduate work, he draws on numerous and widely varying sources. He blends these diverse elements to suggest the possibility of transcending narrow individual and group definitions of identity. One sees this clearly in the Swamp Woman, who represents the first stage of a pattern apparent in Johnson's later work: the presence of an otherworldly teacher who illustrates the process of consciousness transformation that the protagonist must undergo to achieve enlightenment.

Among the most useful elements of Faith's first encounter with the Swamp Woman is hearing the tale of the original searchers for the Good Thing, Kujichagulia and Imani. Their story provides a parable for her journey, as much of the suffering and the pattern of starts and stops in their process resembles what she will encounter. Johnson bases the lovers' story on a Buddhist parable that illustrates how desire creates division in a naturally unified universe. Describing an ideal world where the Good Thing is present and all people understand it, the Swamp Woman emphasizes a commonality of human experience that breeds tolerance. That harmonious existence shatters with Kujichagulia's birth; born to challenge everything he encounters, Kujichagulia is a scourge to the gods wishing to maintain the status quo.

Unwilling to languish in the darkness, Kujichagulia goes seeking the Good Thing. He stops only when he meets Imani, with whom he lives and raises a family. The gods believe their difficulty is resolved, but Kujichagulia's desire is only dormant. Eventually he resumes the quest, casting off his family to climb the mountain where the Good Thing is hidden and dying in its presence. Angered by the eternal child's rebelliousness, the gods punish the entire world by taking away the Good Thing and creating the sense of "bondage" that exists into the present time of the novel (30). Inspired, Faith declares that she will take up the quest. Like Kujichagulia, she is a "restless one," not content with her world as it is and bent on finding out all she can (28). Although she does not yet know it, she also has the benefit of counsel from Imani; she will learn the Swamp Woman's former identity on her return to the cabin, when she finally grasps the value of process as a manifestation of the Good Thing.

When the werewitch finishes speaking, Faith asks whether or not the story is factual. The Swamp Woman offers this striking reply: "'Before you ask if anythin's true, *first* ask y'self if it's good, and if it's beautiful! Was the story good? . . . And was it beautiful? . . . All right!'" (30–31). This statement establishes the standard for evaluating all art in *Faith* (including the novel itself, as the narrator uses almost identical language to close the story). The criteria seem inapplicable, since so much of what happens to Faith is neither good nor beautiful, at least not in conventional terms. But Johnson's stated concern is not social but aesthetic truth, an idea John Gardner articulates in *On Moral Fiction.* "True art treats ideals, affirming and clarifying the Good, the True, and the Beautiful" (133), he says, and Johnson adopts this standard to challenge complacency about art just as he challenges rigidity in all other acts of perception.

In making this claim, Gardner develops I. A. Richards's definition of "good" from his *Principles of Literary Criticism* (1926) as "not really a matter of belief or moral affirmation but rather one of satisfied expectation, tension release—in short, aesthetic pleasure" (Gardner 138). This emphasis certainly fits scenes like Alpha's response to Faith's question about whether or not their affair is acceptable and "good." Instead of reassuring her about the morality of true lovers being together, Holmes identifies a number of pleasurable things, including his story, the meal he has prepared, and sex with Faith, as "good." Gardner's redefinition of beauty further clarifies Johnson's purposes. Much of the world in *Faith* is physically ugly, even repulsive; we see broken, decrepit people, the seedy side of Chicago, and a life filled with disappointment. Drawing on Edgar Allan Poe, Gardner says, "as for Beauty, it should not be conceived only as a matter of technique . . . but as the effect of emotional honesty as well, balance as an expression of the artist's personality maturely realized, for the moment, in the work of art" (145). In these terms, the world of *Faith,* with all its physically repugnant inhabitants, is beautiful indeed.

The concept of truth presents more difficulties, given the human tendency to see truth as synonymous with facts, the concrete evidence of events forming the standard for belief in daily life. Gardner notes the inadequacy of that conception. "When talking about art we use the word *truth* in two ways: to mean that which is factually accurate or logically valid, on the one hand, and, on the other, to mean that which does not feel like lying" (142). Notably, the issue is not empiricism but emotional veracity. When Alpha tells Faith about fighting Big Todd's ghost for the right to woo her, Faith notes several inaccuracies, such as the time of Big Todd's death and the location of his grave. Nevertheless, because of the feeling Alpha's story evokes in her, Faith responds positively to what she knows is not factual. In this train of events, Johnson figures the rest of Gardner's definition of "truth." "What does not feel like lying is that which is true to the essential nobility of the writer's soul, that which expresses what is purest and best in his personality. . . . Its effect is to conjure . . . what the art receiver may have lost touch with, his own best nature, his affirmations" (142). Ultimately, then, aesthetic truth, beauty, and goodness develop from the writer's innate sense of him- or herself both as being and as artist.

Despite what one might say about the artistic beauty of Faith's world and the goodness of her enlightenment, the ugliness of her social realities and questions about the value of liberation through retreat remain. To tell the story of one who overcomes racialized self-hatred is a profoundly hopeful act. Nevertheless, even as he describes Faith's transcendence, Johnson reminds the reader of the legions who remain trapped in the suffering that plagues most of the other characters in the novel. We must also recall that Faith's quest was originally for the good of all humanity, not only for herself. On the way to Chicago, she dreams that she is the Swamp Woman, making up and pouring out a potion that "covered the world. Billions were covered with the brew. And when they managed to smear it all off, they looked like her: the Swamp Woman. . . . And all around the world people looked at each other, winked their yellow eyes evilly, and squealed in harmony: *'Hee hee!'*" (48). The vision is quite positive, as formerly divided people lose sight of external indications of difference. Ultimately, though, she remains in the Swamp, offering her insights to the relatively limited number of people who visit her. This contrasts with her claim that when she finds the Good Thing, "'everyone's bondage will end'" (30). Perhaps disavowing racial uplift is a crucial step on the path toward enlightenment; but if that is the case, why present the catalogue of social evils in such vivid detail? This apparent inconsistency points to the tensions in Johnson's artistic position that increase as his career progresses.

At this juncture, however, his professed interest in uplift concerns breaking down narrow definitions of racial identity. One also sees in this his discomfort with some of the impulses of black cultural nationalism, which is manifest in his use of Swahili for Kujichagulia's and Imani's names. "*Kujichagulia* represents self-reliance and an expression of black identity that comes from within the community, rather than from outside the cultural group," while "*Imani* represents a righteous faith in the history and future of black cultures" ("Kwanzaa" 658). These terms represent two of the seven principles of Kwanzaa, a celebration developed in 1966 by Professor Maulana Karenga that emphasizes "the connection with African culture while recognizing the unique history of African-Americans" (657). The subtext of defining a black communal identity that informs Kwanzaa points to the popular understanding of these terms as indicators of separatist ideology. Johnson takes this up in *Faith* and suggests, through the final disposition of the characters bearing these names, that perhaps black cultural nationalism is not ultimately sustainable.

Kujichagulia's self-reliance effectively causes the world's trouble in this story. His unwillingness to rest in a harmonious universe where all people benefit from the Good Thing represents racial separatism; that he destroys himself and brings suffering to the whole world through his persistent pursuit of his ideal suggests that, in the author's view, such a position is finally not viable. I do not think Johnson objects to the quest itself. Instead, it seems that his principal concern is with the aftermath. Kujichagulia's way of effecting change has a negative impact beyond his personal experience. In terms of Johnson's discomfort with black cultural nationalism, this represents the perpetuation of a sense of suffering not unlike the one that plagues Big Todd Cross, a negative view of self that does more harm than good.

Imani provides an interesting counterpoint. Her obvious devotion to Kujichagulia indicates her faith in the *history* of black cultures, as his seeking represents a necessary stage in the evolution of African American identity. It also demonstrates Johnson's sympathy with Kujichagulia's position as a starting point. Ultimately, however, Imani turns to the synthesis of traditions that defines her conjure practice, putting her hope for the future of black cultures in the notion that intersubjectivity holds more promise than separatism. For Johnson, righteous faith and phenomenological Good Faith appear to be synonymous. This is the lesson that Faith will learn through her own quest: cultural synthesis, rather than division, is her own greatest good. To achieve that wisdom, though, she must first learn the history of black culture that she will overcome, the process that her encounters in Chicago represent.

Her first teacher is Arnold Tippis, whose life story is a tale of frustrated allegiance to a folk ideal transforming into an intellectualized nightmare. His desire to emulate his banjo-playing uncle indicates an early fascination with his folk heritage; the banjo hails originally from Africa and is central to the black folk tradition. Uncle Bud has clearly found value in music, and he attempts to pass that value on to his nephew, as Big Todd has told Faith his stories. Unfortunately, like Faith, Tippis suffers the wrath of a folklore widow. His aunt obviously bears a more active resentment than Lavidia feels toward Todd, and she inflicts it on Tippis, breaking his connection to the folk tradition as she breaks his fingers. Cut off from the potential healing power of a positive view of black creativity, Tippis turns to another conception of blackness. Like Dr. Lynch, with whom he shares a tendency to rely excessively on the intellect, Tippis sees life as tension and release. When Faith counters with a drunken expostulation about the Good Thing, he dismisses her and suggests instead that she "sublimate" her wishes to a more achievable goal, something like "comfortable living" (58), which will soon enough be her substitute for the Good Thing.

Tippis's inability to achieve his desire leads him to practice an ironic form of bad faith. He changes jobs repeatedly, each time assuming the personality characteristics associated with his position. "Tippis's changes were never from within, but only catalyzed from without . . . there was no end to his transformations, to his plastic personality first servile and groveling as a porter's, then jocular and rapacious as a salesman's" (83). Although it might appear that

Tippis engages in Merleau-Ponty's process of self-reformation, his actions all spring from a negative self-concept and a victim's worldview. Where phenomenological good faith celebrates what one can be, Tippis's bad faith focuses continually on what he is not. This sense of victimization makes him a victimizer, an impulse he acts out by raping Faith. By doing so he temporarily transforms himself into a pathetic version of the "bad nigger" and briefly creates the illusion that he has somehow transcended his isolation. When he finishes violating Faith, he departs reciting a folk-style toast celebrating the sexual act, an apparent indication of his fleeting transcendence. As Johnson notes, however, "he looked like one possessed, though momentarily freed, but only briefly, only for a heartbeat." Tippis's false joviality and his parting statement that "he isn't worth a damn" (62) emphasize the depth of his sense of failure.

Worst of all, his self-destructive impulse is contagious. He casts Faith into a state of despair in which she identifies herself with the entire history of racial oppression in the United States. In this moment, she adopts the self-hating mentality that overcame Big Todd. Knowing that her father could not protect her from oppression, she recognizes for the first time in her life how ineffectual his folkways are against larger forces. She also finally understands that his death resulted from his one act of real resistance against the system, an insight that convinces her that "the past was final, irreversible" (65).

Richard Barrett's return offers Faith an opportunity to free herself from bondage. Reversing the events of their first encounter, he seeks her out to pay back her money. Over drinks in a local bar, a setting that reverses Faith's original damaging encounter with Tippis, Barrett describes his quest for the Good Thing. Like Faith, Barrett has devoted himself to seeking the greatest good; that quest has cost him his family, his position, his financial security, and his health. He makes a sincere effort to teach Faith what he has learned, hoping to help her avoid some of his mistakes. As he says, "'We all need a guiding principle . . . that . . . must first . . . exist in some absolute, unsullied, perfect form. . . . But that has problems. If it's a thing we're after, and if that thing is absolute goodness and perfection, then we'll never have it'" (91–92). Although clouded by Barrett's abstract language, this is a critical point for Faith. The philosopher's expression of the dilemma clearly echoes Merleau-Ponty's conception of the right devotional object for Good Faith, and it demonstrates why materialism cannot be the answer. Since no thing can exist in pure form and be attainable, the reasonable response is to choose an object of devotion that is not a thing.

Johnson also makes a point here about what one can gain from such an emphasis, conveying a serious lesson in an offhanded joke about Faith's response to the professor: "Faith tuned Barrett out, studying him from the great distance of objectivity, the way one reads a novel about philosophical ideas, with haste and indifference" (92). Part of Faith's problem results from her uncritical response. She sizes Barrett up too quickly and therefore cannot benefit from his wisdom. When she finally realizes that his approach is valid and hopes to search for goodness with him, it is too late. The description of her rejection and subsequent loss includes a warning about how best to approach the novel. One might well read this story "with haste and indifference," not noting the complex layers of meaning lying immediately beneath its surface.

Johnson emphasizes the transformative value of experience in describing Barrett's "Doomsday Book," which the philosopher claims is his "greatest work." Apparently a blank book, the volume actually enables Faith to conjure memories of Hatten County, images of the goodness and beauty that are her truth: "she saw her father crossing the dung-brown fields behind his farmhouse. . . . Lavidia splitting thick logs from the woodpile by the toolshed . . . Alpha Omega Holmes waving to her . . . the particular magic and music of [that] world" (94–95). What Barrett gives her, in a sense, is her ability to reimagine her past and, by extension, herself. This process requires that Faith reject despair. To see her memories, she must release the sense of victimization that cast a pall over her when Tippis raped her. Setting those blinders aside, she can once again see Big Todd as a folk hero and her mother as the woman she was before Lynch stole her will to live.

The "Doomsday Book" also illustrates another key element of Johnson's aesthetic program: the perceiver's role in creating experience. As Faith recalls the farm, she remembers when her personal purity was unquestioned; this state evokes Merleau-Ponty's "pre-reflective state" of memory, when all thought is suspended in favor of direct experience. Faith's lived experiences influence the meaning she makes on the pages of Barrett's book; similarly, one brings preconceptions and established views to reading that influence interpretation. If, like Faith, the reader can set aside limitations circumscribing the ability to see meaning on the page, then he or she can have a transformative experience with the text.

Johnson extends this approach beyond textual reference in Barrett's comment to Faith that "'people are somewhat like novels (don't make *too* much of that simile)—we operate on beginnings, middles, and ends; subjective aims deposited in ongoing history to be prehended by other subjective aims'" (91). The admonition to not "make *too* much of that simile" evokes the earlier hint about how not to read a philosophical novel, providing a warning to not miss what lies ahead; reading as described in the text might well prefigure a means of living to the fullest. At the same time, the admonition points to the dangers of living too much in the mind. This position seems somewhat ironic, given that approaching racial identity issues in philosophical terms risks the sorts of abstractions that seem problematic in Johnson's fiction. Nevertheless, his jibes at the philosopher's position indicate that even philosophy can be a bad-faith object if the devotee misuses it.

Barrett's experiences in reaching this point equip him to explain the difficulty in finding the greatest good; unfortunately, he intellectualizes suffering. He takes this inability completely to see her world to the grave and beyond. He transcends death and tries to reach her, but his mental games keep them from truly connecting. Bound in the life of the mind while on earth, Barrett becomes a "haint," returning to Faith's room and troubling her in all the ways Big Todd said the spirits would. Unlike other folk "haints," however, Barrett cannot be conjured away. Hopeful that he can save her from his fate, he constantly returns to tell Faith more about his quest. Unfortunately, his methods are still based too much in the intellect. Faith repeatedly awakes, hearing a voice saying, "'You may well be free of Barrett, but not Barrett*eity,*'" and, "'Riddle me this, if you're so smart: Will an arrow ever strike its intended target if, before it can cross that distance, one-half of that distance must be crossed first, and one half of *that,* and one-half of *that,* and one-half of *that*'—" (98). Both comments hold a piece of the key Faith seeks. She must, however, go on the search alone because she lacks the experiential knowledge that would allow her to understand Barrett's mental gymnastics; similarly, he cannot know a better way to tell her because he has no empathy for her suffering.

The idea of "Barrett*eity*" has roots in Husserl's eidetic reduction, which Faith must perform in order to live in good faith. The next step, the transcendental reduction, requires her to ascend to a level of pure experience in preparation for her shedding her skin in the final pages of the novel. Because he retains his philosopher's essence, Barrett the haint cannot explain this any more effectively than Barrett the man could. Intellectually aware of what one must do to achieve the good thing, he cannot balance the life of the mind with the necessary action. Furthermore, because Faith is not sufficiently experienced herself at this point, she cannot yet see how to take the next step that eludes him.

Similarly, she misses the point of the question of the arrow, a version, incidentally, of Zeno's Paradox. The ancient philosopher asks whether or not such an infinitely divisible conception of motion is a valid way of seeing the world. Johnson does value this model of perception, as it emphasizes process over product. Essentially, traveling, not actually hitting the target, defines the path of the arrow. In terms of Faith's journey, the point of searching for the Good Thing is the quest itself. In their last earthly meeting Barrett nearly convinces her of this, but he dies before they can begin searching together for goodness. Unfortunately, under the pressures of her environment, Faith cannot see the value of process. She settles instead for financial security and attaches herself to Isaac Maxwell, in whom Johnson presents his most stinging critique of mental rigidity.

Faith's new suitor's fixation on Will Power contradicts everything she has learned from her father and Barrett. A shy, bookish pseudointellectual with a crippling case of asthma, the pathetic young journalist unsuccessfully attempts to control the world with his will even while showing himself to be completely powerless. He lays claim to Faith much as Tippis did. Faith's response, however, is much more calculating in this instance. Ironically, for all of Maxwell's talk about the place of women and their intrinsically weak wills, Faith's manipulation feminizes him and illustrates how ineffectual his doctrine is. Maxwell cannot defend himself because he cannot see her machinations; at the heart of his theory of Will Power are a series of preconceived notions about power and gender that keep him from understanding his struggle with Faith.

Maxwell's ideology identifies dualistic conflict as the driving force in all situations. Rejecting all collective efforts, most notably those of the people interested in black power, he says that only isolated individuals can effect real change. Ironically, for all his bold talk, Maxwell sees himself essentially as a victim, someone on whom life acts rather than as someone who takes action. From this consciousness, Maxwell's noisy speech about Will Power proves no more useful than Big Todd's folktales or Tippis's toasts. Faith and Maxwell remain locked in bad-faith limbo until they encounter Arnold Tippis. Faced with the threat of his exposing her past, Faith denies Tippis, who protests violently. Maxwell, seeing an opportunity to exercise his will, steps in and savagely beats Tippis. He believes that he comes alive with this action, but his treatment of Faith proves that his violent outburst has irreparably damaged both of them.

Similarly, during the nightmarish first year of their marriage, which Johnson presents in an extended flashback, Faith and Maxwell take the increasing indignities that they suffer out on each other. Maxwell, who expects a promotion for overseeing a weekly human-interest column on a Joliet prisoner, experiences a series of depressing reversals. To make matters worse, he and Faith are in debt because he began spending his new money prematurely; characteristically, he blames these difficulties on Faith. She, in turn, recognizes that this relationship places her among the "dead living"; in response, she gains a great deal of weight and struggles against her body as if it were her enemy. In a sense it is, as she has sold it into bondage to Maxwell in return for security. Although this is not actual prostitution, Faith has a business relationship with

Maxwell, one that on many levels reflects her selling herself to survive. This imagery becomes even more significant when Faith tells Maxwell about her past. Although she hopes for his emotional support, he reacts by renaming her "whore" and that very night, at the company Christmas party, bartering her with his editors in exchange for approval of his prisoner column. Rather than resist, she begins a grim period of satisfying such demands, which Maxwell refers to as her "carrying the ball" (136), an image made all the more striking because of his initial explanation of Will Power as related to football.

Johnson demonstrates the horror of this relationship when Maxwell tells Faith to leave the party with his white boss, Lowell, who "was incredibly drunk, and [whose] pants bulged with an erection as hard as Chinese arithmetic" (137). Maxwell's greatest failing is his inability to understand the experience attached to the label he gives Faith. His actions also modify a pattern from Big Todd's and Lavidia's relationship: Big Todd feels great frustration because he cannot protect Lavidia from the advances of white men, and she hates him for his weakness. Maxwell takes this a step farther, not only submitting to such an arrangement but actually facilitating it, an indication of the depth of his personal corruption. Faith's resignation, unlike her mother's violent hatred, indicates her own psychological turmoil.

This then is the state of Faith's and Maxwell's marriage on the morning of their first anniversary, which is also the day Maxwell will bring Alpha Omega Holmes to dinner. They have a bitter argument, and she screams herself into a catatonic state, visiting the land of Diddy-Wah-Diddy and encountering Big Todd and Lavidia, who have turned into trees. Big Todd tells Faith how to make herself a maple, and she briefly casts off the terror of the previous year. The imagery of a human becoming a tree, which suggests Charles W. Chesnutt's short story "Po' Sandy" (1899), symbolizes a reattachment to one's roots and also an empowerment process that enables one to endure suffering. Most importantly, it signals the revitalization of Faith's sense of heritage and promises some hope beyond the stark outlines of her damaged life. In reconnecting to Lavidia and Big Todd, Faith stands once again, as she did with Barrett's "Doomsday Book," on the verge of escaping her grim existence. Things look even better when Maxwell brings home Holmes.

With his simple clothes, easy speech, and stock of folk tales, he appears as Maxwell's opposite. In his first appearance in the textual present (as opposed to Faith's idealizations of him), Alpha exudes true confidence; ironically, Maxwell almost rejects him for the column because of what he perceives as a lack of Will Power. His preconceived notions about strong prisoners lead him to expect Eldridge Cleaver's militancy. Holmes counters this rigid view of black prison identity with a more fluid conception of selfhood. Building on Big Todd's foundation, he has grown beyond his predecessor's use of the folk tradition, and he shares that vision with Faith when she visits his squalid apartment the next day. He expresses his transcendence of such worldly concerns as his desperate financial situation through his painting. After some discussion, Faith recognizes that Holmes's "conjurations" on canvas resemble the scenery of her "Doomsday Book," and she embraces him and his theory of art as the path back toward her Good Thing. Unfortunately, as she soon tragically realizes, his way of being in the world is as flawed as Maxwell's.

Holmes's vision of painting and selfhood relies on the artist's conception of himself as a created object: "'See, I don't call *myself* an artist . . . a *real* artist is his own canvas . . . someday . . . there won't be a dime's worth of difference between what I'm creatin' and myself . . . my life will be the finished work.'" This ideal of artistry, which promises a continual process of self-reformation, functions in Merleau-Ponty's paradigm as good faith. Significantly, Holmes identifies the Swamp Woman as the best example of his point. She "'didn't need no paints, or stone, or sheet music . . . just ideas. That's what you work on the world with, right? But the trick's in not comparin' the ideas to the world to see if they're right. She compared them to other ideas'" (159). Although Holmes knows how one might live in good faith, he cannot achieve this state himself, because he is ultimately afraid to compare ideas. Until he can make that crucial step, he cannot achieve his creative ideal.

Paternity reveals Holmes's weakness. He responds by shunning all responsibility, even though Faith's child is unquestionably also his. Pressed for a reason, Alpha cries out, "'Honey, I'm different—I can't settle down, or raise kids, or nothin' like that. I'm . . . an *artist*. . . . That means I'm going to suffer, hit means I'm going to be frustrated, and die inside, and wake up in gutters or in hotels with strange women'" (165). For all the pain of Alpha's rejecting Faith, this scene is in fact quite funny. Throughout Johnson's canon, one sees an extension of his initial career as a comic artist, as he uses humor to emphasize the need for a more flexible way of seeing. This instance perfectly illustrates the point: one sees that behind his lofty aspirations, Holmes dreams of living out the conventional starving-artist myth. In clinging to that "ideal," Alpha plummets from the height he and Faith have temporarily reached, saying, as he falls, that he lives his life for "the idea of perfection" (166). This proves that Holmes lives in bad faith; he has a chance to achieve the phenomenological enlightenment that comes from incorporating experience into self-redefinition. Were he to experience the transformative power of the child he and Faith have conceived, then he might well be able to make true art. He voluntarily stops short of that goal, showing that his mind has seized fast to one idea and left room for nothing else.

This shortcoming also heightens the symbolic significance of Holmes's name, which comprises the beginning and ending letters of the Greek alphabet, and which is commonly associated with Christian symbolism. The writer of Revelations refers to Christ as "the Alpha and the Omega, the beginning and the end, the first and the last," a statement figuring both his function as savior and the circular image so prominent in Christianity (22:13). In the novel, Holmes's decision to be an artist is his beginning; his adherence to a rigid idea of what that means is, finally, his end. Similarly, his reappearance ironically promises a new beginning for Faith, a chance to re-form herself and to live with the person she has idealized in her memory over the years since their parting. She will eventually have a new life, but not with Holmes. Rejected by him and losing her dreams of that good and beautiful life in Hatten County, she reaches the end of her path, letting him go free and then suffering Maxwell's rejection as well.

In the wake of Holmes's and Maxwell's rejection, Faith realizes that all the men she has known lack creativity because they cannot bear children. With this insight, Faith grasps the need for a sort of universal harmony that comes not through domination or manipulation but through developing natural potential and recognizing bonds between things. In bearing her child, Faith recognizes her "connection with things, that capacity to dance if the universe said so, to sing if it demanded song" (167). This realization marks her approach to enlightenment.

It also points to another potential inconsistency in Johnson's position: his apparent difficulty in extending his transformative aesthetic vision to issues of gender. Faith's association of reproduction with her quest for liberation represents in many ways a profoundly essentializing characterization of women. In *Being and Race,* Johnson notes a similar tendency in Clarence Major's *All-Night Visitors* (1969), stating that the novel presents "the primitive vision of woman as the vehicle of Being, birth, regeneration, a vision that will horrify feminists, I know, falling as it does into a mystifying of women" (61). This somewhat dismissive response to feminist concerns overlooks the significant fact that the responsibility of reproduction has arguably been at least as limiting as liberating. In the American literary canon two examples, Kate Chopin's *The Awakening* (1899) and Nella Larsen's *Quicksand* (1928), prove that point. Furthermore, this biological vision of womanhood counters the idea of seeing the world, and the people who inhabit it, differently. Given Johnson's strong resistance to any essentialist notions of race, I find this presentation of gender, which reappears in *Oxherding Tale,* confusing.

Unfortunately, the universe tests Faith's newfound sense of connections by immediately claiming her baby's life. Broken, burned, and disillusioned, she returns to the Swamp Woman hoping to find the answer to her quest before she dies. The conjure woman strips her of her last illusions, explains the value of experience to Faith, and spells out the process of self-transformation that is the Good Thing she seeks. Her words also model living in good faith. "'Ya take every path: the oracle's, teacher's, the artist's, and even the path of the common fool, and ya learn a li'l bit from each one. That's life, girlie. Ya keep right on steppin' and pickin' up the pieces until ya gets the whole thing—the Good Thing'" (188). She echoes Barrett's initial explanation of the quest and Holmes's initial explanations of artistry; more grounding in Faith's world and a more carefully examined intellectual framework temper her answer. Drawing from her experiences to explain the Good Thing, the Swamp Woman finds the greatest good that eluded the philosopher. She also helps Faith back onto the path toward her ideal.

Speaking from her perspective as a werewitch, the Swamp Woman cites conjuration as the best way to reach the Good Thing from that path. With this claim, she returns to African American folk culture and identifies this heritage with the process of self-transformation. Conjuration, by definition, involves adopting a different way of seeing; as the Swamp Woman works her spells, she liberates her vision and Faith's from conventional boundaries and engages with the world in terms defined by possibility rather than limitation. With this action she challenges Faith to consider the costs and benefits associated with the folkways she uses. By doing so, she can avoid the bad-faith pitfalls of Big Todd's limited understanding of the tradition. Now capable of creating the story instead of only repeating her father's stories, Faith finally becomes the "true Artist" Alpha describes. In this one sees that the transformative power of these experiences, including reading the text itself, allows one to mount the new path of creator. This knowledge elevates the reader to the status of artist, allows him or her to dress up in the skin of process, just as Faith has, and enables his or her own search for good faith.

• • •

Part of the reader's quest involves examining Johnson's signifying revision of works by black and white predecessors. He uses these antecedent texts to challenge preconceived notions about African American life and literature, making in the process his first significant steps toward the ideal philosophical black fiction he describes in his essays. Among the wide range of references that the novel comprises, its allusions to Du Bois are particularly interesting.

In addition to taking up the issue of double consciousness, a dilemma plaguing all of the novel's major characters, *Faith* also reflects the influence of Du Bois's first novel, *The Quest of the Silver Fleece* (1911). An indictment of post-

Reconstruction economic policy based on the story of Jason and the Argonauts, *The Quest* contains a series of interwoven, sometimes conflicting plot lines. The most important for Johnson's purposes is the story of Zora, the mystical child of a corrupt swamp witch named Elspeth. Unwilling to submit any longer to the passions of the white men who visit Elspeth's cabin, Zora hides in the swamp until she meets Bles Alwyn, a student at the local school for blacks. Motivated by love, she helps him cultivate a cotton crop on a cleared island in the swamp. After he spurns her because of her past, and after the white plantation owner who initially violated her takes the cotton, Zora leaves the swamp for the city, determined to make a new life. When that fails, she dedicates herself to finding the Way that will help her oppressed people. Transformed by her quest, she returns to the Swamp, becomes the spiritual center of the African American community, and regains Bles's love.

Zora's Way and Faith's Good Thing have much in common, as do the young women who seek these ideals. Furthermore, the description of Elspeth's horrific visage and magical powers evokes images of the Swamp Woman (although while Elspeth survives by gratifying the white men's desires, the Swamp Woman apparently lives to frustrate them). And, significantly, each young woman's quest follows a similar trajectory, moving in a circle from the country to the city before returning to the starting point. Both authors also believe that the greater good their heroines seek will benefit the community at large. The differences between the works begin to appear, however, when one considers the nature of these benefits. Faith's position in the swamp limits the good that she can do for the entire community. Zora, however, embodies collective action as she concerns herself with uplifting the southern blacks held in thrall to the economic and social demands of the sharecropping system. As such, her quest represents Du Bois's primary social agenda (Lee 392). In a move that fits Johnson's definition of ideology, Du Bois attempts in *The Quest of the Silver Fleece* to get the community to *do* something. Furthermore, this rallying cry helps perpetuate a strong sense of black identity. For Zora and for her creator, the idea of the Way must be inextricably linked to the history and the future of the race.

By contrast, Faith ultimately realizes that achieving and sustaining the Good Thing means avoiding the vision of racialized identity that threatens her sense of unity. Whereas Zora embraces her blackness and sacrifices herself for the black community's salvation, Faith assumes the role of the Swamp Woman with the understanding that she must overcome, or at least broaden, her idea of race. Her efforts promise not the economic uplift that Zora seeks but a more fundamental, intersubjective human enlightenment. This, then, is apparently the heart of Johnson's signifying revision of Du Bois: he attempts to resist the call of race politics in favor of his philosophical ideal. There are moments in the novel that suggest his ambivalence—the account of Isaac Maxwell's tribulations at work, which reflects real outrage over the difficulties black men face in the modern workplace, is one of these—but in the main, he privileges a vision of the Good Thing that does not turn on the issue of racial identity.

Or does it? Certainly Faith demonstrates her universalist impulses in her intention of telling her first visitors about "Aristotle's Illusion [and] Stackalee's great battle with Lucifer in West Hell" (196). One sees something similar in Du Bois, however, in the description of Zora's bookshelf, which includes works by Plato, Balzac, Spenser, and Tennyson (399). Zora's interest in white Western classics suggests Du Bois's belief that African Americans must not restrict themselves in their pursuit of knowledge, an idea that Johnson suggests with his description of the various sources for the werewitch's magic. Similarly, both books subvert generic classifications by emphasizing literary connections across racial lines (Lee 390). With all of this in common, and given that Johnson transforms his heroine into an archetypal symbol of African American culture, the conjure woman, might one not reasonably infer similar aims for the two authors? Could Faith's return to her Hatten County roots signal that, on some level at least, affirmation of racial identity is an important part of Johnson's program in the novel?

The relative difficulty of answering these questions points to important tensions in Johnson's work, nascent here but increasingly prominent as his aesthetic evolves. For Faith to be a conjurer committed to avoiding the "history of the race" is a tall order indeed. One might well describe her mission to transform perceptions of that racial history as a form of uplift; however, the terms might differ from Zora's at first glance. I am suggesting that perhaps, like Du Bois, Johnson is already acting out the role of the antirace race man, seeking simultaneously to materially aid the black community and to challenge the notion of race as a determinative identity structure (Posnock 5). That conflict accounts for the indeterminacy and inconsistency in *The Quest* that leads critics like Richard Kostelanetz to deem the novel an aesthetic failure (174).

In Johnson's case these tensions between an aspiration to transcend racial classifications and his real concerns for the black community demonstrate the difficulties inherent in celebrating the particulars of African American life as a pathway to the universal (Johnson, *Being and Race* 31–33; Posnock 13). His signifying on Du Bois indicates his effort to shift the balance toward universality, or at least intersubjectivity; and yet, at the same time, he affirms the efforts of his predecessor. Although Faith's swamp is at least characterized as a less racialized space, her sojourn there would be much less rich were it not for Zora's example.

In the same vein, *Faith* also bears the imprint of another Zora who recounts a quest for a different type of good thing. By evoking a transformative view of black folk heritage and leaving his heroine pondering her experiences at the end of her story, Johnson refers to Zora Neale Hurston's *Their Eyes Were Watching God* (1937). Like Faith, Hurston's heroine, Janie, progresses through a series of destructive relationships with men before finally choosing solitude and reflection as the resolution to her quest. Furthermore, for Janie as for Faith, the black folk tradition figures heavily in her development. And, in each novel, the author ultimately raises questions about the value of that folk heritage through the actions of the primary male representative of the tradition. An important difference between the works appears, though, in their ultimate resolutions. Janie's decision to return to Eatonville and retire into her house after circumstances force her to kill her husband Tea Cake in self-defense suggests that Hurston believes this flawed model is the best that the culture has to offer at the moment. Having exhausted its possibilities, Janie must choose isolation to sustain her sense of self. Johnson's revision of this paradigm demonstrates his attempt to remake the meaning of that tradition, to break African American folklife out of the bonds of Otherness and emphasize its universal aspects.

Faith's and Janie's stories follow similar patterns: both young women begin under the domination of an older maternal figure who seeks to control the heroine's future. Departing from home, each character passes into a series of relationships with men that shape her development. Both Janie and Faith become involved with three men, and in each story they pass through a similar arc of experience in the course of those relationships. Logan Killicks and Arnold Tippis, the first of the three men, perpetuate a form of oppression on Janie and Faith, respectively. Where Tippis turns Faith into a whore, Killicks makes Janie a beast of burden, the "mule of the world" (14) her grandmother had told her all black women are. That Janie becomes this mule suggests something important about her relationship with Killicks; a farmer of moderate means, he sees himself as inferior to his white counterparts and lives in the shadow of received understandings of racial identity, as Tippis does in *Faith.* Burdened with such a negative self-understanding, Killicks can only tear Janie down and encourage her to see herself negatively, just as Tippis pushes Faith toward her streetwalking life largely because of his own damaged sense of self.

Both Janie and Faith generally submit to this domination until a second, more promising figure appears and affords them an opportunity to escape. For Faith, that man is Isaac Maxwell; his counterpart in Hurston's novel is Joe Starks, who charms Janie away from Killicks with the promise of a better life. Unfortunately, like Maxwell, Joe proves unable to provide anything truly better because of his flawed consciousness and his limited, destructive self-perception, all of which he brings to bear on Janie.

Both Maxwell and Starks aspire to success defined by and typically reserved for white men; each also has particular ideas about the roles their wives will play in the quest for prominence. Just as Maxwell tries to tell Faith how to behave, Starks puts Janie on a literal and figurative pedestal when he forces her into bondage on the high stool in his store. Cut off there from the rest of the community, she begins to crumble under the weight of her husband's oppression. Finally, unable to submit any longer to his taunts and abuse, she lashes out, figuratively emasculating him and destroying his carefully crafted public image. As a result of his shame, he loses his will to live. Unable to exist except in the terms he has defined for himself, Joe Starks cannot continue after Janie's outburst destroys his fragile sense of self.

Numerous significant parallels exist between Joe Starks and Isaac Maxwell, and through these characters each author teaches readers a lesson about individual and group identity formation. The most powerful parallels occur, though, in the "savior" figures that come to liberate Faith and Janie, Alpha Omega Holmes and Tea Cake Woods. Like Holmes, Tea Cake is the classic folkloric tough, a good talker as well as a great musician. He also breaks the formerly suffocating heroine out of a loveless life and reawakens her appreciation for the folk culture that takes a central position in his identity-formation process. Furthermore, Tea Cake and Alpha are bound less by conventional morality than by a devotion to pleasure and aesthetic satisfaction. As Alpha finds joy in his painting and adopts it as his standard of goodness, Tea Cake lives for the joy his guitar playing brings. He uses that pleasure as his guiding principle, especially in the scene where he takes Janie's hidden money and stays out all night, using her cash to subsidize a party that she is not invited to.

That last action, along with his beating of Janie, indicates the other important similarity between Woods and Holmes: their function as challenge to the idea of a narrowly defined vision of black folk culture. Both of these folk "heroes" mistreat the women who turn to them for liberation. Woods's abuse is more overt; Holmes's only manifests itself when he rejects Faith to pursue his dream. Nevertheless, in each case, these character flaws raise important questions about the identity models that these men operate from. Hurston further emphasizes her reservations about Woods in noting his occasional loyalty to white values, as in the decision, which ultimately costs him his life, about when to leave the muck. This inconsistency in his self-definition suggests Holmes's speech about dying in his lonely garret, although the comic irony of Johnson's version is distinctly absent. And that absence characterizes the final disposition of these two novels. As inadequate as he is, Tea Cake proves to be the best of the options open to Janie in a world riven by racialism. Hurston's dissatisfied and in some ways unsatisfactory acquiescence to that vision of the world leaves Janie alone in her house and critics debating the precise nature of the novel's impact on the evolution of African American literary identity in the twentieth century.

Hurston's work appeared at a moment when African American writers were struggling with the question of how to represent themselves and their race. It is, therefore, crucial as a celebration of African American folk culture and an important text for a great many writers who have followed her, including Toni Morrison and, most notably, Alice Walker. Walker's appreciation for Hurston led her to resurrect the author from relative obscurity as the women's movement and the Black Arts Movement were gathering energy in the late 1960s. Johnson does not deny Hurston's importance; in fact, in *Being and Race* he praises the elaborate detail with which she infuses her fictional life-world. At the same time, he recognizes that the conception of folk culture Hurston presents in *Their Eyes* remains grounded in a sense of racial otherness and separation—something that he attempts, at least, to avoid. In an effort to emphasize that difference and advance his views, he modifies her position by integrating elements that suggest a new way of understanding black culture and the process of identity formation.

Johnson balances his effort to modify conceptions of the African American folk tradition with a revision of key American literary naturalist principles, which he has referred to as "an explanatory model that strip[s] experience of its richness" (e-mail, 3 Nov. 1996). This resistance to determinism particularly applies to his vision of race, and he pointedly addresses classic black naturalist novels as part of his effort to forge a new sense of African American selfhood. Here, as in his subsequent fiction with urban settings, he focuses on the economic and social forces threatening the community and shaping its individual members' perceptions of themselves as victims. As Jonathan Little demonstrates, Johnson rewrites Wright's *Native Son* in *Faith and the Good Thing* (*Charles Johnson's* 77–79). Furthermore, one sees an interesting comparison between Faith Cross's experiences and the story of Lutie Johnson, the heroine of Ann Petry's *The Street* (1946). Plagued by circumstances resonant with Faith Cross's experience but convinced that she is a victim, Lutie cannot transcend the environmental forces threatening her and her son, Bub, in their Harlem home. The novel closes with an image of the "grime and the garbage and the ugliness" of her world (436), precisely the sort of landscape of despair Johnson revises in his final images of the beauty of the swamp.

In addition to addressing the idea of race in his critique of naturalism, Johnson also considers issues that are not necessarily racially defined. Chief among these is desire, which he identifies as one of the primary forces dividing society. This attitude arises from his interest in Eastern religious thought. The reasoning goes as follows: a sense of desire for something means one has a sense of separation from it, an awareness of individuality that counters any impulse toward overarching unity. Pursuit of such desire creates *karma,* the cycle of suffering in which individuals exist until they achieve enlightenment, which one experiences as a sort of fusion with the whole. He explores this idea in all of his fiction, treating it most extensively in *Oxherding Tale,* the most Buddhist of his novels; in *Faith and the Good Thing,* he takes an important first look at the issue.

In treating desire this way, Johnson distinguishes himself from most of his African American literary predecessors. As Claudia Tate notes in *Psychoanalysis and Black Novels,* "traditional African American criticism has been much more invested in defining desire as . . . the consolidated aspiration for black civil rights than appreciating desire as the performance of existential freedom" (10). She sees writers like Du Bois, Hurston, and Wright as concerned with this broader notion of desire but still seeing the issue in racialized terms. Johnson certainly addresses the idea of freedom in existential terms, both here and in his subsequent fiction. His hope, however, is to look at desire as somehow above race. Although desire informs both *Native Son* and *The Street,* and Johnson speaks to that in his revision of those texts, he also turns to an earlier, archetypal American naturalist novel: Theodore Dreiser's *Sister Carrie* (1900).

Carrie's flight from Columbia City to Chicago resembles Faith's journey, although Carrie's good things are more sensual than cerebral. Furthermore, her relationships with Charles Drouet, George Hurstwood, and Robert Ames evoke comparisons with Tippis, Maxwell, and Holmes. Carrie, like Faith, experiences degradation with the first man, an elevation in status with the second that has negative consequences, and an unrealized hope for liberation with the third. Both women temporarily fix on materialism as the solution to their dissatisfaction, and both end up alone, staring out of windows. Other minor parallels, such as the reoccurrence in both texts of twenty dollars as the figurative price for the heroine's life, or at least her freedom, intensify the sense of intertextuality. And yet, in signifying on Dreiser, Johnson works a profound change on the naturalistic paradigm.

Dreiser says of Carrie, "In your rocking-chair, by your window dreaming, shall you long, alone. In your rocking-chair, by your window, shall you dream such happiness as you may never feel" (369). The clear message here is that desire is a deterministic force that Carrie cannot defeat. Unlike Carrie, who ends her journey aware that she must "have a good deal more" but unsure of how to get it, Faith lays down the way of the young innocent and takes up the path instead of the Swamp Woman herself. Where Carrie looks out her window, a symbol of her confinement, and feels a gloominess that comes from her unsatisfied desires, Faith looks confidently forward to an endless round of process, recognizing that the endless number of changes awaiting her will be important to her development. The promise of liberation from desire and the subsequent transcendence of the world are the premises of the antinaturalistic impulses in Johnson's aesthetic.

But, as the novel's positions on questions of race and gender roles demonstrate, *Faith and the Good Thing* does not represent the realization of that ideal. The novel's use of African American folklore means that Johnson still adheres at this point to a racialized creative consciousness. Furthermore, although this folklore does allow for a different way of seeing the world, it supports the fundamental conventions of Western cosmology, physiology, or linguistics. Johnson's attempt to engage those issues will move him to create the Allmuseri, who push beyond the boundaries that contain the Swamp Woman. This effort, combined with his reassessment of the social and economic forces marshaled against blacks by American society, informs his writing as he works to articulate his aesthetic vision in *Oxherding Tale.* One sees the fruits of this interim labor in *The Sorcerer's Apprentice* (1986), which consists of the short stories he wrote while composing that novel.

4 Lumber for the Platform: *The Sorcerer's Apprentice*

Johnson's first collection of short fiction, *The Sorcerer's Apprentice: Tales and Conjurations* (1986), comprises eight stories, written between 1977 and 1982, which are connected thematically with his second novel. As he notes, "when I couldn't do *Oxherding Tale* . . . I'd do a short story that would take up some of the same questions of freedom and personal and cultural identity." In his view, then, "the stories in *The Sorcerer's Apprentice* were written . . . because that one novel was such a difficult project to maintain" ("Philosopher" 14). As he sought to articulate his aesthetic in his Eastern-influenced neo–slave narrative, Johnson struggled with the form and content of his fiction. Applying lessons from John Gardner, he worked to master a broad range of story types. He also wrestled with the difficulties of challenging conventional conceptions of black literature. This forced him to push beyond Gardner's definition of moral fiction; it also demanded that he refine the ideas about racial identity that he presents in *Faith and the Good Thing*. As a result, *The Sorcerer's Apprentice* turns on three interrelated ideas: the importance of form to the meaning of fiction, the relationship between literary master and student, and the liberation one finds by embracing new ideas about racial identity.

The collection contains two historical stories, a beast fable, a stream-of-consciousness narrative, and four stories of "contemporary" life told from divergent perspectives. For Johnson, each of these literary forms offers a new way of interpreting experience because a "vision of the world that is appropriate to its particular universe" informs it (*Being* 48). He notes, for instance, that one cannot convincingly tell a social realist story as a folktale because of the differing demands of each form, offering the contrast between the worldviews presented in Wright's *Native Son* and *Faith and the Good Thing* to make the point.[1]

The logical end of this reasoning is that if one wants to explore numerous experiences of blackness, one might employ several forms to tell varying stories about black experience. Johnson uses this method effectively in the twelve short stories he wrote for *Africans in America* (1998), the companion volume for the PBS series of the same name. Each presents an element of America's history during the slavery era, and Johnson tells them all in different forms. The collection, subsequently published in *Soulcatcher and Other Stories* (2001), includes first-person and full omniscient narratives, an epistolary story, a third-person monologue, and a fictional newspaper article. As Johnson filters components of the same history through these various forms, he enriches our understanding of the slave experience.

This collection, like *The Sorcerer's Apprentice,* also illustrates the literary value of this approach to writing. By opening up the number of ways one can tell black stories, one can broaden the scope of black literature. In *The Sorcerer's Apprentice,* Johnson's experimentation with form takes him beyond the typical boundaries of the African American canon. To be sure, one sees the imprint of his African American literary predecessors in stories like "The Education of Mingo" and "The Sorcerer's Apprentice." These stories, which frame the collection, recount the psychological costs of slavery for black and white survivors and their descendents, a recurrent theme throughout the African American canon. One might, for example, think in this context of works by William Wells Brown, Jean Toomer, Ralph Ellison, Ernest J. Gaines, Toni Morrison, and John Edgar Wideman.

But the stories in *The Sorcerer's Apprentice* are about more than physical bondage. They exemplify Johnson's struggle to write stories that fulfill the potential he describes in "Philosophy and Black Fiction" and "Whole Sight."[2] None of these stories are about writers per se, but several engage the basic issues of the author's evolving aesthetic. For example, the frame stories examine master/slave relationships and consider each participant's responsibility when the connection influences either person's creativity.[3] In the story of a slaveholder's tragic attempts to reeducate an Allmuseri tribesman, "Mingo" comments on the relationship between white "master" authors and black "apprentice" writers who internalize their lessons. The title story, by contrast, illustrates the dangers facing young black writers who adhere too strongly to the examples of their predecessors within the African American tradition. "China," which is arguably the most important story of the collection, metaphorically presents Johnson's efforts to weave black life and Eastern religion together as he worked on *Oxherding Tale.* With its specific relationship to Johnson's personal project, "China" brings the fundamental issues raised in "Mingo" and "Apprentice" into focus. To varying degrees, the other stories in the collection serve these same purposes. I am concentrating on the frame stories, "China" and "Exchange Value," because they most clearly illustrate the evolution of Johnson's aesthetic as he prepares to write *Oxherding Tale* and as he works to resolve the tensions that complicate his message in *Faith and the Good Thing*.

In "The Education of Mingo," a lonely, childless white farmer named Moses Green buys a slave, Mingo, and attempts "the evaporation of one coherent, consistent, complete universe and the embracing of another one alien, contradictory, strange" in training him (6). Green thinks he has his chattel's best interests at heart, and he takes pride in Mingo's progress, despite warnings from Harriet Bridgewater, a highly educated spinster whom Moses hopes to marry. Soon, though, Mingo reverses Moses's lessons about being kind to strangers and killing chicken hawks by murdering a local farmer and Harriet Bridgewater. Forced to choose his creation's fate, Green recognizes his responsibility for these crimes, lets Mingo live, and flees west with him, toward Missouri.

Moses's innate sense of superiority taints his efforts at remaking Mingo. Although he seeks companionship, he needs that sense of separation to appreciate what he has accomplished. As Johnson tells us, Mingo "was all Moses wanted him to be, his own emanation, but still, he thought, himself. Different enough from Moses so that he could step back and admire" his creation (11). This fixation ultimately proves to be Moses's undoing. After the murders, Moses realizes that he cannot execute Mingo because his slave's existence affirms his worldview. Their relationship mirrors the terms of the philosopher Georg Wilhelm Friedrich Hegel's master-slave paradigm (Hegel 404–5); in many ways, it also presages Flo Hatfield's need for "epidermalized Being" at Leviathan. So long as Moses needs a slave to define his existence, freedom is impossible. Like Mary Shelley's scientist, whom Johnson references in a passing remark about Harriet Bridgewater's reading, Moses has created a monster he cannot control.[4]

On a literary level, "Mingo" raises interesting questions about Johnson's changing relationship with black cultural nationalism. One might see remnants of his loyalty to that ideology here, as the story's indictment of a narrow view of black being suggests difficulties that African American artists have faced for decades. With his fixed sense of Mingo's slave identity ("'Mingo, you more me than I am myself. Me planed away to the bone!'" [22]), Moses resembles white modernist authors such as Carl Van Vechten and Eugene O'Neill who assigned blacks the role of "primitives" as a means of defining themselves as superior beings. In articulating this relationship and in describing Mingo as "strangely elemental" with skin that "had the texture of plant life" (21), Green illustrates what his understanding of Mingo as subhuman means to him. One might also think in this context of Green's resemblance to Charlotte Osgood Mason, infamous "Godmother" to Langston Hughes and Zora Neale Hurston, who pushed her beneficiaries to create primitive art and then, in Hurston's case at least, claimed control over the products.[5] She was, in a sense, a creator herself as she attempted to mold her charges into the vision of black selfhood that best suited her needs.

I would not push that specific analogy too far; these white authors were to a person more sophisticated and subtle than Moses Green, who cannot grasp the most basic philosophical argument without help from Harriet Bridgewater. What he does share with them, however, is the essentialist blindness associated with a racialized, dualistic model of the world. This does not mean that the process of slave reeducation might ever be construed as laudable. But Johnson suggests that the white writer who defines his project entirely in terms of a binary opposition between himself and his black subject cannot see that subject clearly or completely. This clarifies Green's particular shortcomings; he persists in believing Mingo to be ignorant even when the Allmuseri grasps philosophical subtleties about property that elude him.

And yet, at the story's end, Moses has no intention of making Mingo anything more than the extension of himself. His need for the slave as other saves Mingo's life, perhaps, but it circumscribes his, and Moses's, being. And here is where a nationalist agenda might be identified. In artistic terms, Green remains the creator who sees the world in binaries. From this position, he cannot envision other modes of working; neither can he allow Mingo, who resembles the student bound too closely to his domineering master, to fulfill his individual potential. Like the black artist hampered by a white-defined view of artistry, Mingo cannot create anything sustainable on his own terms. He experiences the "cultural strangulation" that Addison Gayle describes; clearly, for Johnson this position is untenable. Like Huck Finn before them, Moses and Mingo "light out for the Territory" (Twain 362), but they will find no freedom when they arrive. Jonathan Little sees the story this way, calling it "anti-integrative" and arguing that the tragic failure of Moses Green's experiment means that Johnson values "the maintenance and preservation of separate cultures for the healthy survival of all who participate in the frightening dance of racial relatedness" (*Charles Johnson's* 112).

By contrast, I believe that Johnson resents *and* resists the power of the narrow view that he presents here. For all that the story shares with the principles of black cultural nationalism, Johnson does not rest in that position. In the midst of the story's nightmarish vision, he softens the horror and challenges the stridency of cultural nationalist rhetoric. The description of Mingo and Moses as ventriloquist's dummies, wired together and "hauling hips across a cold black countryside" (16) that Little calls "horrific" (111) offers but one in a series of humorous touches that characterize the story. The resulting lightness subverts any thoroughgoing indictment of Moses's vision in a manner not unlike Johnson's visual treatments of black identity politics in *Half-Past Nation Time.* His mockery of Moses's plan, which is actually not truly integrative but rather assimilative, undermines both it and the separatist forces marshaled against it.

Johnson's play with identity issues here presages his more thorough exploration of them in *Oxherding Tale.* Like Mingo, Andrew Hawkins is a slave beset by masters who would reform him in terms of their identities. Also, Andrew's slightly less gory experiences share the nightmarish quality one sees in "Mingo." Johnson's creative evolution, and particularly his growing interest in Buddhism, leads him to resolve Andrew's fate rather differently, though. As I shall demonstrate, the novel's version of the master-slave dilemma promises a liberation that this version lacks.

The story makes a step toward that ideal in its signifying on Edgar Allan Poe's "William Wilson"; Johnson uses Poe's image of the doppelganger to inform his discussion of otherness and interdependence. In killing his double, Wilson takes the one step that Moses Green cannot; nevertheless, the action brings him no more relief than Green's sparing Mingo does. In both cases, the creators absolutely need the other to feel alive. And in both cases, blackness marks that other. In Poe, the William Wilson whom the narrator fears often appears shrouded in darkness, and we see him finally with "a mask of *black* silk entirely covering his face" (260, emphasis added). I see Poe using this story to express his anxieties about the threatening presence of blacks in the South and the concomitant need whites have of them in formulating a sense of regional and racial identity, much as Harold Beaver says he does in *The Narrative of Arthur Gordon Pym of Nantucket* (Beaver 14–18).

William Wilson's self-murder brings forth the horror in Poe's vision; for Johnson, such destruction is not even possible at this point. As he detaches himself from Western conceptions of identity, though, it will become an ideal of sorts. In *Oxherding Tale,* losing the illusion of selfhood enables Andrew to gain his final freedom. His role models for this lesson are Horace Bannon and Reb. The Soulcatcher, who effectively becomes the doppelganger of every slave he hunts, repeatedly reenacts actual self-destruction in his work. The Coffinmaker, also an Allmuseri, lives out his denial of selfhood by consistently refusing to acknowledge any separation between himself and his environment. Mingo shows nascent signs of that awareness in describing his relationship with Moses. "'What Mingo know, Massa Green know. Bees like *what* Mingo sees or don't see is only what Massa Green taught him to see or don't see. Like Mingo lives through Massa Green, right?'" (15). At this point he does not fully grasp the notion; this figures in the difference between his two murders and Bannon's holy killing. The differences between Mingo and subsequent members of the Allmuseri tribe emphasize the evolution of Johnson's aesthetic. Little more than a name at this point, the tribal identity will become the hallmark of his creative ideal in *Oxherding Tale* and *Middle Passage.* Ultimately the prophets who model absolute intersubjectivity, in Mingo the tribe represents only an especially odd example of otherness. One could say that with this story Johnson identifies one of the major problems he will treat throughout his canon, but he has not yet satisfactorily determined how to address it.

The heart of that issue is the difficulty of reconciling ideal and application when challenging dualistic models of racial identity. And yet, even as Johnson wrestles with this dilemma, one can see him striving toward a hopeful resolution. Moses's recognition of his need for Mingo and his inability to counter it suggests that he is as trapped in this relationship as Dr. Henry Popper is in the spaceship at the end of "Popper's Disease." Although humorous in its own right, as the description of the alien as "what you might expect to find on a seafood platter in a decent restaurant" indicates, with its final twin nightmare messages, *"It's the Self"* and *"There is no Cure,"* "Popper's Disease" may well be the story that "subverts the life-affirmation of Johnson's novels and some of his short stories like no other story in *The Sorcerer's Apprentice*" (Little, *Charles Johnson's* 125). The presence of "Mingo" and "Popper's Disease" as well as "Menagerie" and "Exchange Value" in the collection illustrates Johnson's further confrontation of the issue of the "history of the race" that surfaces at the end of *Faith and the Good Thing.* These stories represent his lasting resentment over the legacy of racialism and his "focus on the pain and suffering of African American existence, unalleviated by the possibility of spiritual transcendence" (Little, *Charles Johnson's* 109). They do not, however, convey all of his opinions on the issue. He balances the negativity of these stories with more hopeful perspectives in "Alethia," "China," and "The Sorcerer's Apprentice." Although he never fully resolves this conflict, these stories all hopefully suggest that racialism can be transcended. This position, which Johnson will embrace in *Oxherding Tale,* shapes not only his social but also his literary message in the short fiction.

"Mingo" focuses on the consequences facing an artist who creates irresponsibly and who perpetuates narrow racialized views of the world in his art. Although charged with humorous elements, the story sounds a mostly grim warning for artists standing in danger of falling prey to the "deadly upas of race and relationships" (21). Johnson balances that view with "The Sorcerer's

Apprentice," a story that further illuminates his growing discomfort with the Black Aesthetic. In this case, the literary problem is tension between generations of black writers, and the resolution is much more hopeful. Johnson describes a young black artist's desire to emulate his teacher, his failure at duplicating his mentor's success, and his final recognition of his ability to do things his own way. In the liberating moment of that final realization, the Apprentice makes his most significant art. The story simultaneously suggests something profoundly personal about Johnson's own struggle and provides commentary on the struggles he sees facing all modern black artists.

Drawing on Goethe's "Die Zauberlehring" and adding some of the texture of Jean Toomer's *Cane,* "The Sorcerer's Apprentice" describes Allan Jackson's adoring dedication to Rubin Bailey, a revered Allmuseri magician who had once healed Allan's father, Richard (Griffiths, "'Sorcery'" 527). When the wizard begins to fear death, he takes Allan as his student and sets about teaching him his magic. Unlike Moses Green, Bailey does not want to make his pupil exactly what he is; rather, he seeks to communicate his acquired knowledge for his apprentice's personal development. Unfortunately, Allan believes that he need only copy his master's actions to be like him. When faced with his first client, the apprentice cannot perform the healer's tasks. Believing himself unable to fulfill his new role, Allan remembers a spell that will "bring forth demons—horrors that broke a man in half, ate his soul, then dragged him below the ground, where, Allan decided, those who could not do well the work of a magician belonged" (161). Fortunately, his father appears and stops him from submitting to the demons. Finally, feeling "the first spring of resignation, a giving way of both the hunger to heal and the anxiety to avoid evil," Allan steps out of the "loneliness of a life devoted to discipline and sorcery" (168) into a world where his ability to love gives real power.[6]

Allan's failure arises from his slavish imitation of Rubin Bailey's methods. His teacher tells him explicitly that a successful magician must personalize the spells. Rubin, for instance, has made accommodations for his arthritis in the way he does certain movements, despite a warning from his former teacher that his modifications are wrong. Bailey also tries to tell Allan that the magic is not fixed. When he first speaks of magic to his new apprentice, he warns him: "'There is no certainty these things can work for you, or even for me, a second time'" (151). Blind to these admonitions, Allan copies Rubin's movements exactly, even after the sorcerer explains about his arthritis. He also shudders when, in the course of complimenting him for a successful conjuration, Rubin suggests that he be prepared for the idea that he can never work that same spell so well again. The sorcerer means no harm; in fact, he is trying to teach his apprentice the greatest lesson of all: one must view conjuration as a fluid process rather than a fixed product. With this message, Johnson achieves another important step in the articulation of his master symbol. Not only does Rubin possess greater awareness than Mingo, something closer to the insight that subsequent Allmuseri will show, he is also more successful at sharing this with his pupil.

Sorcery aptly symbolizes writing in this story. Bailey represents the black author who knows he must do things his own way to make effective, powerful art. He has learned his master's lessons well, but he knows that this alone will not suffice. When he modifies his hand motions to compensate for his arthritis because that is how the magic "works best" for him, Rubin changes the tradition in order to invest it most effectively with what he has to say (155). In the terms of Johnson's discussion about writing in *Being and Race,* Bailey "honor[s] the form" (47). Allan, by contrast, determines that copying his predecessor's accomplishments exactly will yield him the same results. Despite everything he hears from his teacher, Allan remains unwilling to explore what his own creative voice might have to offer. His failure represents another cautionary tale from Johnson about what can happen to writers who cling too tightly to others' standards when defining their careers. One thinks in this instance of the author's apprentice period and his efforts to break out of slavish imitation of African American master authors in his writing.

Significantly, unlike "The Education of Mingo," this story offers some hope and suggests that this is perhaps a problem that is more easily fixed than the one plaguing Moses and Mingo. Allan does finally do one great thing: he enables his father to express his emotions and to break through the psychological limitations imposed upon him by slavery. Richard's stoicism is his most noteworthy feature. Throughout the story, Allan reflects on what it would mean to him to hear praise from his father; he also ponders what might have made his father so reserved. Like Andrew in *Oxherding Tale,* Allan concludes that slavery scarred his father and left him unable to show love. Richard's reserve ultimately dissolves, however, under the power of Allan's right-handed touch. Finally doing things his own way, Allan can make art that heals his father's pain. In this moment, he achieves Rubin Bailey's level of success and becomes a sorcerer in his own right.

That sorcery has a literary analogue as well. If one takes Richard's scars from slavery to symbolize the psychological damage that bondage worked on the African American psyche, then Allan's final action becomes a means of freeing his father, and by extension the community, from that constricting vision of blackness.[7] Allan learns the lesson that Johnson argues all African American writers must embrace if they are to transform perceptions about what black literature can be. With Rubin Bailey, the author pays tribute to preceding generations of black writers who pushed the boundaries of the canon for the sake of healing skewed perceptions about black literary and personal identity. Perhaps, as Griffiths suggests in noting resonances with *Cane,* Bailey stands for Toomer ("'Sorcery'" 528–33).

Alternately, one might read Bailey as representing Ellison. I find the relationship between the narrator of *Invisible Man* and his grandfather, the former slave, a provocative analogue to Allan's experiences with Richard. Both former slaves are essentially enigmatic, and both younger protagonists must unlock the riddle of their ancestor in order to be free. Where Invisible Man must reject the dominant values of the state college for Negroes, Allan must escape the dual burdens of slavish imitation of his master and the emotional coldness of his father's house. In resolving this dilemma, however, Johnson goes a step further than Ellison. Where Invisible Man is pondering coming out of his hole at the end of his story, Allan makes the final connection with his father that enables their mutual healing. With this important variation, Johnson fulfills the terms of his own message.

As in "Mingo" and the novels, he expands conceptions of black literary artistry by fusing black and white influences. With Poe and Toomer, Johnson draws on two significant practitioners of the American short story who shape his own creativity in the form and enrich the meanings of his short fictions. He invokes yet another master of the American short story by weaving strands from Nathaniel Hawthorne's "The Artist of the Beautiful" into the fabric of "The Sorcerer's Apprentice." Hawthorne's story of a young watchmaker obsessed with creating beauty echoes in Allan Jackson's rationale for becoming a sorcerer. Unlike Hawthorne's protagonist, Owen Warland, however, Allan ultimately learns that the greatest beauty lies in human connection.

The idea that making beauty is ennobling has a certain undeniable appeal. One would expect an author, whose professional life turns, ostensibly at least, on the successful making of beauty, to see it as such. In these terms, making beauty becomes a form of doing good, which is Allan's greatest desire. (Recall the interrelationship of goodness, beauty, and truth in *Faith and the Good Thing,* which also appears in the short story "Alethia.") The difficulty with this is that obsession with beauty as an absolute has negative consequences, too. As Rubin warns Allan, "'you can't be too faithful, or too eager, or the good becomes evil'" (150). This remark suggests that Johnson interprets Owen Warland's choice of beauty over human relationships in these terms. Warland ultimately has made beauty, but it is something only he can understand. The destruction of his artifact means little to him because of what he has learned, but it marks the end of his effectiveness as a communicator. He cannot give of himself as Allan finally can when he chooses love over sorcery. If Allan lived entirely by Owen's rules, he would surrender to his demons for the sake of his art. In doing that, the apprentice could only do harm, and his life would be lost in vain. Johnson brings this image of artistry into his tale to illustrate his desire to make useful beauty. His goal of creating a healing literature makes it crucial that his artist of the beautiful understand that the love is more important than the butterfly.

Johnson matches the literary trajectory of *The Sorcerer's Apprentice* with commentary on contemporary socioeconomic concerns. As he moves from negativity to a qualified hope, he suggests that the harsh social forces that reinforce a sense of victimization within the African American community must not bind individuals. And yet what he describes is, by definition, a limited response. This pattern of change, while beneficial to the individuals who adopt it, does not materially affect the environment. Johnson's recognition of that reality accounts, I believe, for his steps toward this social position being more tentative than his literary strides. By the time he publishes *Dreamer,* his concerns over social injustice will push him back from the view that he adopts during this period. Within the parameters of the collection, though, he addresses these issues as a part of his sincere effort to resolve the racial dilemma.

He presents the dark end of the spectrum in "Exchange Value." This story, narrated by a young African American man named Cooter, describes his and his brother Loftis's experiences with the fortune they steal from one of their South Side Chicago neighbors. A combination of a crime story and a horror tale, it also makes an important statement about identity. From the start, the money gets tied up with the brothers' views about race, and their blackness shapes their relationship with their new things. The older of the two, Loftis, seems doomed to suffering and dissatisfaction; Cooter has perhaps a minimal chance of surviving the burden the money and his race place on him. The indeterminacy of the story's ending makes this a qualified hope, though. What seems clearer and more likely is that history, complete with the racialized sense of suffering that eventually marks both their victim, Miss Bailey, and Loftis, repeats itself.

Loftis reasons that Miss Bailey, a single, elderly woman who lives like a miser, should have "some grandtheft dough stashed inside, jim, or leastways a shoebox full of money, because she never spent a nickel on herself, not even for food" (27). When several days pass without them seeing her, the brothers go in through a window. Bypassing her crude booby traps, they enter a living room filled with money, stocks, furs, paintings, books, food, liquor, old newspapers, rags, a car, and a dead tree. Although Cooter senses something amiss with this bizarre collection, Loftis insists that they move the horde into their own apartment. After they have taken possession, strange things begin to happen. Cooter understandably wants to celebrate their newfound wealth and heads out with a pocketful of money to eat, shop, and go sightseeing. While he is gone, Loftis stays behind and booby-traps their apartment. When Cooter returns, his older brother beats and berates him for wasting the potential of the money he spent. "'As soon as you buy something,'" he tells Cooter, "'you *lose* the power to buy something'" (36).

Loftis rapidly transforms into a younger version of Miss Bailey. He begins picking through other people's garbage for things of value, bringing home refuse to add to the pile and resisting any impulse (even hunger) to deplete the stash. To make matters worse, the brothers begin having the same maintenance problems Miss Bailey did, and like her they cannot call a repairman for fear of exposing the stash. Their world and hers flow together, and they stand on the verge of being lost to the same forces that destroyed her. At the story's end, Loftis returns home from four days of wandering the streets inspired by his chance finding of a penny on the way from work, a development that terrifies Cooter. He wants desperately to believe that he and Loftis can escape; nevertheless, he ultimately submits to their fate, albeit uneasily.

Even as Cooter struggles to free himself and Loftis, he knows what really killed Miss Bailey: "that special Negro fear of using up what little we get in life . . . believing in her belly, and for all her faith, jim, that there just ain't no more coming tomorrow from grace, or the Lord, or from her own labor, like she can't kill nothing, and won't nothing die" (37). This attitude, a version of the victim mentality that plagues Big Todd Cross and George Hawkins, destroys Miss Bailey's sanity; it similarly threatens Loftis and Cooter, who describes himself as "thinking that even if I ain't had all I wanted, maybe I've had, you know, all I'm ever gonna get" (30). This racially informed worldview controls Miss Bailey's response to the money; having felt powerless all her life, she takes the power in her horde, the financial piece of which she inherited from a former employer, as a source of strength. Once she has that power in hand, better to stop living than to let go.

Loftis shows all the signs of Miss Bailey's affliction. He thinks himself above her "'backward ways'" and expects to do better with the money than she has (33). He has more education than his brother, including success at DuSable High School, classes at the Black People's Topographical Library, and a steady diet of the journal *Black Scholar.* He also understands the Marxist concept of exchange value, which appears in the *Economic and Philosophic Manuscripts of 1844,* well enough to explain it to Cooter after his initial shopping spree. For all that, he still suffers from his own fears about blackness and powerlessness, and he falls victim to the same illusions that destroy her.

Two details in Cooter's description tip the reader off to a deeper commentary associated with Loftis's position. *Black Scholar* was founded at the height of the Black Arts Movement and informed, at least initially, by its principles. The Black People's Topographical Library is a thinly veiled reference to the Black People's Topographical Institute, a nationalist organization that was active in Chicago in the late 1960s. The institute offered lectures illustrating how urban blacks were largely confined to ghettos so that the state might better contain them in the event of any national assertion of white supremacist politics. As an alternative, the institute advocated blacks leaving major urban centers for the American South, where they could form their own nation-state (Royster). In a move that details his growing discomfort with black cultural nationalism, Johnson uses both symbols to convey Loftis's intellectual shortcomings. Although Cooter cannot see it, the actions and attitudes of these racial essentialists limit his brother's quest for power. Though his motives are somewhat different from Miss Bailey's, his destiny resembles hers. So long as he adheres to a limited notion of his racial being, especially one grounded in a long-standing sense of oppression and injustice, he cannot escape the lure of power trapped in the money.

Even in this instance Johnson's critique is not entirely unsympathetic, however. Cooter's final ambivalence clearly indicates the author's awareness that Loftis does not imagine his oppression. To some extent, Cooter demonstrates these miserly behaviors himself, and Johnson suggests that his arrival at these conclusions is *not* political indoctrination but rather the result of trying to negotiate an environment set up to perpetuate his suffering. His early statements about what he has had and what he wants suggest that he does reasonably feel some sense of victimization. Furthermore, as he ponders Miss Bailey's corpse on its way down the stairs, he demonstrates insight and understanding with regard to her motives. He even begins to act like her while Loftis is gone, adopting her habit of begging food from a local restaurateur rather than eating anything in the horde. His transformation occurs more slowly than Loftis's, because it arises from experience rather than training; nevertheless, he starts on the way toward his own mental dissolution during his brief period of forced isolation.

And yet, even as he chronicles the horror of this landscape, Johnson cannot rest comfortably in that negativity, which so powerfully counters the unifying impulses of his aesthetic. Like Nella Larsen's Helga Crane, his inability to either conform or to be comfortable in nonconformity with regard to racial matters puts him in a difficult position. In this case, that struggle results in the indeterminacy of the ending. Throughout his ordeal, Cooter maintains some awareness of the need for something different from him and Loftis. Although Cooter knows the stakes, he cannot necessarily do anything about it at this point. His last thoughts suggest the difficulty of his position. "I wanted to tell Loftis how Miss Bailey looked four days ago, that maybe it didn't have to be like that for us—did it?—because we could change. Couldn't we?" (40). He has an impulse toward change, even though he doubts his chances of making it happen.

Cooter's responses embody the challenges Johnson faces as he struggles to refine his aesthetic. His profound awareness of environmental pressures makes him resist easy answers. Cooter's indecision is a cry from the heart, a recognition that he cannot make a blithe promise of sweeping change even to himself. His decision to put the penny "away carefully, for now, with the rest of our things" illustrates his, and Johnson's, dilemma (40). "For now" indicates a desire for something else; "our things" shows to what extent he has already succumbed to the power of the treasure. By leaving Cooter's dilemma unresolved, Johnson reinforces his indictment of the socioeconomic realities under which African Americans must labor. And yet, at the same time, he also uses this scenario as a platform for the philosophical ideals that interest him. Cooter may indeed have all he is ever going to get, but in the recognition of what else he wants, Johnson offers some glimpse of the transcendence he wishes were available to Cooter and the community he represents.

Cooter's last look at Miss Bailey's corpse sets him to contemplating how in an ideal world he might change. This transformative encounter with death reflects one of Johnson's key philosophical influences: Martin Heidegger's idea of *sein-zum-tod,* or "being toward death." Heidegger argues in *Being and Time* that recognition of death allows subjects, with awareness of their history and the potential of their future, to make different choices about their actions. This makes sein-zum-tod *"that perspective from which one sees the whole or totality of human existence"* (Gelven 143). Although he treats this notion more extensively in *Oxherding Tale* and *Middle Passage,* he lays the groundwork here. Cooter embodies this ideal as he tries to understand Miss Bailey's passing and to make choices based on it that are healthier and more life-affirming than hers.

Cooter also has a revelation about time that indicates he is moving away from the rigidity of Loftis's model of perception. When he and his brother are moving Miss Bailey's stash into their apartment, it occurs to him that the property is both the past and the future. It contains the energy of its former owner, he realizes, and it also is the key to his and Loftis's security. The idea comes to him suddenly, a burst of enlightenment that he stumbles into as the student of Zen sometimes experiences an epiphany (Watts 158–59). That analogy is particularly appropriate, as the idea of simultaneity that describes this view of time reflects the tenets of Buddhism that Johnson embraced while writing *Oxherding Tale.* Cooter's momentary recognition of the confluence of time, like his stepping outside the racialized view of property, shows he is developing more flexible perceptions than his brother's. He can see things differently from Loftis, which means he might break the cycle of destruction that they have entered. The "for now" of his final statement leaves open that possibility, however slim it might be. Or at least so it appears. I do not see real hope for Loftis or Cooter in this story; both seem doomed to repeat the suffering that destroyed Miss Bailey. The narrow gap of Cooter's "for now" represents the toehold that philosophy has on the situation, the scant chance for liberation that represents Johnson's ideal. At this point, however, it seems that not even he sees how that ideal might be sustained in such an environment.

He adopts a more qualifiedly positive position in "Alethia." Once again, Chicago's South Side provides the backdrop for a significant portion of the action. In this instance, though, the narrator returns to the community by choice. Furthermore, his return, rather than harming him, provides the insight he needs to heal his psychic wounds. The ghetto becomes, in short, a healing place rather than a destructive zone. That one can do better than Cooter's "for now" in the ghetto suggests a more tangible, more nearly attainable possibility of liberation than Johnson offers in "Exchange Value." Significantly, as in that story, one sees the mind and the street in conflict. In "Alethia," though, Johnson modifies his original position, suggesting the necessity of balancing apparently disparate elements.

"Alethia" tells the story of an unnamed black philosophy professor who, like other philosophers in Johnson's fiction, realizes that the life of the mind no longer satisfies his desire for happiness. His dissatisfaction arises from the following words of Max Scheler: "'Contemplation of essence, the fundamental approach to Being peculiar to metaphysical knowledge, demands an attitude of loving devotion.'" Brooding over this notion while lecturing on Kant in his graduate seminar, the professor finds the embodiment of Scheler's abstraction in a student named Wendy Barnes. As she comes in late, he sees her "with the flash of clear vision, the focus, the gasp of recognition that slaps you, suddenly," a burst of insight much like what Cooter experiences when he finds Loftis's latest treasure (100–101). Frightened by the revelation and ashamed of being attracted to a student, the professor flees to the safety of his office.

The problem with his strategy, in narrative terms at least, is that the object of his desire follows him home. Barnes has no love for the professor, but she needs a B to keep her scholarship and stay in school. She comes to his office, therefore, to threaten him with a sexual harassment claim unless he guarantees her the required grade. Terrified of what she might do to his hard-won reputation, he agrees to go somewhere off campus to discuss her dilemma. She takes him to a raucous South Side party, where he takes a mix of drugs and sinks into a contemplative trance. He awakes from the haze of that long night to a bright morning in which he and Wendy Barnes find mutual satisfaction.

The trip to the South Side proves crucial in the professor's journey to enlightenment. Before Barnes arrives, he has been mulling over another idea from Scheler: *alethia,* which translates as "to call forth from concealedness." The term suggests that "each man, each moment, each blink of the eye, was responsible for obliterating [ugliness and pain] and conjuring only those visions from perceptual chaos that *let be* goodness, truth, beauty" (104). For the narrator, that ugliness is the poverty of the Chicago ghetto, from which he escaped into the academy. Barnes's appearance in his office forces him from abstraction to engagement. Under her guidance, he must reenter that world and come to terms with what it means to his own experience.

To reconcile himself with that community, he must overcome the sense of separation that he feels as a black academic. The professor, who describes himself as favoring "that towering sociologist W. E. B. Du Bois," suffers under the burden of double consciousness. The professor's experience in academe echoes the description of Henry Popper's medical school training. He describes his education as stealing "crumbs of thought from their genuine context" and denying difficulties like Hume's racialist attitudes to embrace the good conveyed in his "reasoning of the self." In addition to deepening his sense of dualism, this approach threatens his eventual disillusionment. As he puts it, the black college student (i.e. him in his youth) "embraces—and this is the killing part—the lofty balderdash of his balding, crabbed-faced teachers about sober Truth and Science when they, shaken by Wittgenstein, had in fact lost faith and were madly humping their teaching assistants" (102). As he ruminates on his frightening encounter with Barnes, he fears himself on the verge of surrendering to that despair. Despite his efforts to live his philosophy devoutly, he recognizes, with Scheler's help, that life without love is useless, even wrong; Barnes seems to offer a chance to correct his error. With this realization, the professor prefigures the moment of enlightenment Ezekiel Sykes-Withers experiences in *Oxherding Tale* when he devotes himself to serving Althea Moses (note the similarity between her name and Scheler's concept). Fortunately for the professor, though, that insight frees him rather than destroying him, as it does Ezekiel. The difference between their fates arises from his having the opportunity to implement the lessons.

Returning to the South Side life he both hates and yearns for, the professor can confront what has become to him an essential separation between his life and the lives of those in the black community he fled. The journey back to his roots helps him reconcile his most basic dichotomy. With the help of several psychedelics, which guide his quest for a liberation of perception, the professor finally sees the unity behind things. His view of the partygoers, who vary in appearance from an ugly Rastafarian to a Joe Frazier look-alike to the beautiful Wendy Barnes, blends into a vision of the transcendent Whole. Furthermore, he knows all of the other people at the party to be himself, as he overcomes dualism and with it the racialized consciousness that has plagued him for so long.

The professor's real success, though, is not an abstract realization of intersubjectivity. Rather, it is his ability to embrace that life, to be in that black world and to "let [his] mind sleep" (112). Perhaps ironically, his descent from the ivory tower of philosophy into the squalor of Wendy's apartment illustrates the foundation of Johnson's philosophical system. In surrendering to experience and thereby distancing himself from the preconceptions and distinctions associated with his academic life, the professor enacts Husserl's epoché. Johnson describes phenomenology as "something you *do,*" an applied way of looking at the world that yields new, potentially life-altering modes of perception (interview, 23 Mar. 1991). "Alethia" illustrates that idea. In the process, the author refines his response to the societal problems that racialism causes. Rather than resting with preconceptions about racial identity, one must forge new ways of understanding life in a racially fragmented environment. Accessing that heightened awareness frees the enlightened individual from the trap of double consciousness and allows him or her to transcend feelings of outrage or victimization.

Although Johnson eventually returns to the notion that an individual's gaining mental freedom fails to resolve the community's ills, at this point that represents the fulfillment of his design. He privileges the individual's quest over the community's needs even more radically in "China," which has a more overtly personal component than most of the other stories in the collection. In addition to commenting on Johnson's evolution as an artist, the story also presents the most complete articulation, save *Oxherding Tale,* of the relationship between Eastern philosophy and his ideas about race.

Rudolph Lee Jackson, a fifty-four-year-old African American postman in Seattle, lives a life burdened by definitions of blackness that emphasize his inability to break out of the socially cast mold his race relegates him to. Together with his wife, Evelyn, he has settled down to a boring, disappointing existence characterized chiefly by their shared sense of victimization. Rudolph's life begins to turn around when he sees an advertisement for a kung fu movie one night when he and Evelyn are out together. Despite her salty rejection of the onscreen action as impossible, he goes to see the film, meets some practitioners of the art, and begins training. His experiences at the kwoon, or training hall, are transformative. In addition to the physical benefits of the exercise, he embraces the philosophical foundations of the martial art, begins meditating, and finds a way to escape the racial oppression that has held him back for so long. The only major difficulty in his life at this point is that Evelyn does not understand the changes she sees in him, and she tries to turn him back into the broken man she has become comfortable living with.

Evelyn's lack of understanding arises from her strict adherence to a circumscribed notion of her life's possibilities. Deeply rooted in the traditions of the black church, she expects that she and Rudolph will grow old together and die—him first, so that she can have some years of peace to make up for her suffering. The rigidity and inefficacy of her worldview figure in her incipient blindness. On every level, she cannot see the good in the new Rudolph. His new hobby, as she characterizes it, frightens and confuses her. In response, she undercuts everything he does, hoping to get a rise from him that will allow her to browbeat him into submission. Although Rudolph breaks down stereotypes, to some extent Evelyn reinforces them. Filled with the inner harmony that comes from meditation, however, Rudolph refuses to fight. Instead, he asks her to come to the Kingdome to support him as he fights in a tournament. She hesitates but finally relents, arriving at the arena in time to witness Rudolph's success. The vision of him leaping high into the air, figuratively transcending the limitations of all he has been before, convinces her of the value of his new approach to life.

The tension between Rudolph's Eastern beliefs and Evelyn's African American religion mirrors a conflict Johnson must resolve in progressing aesthetically from *Faith and the Good Thing* to *Oxherding Tale.* Her Christianity is on the order of Lavidia Cross's, a manifestation of traditional black culture and an important element of the African American folk tradition. Although that tradition proved a fertile ground for his initial philosophical exploration, and although *Faith* itself bears some important Buddhist inflections, this conception of religion was too limiting for Johnson once he began a more systematic study of philosophy. In order to pursue his aesthetic goals effectively, he needed to represent Eastern thought more completely in his work. Unfortunately, his new intellectual and artistic aspirations were the source of some unexpected conflict. As he explains, Johnson felt that Gardner "wanted me to write another book like *Faith.* . . . But once finished with that novel, I wanted, needed something else: a neo–slave narrative that explored fundamental questions about the (black) self, and deployed Eastern philosophy in the process. . . . I desperately needed to push beyond his conception at the time of what black literature, culture, (and Charles Johnson) should be" ("John Gardner" 623). In an effort to explain his feelings and his motives to Gardner, Johnson wrote "China."

Rudolph's exploration of black being and his expanded understanding of what that term can mean perfectly represents Johnson's own creative struggle. By recognizing a new source of identity that opens up numerous possibilities for understanding black being, Rudolph achieves Johnson's ideal fusion.[8] And although her sight is not yet whole, Evelyn appears to be on the way to grasping what her husband has learned. Her enlightenment has further literary implications, as one of the things she mentally permits Rudolph to do if she predeceases him is to throw out her old books, an action that symbolizes her recognition and rejection of the aesthetic arm of her narrow, restrictive worldview. In this moment, she makes the first step beyond their lessons, as Johnson is trying to show his teacher a way beyond the limitations that Gardner would place on him.

Rudolph's situation, or perhaps more properly Johnson's as apprentice to John Gardner, apparently reverses Allan Jackson's dilemma.[9] Rather than loving the master too well, Johnson seeks a liberation that comes only when he makes what the master has demonstrated his own. Although the apprentices approach the lessons from different perspectives, they reach the same conclusion. Through the description of Rudolph's evolution as a martial artist, Johnson reaffirms Rubin Bailey's point to Allan about finding his own way to be creative. He also emphasizes the healing power of the artist's enlightenment again in "China," this time by having Evelyn regain her sight in time to witness the apex of Rudolph's flight. Although the terms are greatly changed, the criterion of using art as a means of healing old wounds or assuaging old pain remains central.

In addition to commenting on his relationship with John Gardner, the martial arts imagery has another deeply personal connotation for Johnson. He has practiced a martial art for more than thirty years, most recently studying and teaching choy li fut kung fu; the mental transformation his characters undergo has deep roots in his personal experience. His active interest in the martial arts dates to the summer of 1967, after his freshman year at Southern Illinois University. He was admitted to Chi Tao Chuan of the Monastery, a martial arts school on the South Side of Chicago, which he describes as "an early martial arts studio . . . devoted less to learning elegant forms and tournament competition than to animal-like fighting that involved its practitioners forcing themselves into a nearly trance-like state" ("Charles" 233). As he embraced this "discipline of the body that also required an ongoing testing of the spirit" (232), he internalized the life-changing possibilities that the art offers and blended them with his growing interests in art and philosophy. This personal commitment to kung fu also fueled Johnson's creative ambition. His experiences in Chi Tao Chuan of the Monastery were the source for his first "apprentice novel," originally titled *The Last Liberation,* a story of a young black man's struggle and enlightenment through martial arts training. Although Johnson has never published that first manuscript, the notion that kung fu might offer some way to racial enlightenment continued to haunt him. He revisits the theme in "China" and takes it up again in two subsequent short works, "The Green Belt" and "Kwoon."

Under the influence of his training, Rudolph sees that he can transcend limiting racial categories to have a fuller, more empowering life. He also understands that failing to grasp that transcendent view dooms him. Crawling home, too sore to stand erect, from his first lesson at the kwoon, Rudolph explains to Evelyn what makes this so important to him. "'Gung-fu means 'hard work.' . . . I don't think I've ever really done hard work in my life . . . something that asks me to give everything. . . . I've never been able to give everything to anything. The world never let me.'" In addition to recognizing how he has been constrained, Rudolph also explains why these limitations terrify him: "'sometimes I get the feeling that the unused part . . . spoils. . . . Don't ask me to stop training. . . . If I stop, I'll die'" (76–77). Rudolph has already had his own experience of being toward death. This is crucial to his successful resolution of his difficulties. Of course, he might well not physically die if he stops training (although his health will continue to decline), but after one lesson he already sees the danger of spiritual death inherent in surrendering to his limited world. In turning to the East through kung fu, he finds a way to break free from the oppression of Western culture.

Evelyn, angered by the change in Rudolph, embodies Western culture, especially its traditional attitudes about blackness and black experience that he finds so harmful. A devout Christian, Evelyn compares everything Rudolph does at the kwoon to the traditions of her church. "'You grew up in Hodges, South Carolina, same as me,'" she tells him, "'in a right and proper colored church. If you'd been to China, maybe I'd understand'" (90). For Evelyn, the limits of her understanding stretch only to the boundaries of a racialized worldview. She sees her blackness in essentialist terms and embraces the related limitations as inevitable. Even as she sees her husband trying to break out of these boundaries, she reminds him of his racial heritage. Furthermore, she even relegates his attempts at transcendence to racial terms, telling him that he cannot "be Chinese" no matter how hard he tries (91).

As Rudolph patiently explains, he does not aspire to "be Chinese"; the suggestion, in fact, strikes him as ludicrous. What he understands that Evelyn cannot yet grasp is that the racial categories she assigns to being are false.

Rudolph's being *Chinese* is not the issue; his *being* is what is at stake, and he has learned that the definitions that make the world comfortable for Evelyn place unbearable limits on him. This new way of seeing also extends to the burdensome sense of blackness as a limitation. He does not feel the ties to a black heritage that Evelyn cites because he has learned that he can see and be in the world differently, beyond the parameters of a racialized identity.

By contrast, Evelyn's experience severely distorts her conception of the world. Johnson emphasizes her flawed way of seeing by noting, "her retinas were tearing like soft tissue. At these times the world was a canvas with white-out spilling from the far left corner toward the center. . . . Someday, she knew, the snow on her eyes would stay" (64). This overpowering onset of whiteness symbolizes the racially circumscribed nature of her vision of the world. The limitations she attaches to herself and tries to attach to him, and her understanding of them as defined by their common racial and religious experience, show how much her sense of black being determines her reactions to the world. The whiteness that will ultimately blind her marks the culmination of her submission to the demands of the white-defined world that she has allowed to control her for her entire life.

The imagery of Evelyn "always nibbling" (83) as she watches Rudolph train illustrates the weakness of her way of life; her constant hunger, which symbolizes her unfulfilled desires for something better, makes a sharp contrast with her husband's calm. However, consistent with his idea that anyone can transcend limitations, he does not leave her hopeless. In the final moment of the story, Evelyn realizes this art's great potential for transcendence. Momentarily blinded, she recognizes that hers is the passive way toward death characterized by "her sour, rotting smell" (95), a reference that evokes Rudolph's idea about "unused life" spoiling. From that comes the awareness that Rudolph's transcending her desire for death—beautifully figured in his leaving the floor to throw a flying kick just as her enlightenment bursts upon her—is a wonderful thing. Only then, finally able to see her husband as both postman and martial artist, does her sight return, "and the fighting in the farthest ring, in herself, perhaps in all the world, [is] over" as she and Rudolph share a certain balance and harmony in their approach to life (95).

That "perhaps" resonates a bit with Cooter's "for now" in "Exchange Value" and suggests some qualification to Johnson's hopeful vision in the story. Although a surface similarity does exist, I see an important distinction. Rudolph has changed, and Evelyn can; their transcendence marks an achievement that far outstrips Cooter's hesitant steps toward liberation. What "perhaps" indicates is the hope that their enlightenment has broader implications, that this might be a way to heal social suffering, much like Faith Cross's dream of being the Swamp Woman.

Of course, in this story as in the first novel, questions remain. First of all, there is the obvious other reading of "perhaps," which suggests that it might not be possible to stop worldwide fighting over race. Compounding that, one must also consider Johnson's characterization of Evelyn, which relies heavily on broadly accepted negative notions of black womanhood. With her fierce loyalty to the church and her cutting disapproval of her husband's efforts to assert himself, she is a stock figure from the African American tradition. Translating the symbol into popular cultural terms, she resembles, in her harshest moments, Aunt Esther from the television show *Sanford and Son.* That Johnson turns to this stereotype in the midst of this story about transcending preconceptions suggests his continuing difficulty in applying the fundamentals of his aesthetic to questions of gender. In addition to this significant concern, the story also raises the issue of applicability that proves so troubling in *Faith and the Good Thing.* What value can one find in retreating to the kwoon when the world outside its doors remains rife with racial oppression and economic injustice?

Johnson attempts to address this latter issue directly in his two other martial arts stories, "Kwoon" and "The Green Belt." "The Green Belt," a teleplay that Johnson offered to PBS in 1982, draws on the story line of *The Last Liberation* and chronicles young Wyatt Franklin's struggle to transcend his South Side Chicago heritage by studying karate. He avoids numerous temptations, most notably gang violence, and remains true to himself and his sense of the art. The message is one of resistance to social pressures, as Johnson offers the martial arts as an alternative to harmful influences such as drugs and violence. Wyatt's blackness, Johnson says, need not be negatively defined by his impoverished life, and he can negotiate that landscape with help from his training. As Wyatt struggles to mediate the tensions that press on him, he must contend with several models of black male identity. Johnson offers an array of portrayals of black manhood that span a spectrum of stereotypes and address various contemporary limiting views of raciality. These representative men, each of whom has something to offer Wyatt, provide a broader perspective on black being that transforms the story from an account of one adolescent's struggle with himself to the African American man's struggle with definitions, an issue that Johnson revisits repeatedly throughout his work.

The most pressing identity model that Wyatt must examine comes from his best friend Smoky, a member of the Comanchero street gang who wants Wyatt to use his martial arts skills against their arch rivals, the Apaches. As

Wyatt struggles with the physics lesson that he must master to get his green belt promotion, Smoky argues the futility of education and the value of loyalty. "All them teachers . . . that be tellin' you, 'Don't be no fool, stay in school'—man, they was talkin' to some white boys . . . or to nigguhs that got some money. People like you and me ain't got nothin', Wyatt, nothin' but each other" (565). Smoky's logic, grounded in a harsh view of racialized economic injustice, confines his ambition to gang membership. Furthermore, when the gangs clash and Wyatt refuses to fight, Smoky rejects him in favor of the Comancheros. Though that loyalty lands him in a hospital bed, in Smoky's worldview the fight and the family are all that matter to him, because they are all that he can see for himself.

Wyatt's refusal to participate in the Comancheros' battle casts an important light on his commitment to karate in its purest form. He carries a burden of rage more or less equal to those of the gang members. Nevertheless, as Wyatt ultimately knows, and the story tells us explicitly, the goal of his martial arts study is not the ability to fight; instead, karate offers him a way of transcending the violence that mars the Comancheros' lives. If the story were merely the tale of a conflict between the chaos of the streets and the order of the dojo, though, it might descend quickly into cliché. Johnson complicates its take on identity and violence by introducing several male role models whose ways of being black in a white world complicate Wyatt's quest for his own sense of self. At home and at work, Wyatt confronts two men whom he sees as representing all that he does not want to be: his father, David, and his co-worker, Norris. With his adolescent rage as his driving force, Wyatt makes early appraisals of both men that prove inaccurate, or at least incomplete, once he has broken with the limited model that Smoky and his peers offer him.

David Franklin appears in the story as a serious man who never stands up for himself. Wyatt sees him as a *"strange, hard-working black man whom he loves but whom he doesn't want to become"* (575), because he thinks there is no fight in his father; he further believes his mother was right to leave them because of David's weakness. All of these feelings come to a head symbolically for Wyatt when David goes to work on what was supposed to be his night off, keeping his white boss happy at his son's expense. Johnson's portrait of this character contains both gentleness and criticism. David obviously cares for his son and intends to be supportive. At the same time, he sees himself as limited by the economic and social realities of his position. He knows he must keep his job in order to give financial support, and he does whatever is necessary to preserve his position. Unfortunately, his determination to provide for Wyatt creates an appearance of self-negating compliance that makes his angry son determined to be different. Wyatt does not take his father for granted; nevertheless, he also does not really understand him, as his frustration and resentment suggest.

Wyatt has another father figure whom he also does not understand, although because their relationship is purely business, he feels no compunction about acting out his hostility toward Norris. Not surprisingly, Wyatt's older co-worker resents the young man's irresponsible attitude toward his job and seeks to make him accountable for his actions, reporting him when he breaks a case of cologne and demanding that Wyatt work his full shift at the store. We know, although Wyatt cannot see it at first, that Norris's motives are good and that he is not merely the Uncle Tom Wyatt believes him to be. As Norris expresses his concern over Wyatt's involvement with the Comancheros, he represents an elder generation of the black community unhappy with the threat the gangs present.

Norris initially seems to be a replica of David Franklin, and Wyatt offers him little respect. Finally, Wyatt attacks Norris when the older man threatens to report him for leaving work early yet again. Surprisingly, the youth cannot touch the older man, who responds to his imperfect karate with a series of Golden Gloves boxing moves. Impressed with the older man's physical ability, Wyatt finally listens to him. Norris offers the young man a crucial piece of advice: "'Ima tell you somethin', though. You got too much *inertia,* boy. . . . You ain't light on yo' feet in a wide stance like that'" (575). Norris's comment also points to the weaknesses in the young man's approaches to the world. Though he has acquired some of the tools the martial arts can offer him for self-defense, he has not yet fully adopted the philosophical stance that supports those physical accomplishments. Norris is a fighter who chooses not to fight. He adopts a harmonious approach to existence, achieving the synthesis of elements in his environment that allows him to be peacefully in the world that Wyatt still wants to whip into submission.

In addition to his two fathers, Wyatt examines the examples of racial identity offered in the lives of two instructors: Mr. Tilden, his harried physics teacher, and Al Baker, his karate *sensei.* Tilden means to do his job well, but he must deal with students who bully him, members of the Comancheros too stupid to pass the course on their own but smart enough to terrorize their teacher into inflating their grades. Like David Franklin, Tilden has no fight left in him. Oppressed by the circumstances of his position, he surrenders to the "might makes right" idea that comes from and perpetuates economic and racial victimization. He fails doubly as a teacher because he believes in the power of the Comancheros and lets them intimidate him. By giving in to their terrorism, he affirms their way of being in the world, which foregrounds the black male's right to be brutal because the system has nothing for him.

Al Baker presents a sharp contrast to that notion. In keeping with his teaching that his students' most important weapons are their minds, he demands that Wyatt learn his academic lessons, train hard to develop physical strength, and avoid any trouble on the streets. By doing so, he demonstrates what Johnson sees at this point as the best response to the pressures of a racialized society. Although not immune to the terrors besetting his students in their ghetto environment, he believes completely in his response to them as the path to liberation. And that conviction makes him a demanding master. Baker knows Wyatt's anger, and he sympathizes with the young man's situation; he also understands that the situation is no excuse for condoning behavior that subverts the purposes of his lessons. Even more importantly, he knows that Wyatt must resolve the conflicts between school, work, home, and the street himself. In putting Wyatt on probation, he forces him to address the tensions fragmenting his experience and undermining his progress.

This synthesis marks the final phase in Wyatt's development, in which he also gains a double promotion, moving past the green belt to a brown in one night. This promotion comes because he has found a way to integrate the various parts of his life, a process that is the fundamental goal of traditional martial arts training. Like his sensei, Wyatt uses his art to break the mold of victimization and frustration that holds Smoky, Tilden, and his father down. Rather than surrendering to an idea of self defined by negative experiences of black identity, Wyatt finds a means of transcending those boundaries and seeing himself differently. He still exists in the same world, but through his martial arts training he has found a new way of being in it, a process that enables him, like Rudolph Jackson before him, to stop fighting. And, since his refusal to fight includes his returning Smoky's Comanchero gang jacket, we can infer that his liberation from this world might eventually be physical as well as mental, an application of lessons from the dojo that has immense practical value in his socioeconomic environment.

The world of "Kwoon" (1991) is similarly grim, a South Side neighborhood so dangerous that even the most experienced members of the school fear the walk from their cars to the door. Clearly modeled on Johnson's own original kwoon, this storefront sanctuary becomes the testing ground for the ideals of David Lewis, the sifu who sees his training as a higher calling. Reflecting on his students' naïve desire to become fighters, Lewis notes his sense of being "duty bound to lead them, like the Pied Piper, from Sylvester Stallone movies to a real understanding of the martial arts as a way that prepared the young, through discipline and large doses of humility, to be of use to themselves and others" (578). In his convictions, one sees the complete answer to the applicability question: the kwoon builds better citizens who overcome the difficulties of their environments by eschewing preconceptions about themselves. The challenge to this notion comes from Ed Morgan, a bitter, violent veteran of scores of schools around the world. He comes to this kwoon convinced that, like all the others he has found, it mocks the true ideal of the art and serves only as a backdrop for Lewis's boasting and egotism. Eager to destroy a stranger that he thinks he knows, Morgan savagely beats Lewis during a sparring session, shaking the sifu's confidence and forcing a reassessment of his commitment to the art.

To Morgan's surprise, Lewis emerges from his period of convalescence and contemplation more interested in preserving the art's ideals than he is in proving his sparring skills. His egoless recognition of Morgan's superiority on the mats makes him the master the angry fighter has been seeking, the teacher he can respect. It also grounds the spirit of the kwoon, emphasizing the crucial notion that the group is more important than any single member. Morgan sees this on his return to the school for a final confrontation; Lewis's remaining students help him to the mat, and the touch of their arms on Lewis's sore body symbolizes the transcendent linking of their selves. This sense of harmony illustrates the kwoon's greatest value. In many ways, it presents a small-scale fulfillment of Faith's dream and Evelyn's hope. Morgan realizes that to "prove the system, the teaching here, false, he would have to strike down every one of them. And still he would have touched nothing" (586). For him, the man who has been all over the world, the fighting *is* finally over, a fact symbolized in his uncoiled right fist. By helping Morgan past his disillusionment and rage, the kwoon fulfills Lewis's ideal of serving others. Softening even the qualification of Evelyn's "perhaps," this story suggests how this community ideal might apply to efforts to effect meaningful change.

Johnson attempts to extend this message more specifically to the alienating outrage of racialism; the world that the kwoon builds supposedly stands above racial divisions, although historically that has not always been the case. But in Johnson's fictional kwoon, at least, that ideal seems at first glance to prevail. Several times throughout the story he emphasizes the linkage of cultures inherent in martial arts practice, reminding the reader that kung fu in its purest form embodies his intersubjective ideal. Furthermore, as he explains it, he deliberately omits overt racial identifiers from his descriptions of every character, reinforcing his claim that the issue of transcending the ego is a human rather than a racial dilemma. The description of Morgan as having a physique to rival Marvin Hagler's might be seen as offering a clue to his racial identity, as does one of the students' calling Lewis *"bwana"* (580), but these are as close as one comes to any clear identification. As in the case of Henry Popper's extraterrestrial patient, the malady proves to be the Self; this time, though, there seems to be a cure.

Despite this noble ambition, Johnson's effort to fulfill the ideal breaks down. Another relevant note from Popper's tale resonates in "Kwoon" as well. Describing his nights playing poker with the white judge and mayor of his small Illinois town, Popper remarks that they "so cautiously avoid the topic of race during [their] get-togethers that the conversation seems to be about nothing but race" (129). This tension, although not so extreme as in Popper's case, exists in "Kwoon" as well. Its presence in the story complicates Johnson's effort at antiracialism. The conflict manifests most clearly in the description of the neighborhood, which is even grimmer than the landscapes of "Exchange Value" or "Alethia." Even in the context of telling a story supposedly "above" race, Johnson reminds the reader of the harsh realities of an environment largely reserved for, or inflicted upon, African Americans. Simply put, one cannot read "Kwoon" without reflecting on the horrors of South Side Chicago life. The "kwoon" might be an ideal world, but all of its members have to leave the sanctuary at some point and negotiate the pitfalls of the dangerous, damaging environment surrounding it. In the context of Johnson's canon that environment symbolizes African Americans' oppression. Although he tries specifically to make this story not about race, he cannot silence his call for social and economic justice.

In the final analysis, I do not believe that Johnson wishes to fully transcend the racial dilemma in "Kwoon." The story dates to the period of his composing *Dreamer*. In that novel, Chaym Smith presents a forceful indictment of American racism that makes Ed Morgan his twin, spiritually if not figuratively. Both men have traveled the world in search of enlightenment, specifically freedom from a profound sense of personal futility and isolation, and both find only reinforcements for their negativity. Smith's potential salvation comes in serving his physical twin, Dr. King; apparently, Morgan can hope to gain liberation by joining Lewis's kwoon. In both instances, however, the significant social ills facing the black community remain, and Johnson commits himself to keeping them, and the accompanying need of fighting them, in his reader's consciousness. Success in that endeavor demands that race cannot be forgotten.

In *The Sorcerer's Apprentice,* however, one sees Johnson testing various responses to that dilemma. Rudolph's experiences in "China" and Allan's in "The Sorcerer's Apprentice" suggest that Eastern thought and conjuration offer him the best means of overcoming it at this juncture. He will interweave these strands in *Oxherding Tale* as he more fully addresses the impact of slavery on black consciousness. The argument he makes there for liberation has important literary notes as well, as that text embodies his most sophisticated signifying assault on the American canon. And that success, like the strength of his comment on racialism in the novel, begins here. In a sense, the stories of *The Sorcerer's Apprentice* are Johnson's literary gung-fu, the hard work that enables the transcendent flying kick of *Oxherding Tale.*

5 "There Is a Foundation for the House I'm Building": *Oxherding Tale*

Nothing else in Johnson's corpus proves so challenging and so rewarding as *Oxherding Tale* (1982). The novel, which recounts Andrew Hawkins's progress from slavery to freedom, blends the conventions of the slave narrative with an extensive survey of Eastern and Western thought about being. With this amalgamation, Johnson refines the speculations about personal and racial identity that inform his earlier work. Whereas Faith Cross, Allan Jackson, and most of Johnson's other characters to date (excluding Rudolph Lee Jackson) labor ceaselessly within the confines of a black definition of selfhood, Andrew engages the problem of identity from both of the racial perspectives that his racially mixed heritage comprises. His successful reconciliation of his internal racial conflict illustrates Johnson's complete commitment at this point to an idealized vision of humanity functioning outside the boundaries of racialist dualism. Building on notions first presented in "The Education of Mingo," "The Sorcerer's Apprentice," and "China," Johnson emphasizes his distance at this juncture from his earlier interest in cultural politics, especially black cultural nationalism.

In *Oxherding Tale,* he counters the separatist impulses of the Black Arts Movement and the Black Aesthetic by trying to write the black philosophical fiction that he calls for in his essays. As he struggled to realize his aesthetic, the project took on epic proportions. In his introduction to the novel, Johnson notes that "black fiction as I envisioned its intellectual possibilities—hung in the balance. . . . I often referred to it as my 'platform' book (a playful reference to the zen 'Platform Sutra of the Sixth Patriarch'), meaning that everything else I attempted to do would be based upon and refer to it" (xvii). The "intellectual possibilities" he refers to include the fusion of literature and philosophy and a continuation of his signifying revision of the American canon. The first involves supplementing his application of phenomenological principles with specific treatment of a range of Western philosophers. He fulfills the second by interweaving references to Frederick Douglass's *Narrative* (1845), Herman Melville's *Pierre* (1852), Ralph Waldo Emerson's essays, and the passing novel into his story.

In taking up the neo-slave narrative model, *Oxherding Tale* invites comparison with Ishmael Reed's *Flight to Canada* (1976). Johnson and Reed share an interest in experimentation and an impulse to redefine the idea of slavery that in some ways sets them apart from other twentieth-century African American novelists who have adopted the form of the slave narrative.[1] Both incorporate conventions of the form and signify on works by prominent nineteenth-century white authors; in *Flight to Canada,* Reed pointedly references Harriet Beecher Stowe's *Uncle Tom's Cabin.* Both also suggest that mental freedom should be a primary value for the contemporary African American community. Despite these commonalities, Johnson's and Reed's differing claims about black literary identity shape their disparate interpretations of liberation. True to his New Breed principles, Reed uses Stowe to illustrate the threat of white mental dominance over blacks. Freedom for him comes only when one overthrows the oppressor and embraces a positively constructed black identity. By contrast, Johnson affirms interracial connections between traditions. Less interested than his predecessor in mocking their common literary ancestors, black and white, Johnson uses them to demonstrate how an excessive fixation on distinctions circumscribes one's experience. For him, freedom is not a matter of "othering" the oppressor; instead, it is a matter of recognizing that the very idea of "otherness" generates oppression.

In his vision, this notion applies to literary *and* personal questions. The ghettoization of canons that is challenged by his intertextual references corresponds to his rejection of social divisions between racial groups. Although he will qualify the position in his later work, in *Oxherding Tale* Johnson aspires to full transcendence of racialist principles, positing instead the conviction that humanity can overcome a history of injustice and social violence to recognize the completeness of our intersubjective relations. This creative program, which resonates with Eric Sundquist's vision of American literature in *To Wake the Nations* (1993), manifests itself in Andrew's struggle to reconcile his own personal and intellectual identity crises.

Andrew's conflict can be traced to his origins as the product of a drunken scheme that Jonathan Polkinghorne, the owner of Cripplegate plantation, cooks up with his black butler, George Hawkins. After a long, riotous evening on the verandah of a South Carolina plantation house, Jonathan proposes that he and George trade beds for the night. Somewhat confused but conditioned to obey his master's will, George visits Anna Polkinghorne's bedroom. Their sexual union results in George's demotion to field hand, Jonathan's permanent exile to the lower floor of the house, and Andrew. In a striking reversal of the typical slave-narrative pattern, where the speaker's ignorance of his origins indicts white slaveholders' sexual practices, Andrew tells this humorous account of his conception. That choice advances Johnson's program as it opens a unique perspective on the identity issue. Andrew's knowledge of his origins complicates his sense of self; to achieve some relief from his psychological torment he must negotiate the tensions between racial groups. As he moves from black world to white world, he encounters various teachers, most of whom are driven by some essentialist agenda. Freedom can come only when he reconciles their various lessons.

The education Jonathan provides Andrew proves to be an exercise in balancing conflicting modes of thought. At the feet of Ezekiel Sykes-Withers, his crazed transcendentalist, abolitionist tutor, Andrew learns "everything western intellectual history could offer" and many fundamentals of Eastern thought (xiv). Not surprisingly, his education spoils him for servitude. It also transforms him into a romantic; a sexual encounter with Minty, another Cripplegate slave, brings this to the surface. Inspired by love and pained to realize that he cannot possess her so long as he remains enslaved, Andrew asks Jonathan for freedom. Instead, Jonathan sends him to work for Flo Hatfield at Leviathan plantation. She forces him into a demanding sexual servitude that threatens to destroy him, mind and body.

Probably the only thing that saves Andrew is his friendship with Reb, also known as the Coffinmaker, an Allmuseri craftsman living on the plantation. Reb's every action demonstrates his sense of unity with the environment, which enables him to largely transcend the chaos of Leviathan. When Andrew inevitably displeases Flo, she sends him and Reb to work in her nearby salt mines. The two men escape by posing as a white gentleman and his body servant. The fugitives must elude the Soulcatcher, Horace Bannon, a bounty hunter who "plays upon black fears—and a rigid, essentialist notion of the self—to trap his prey" (Johnson, Introduction xvii) and who believes so completely in this method that he vows to retire if he ever meets a slave he cannot catch.

Meanwhile, Andrew and Reb settle in Spartanburg, South Carolina, where Andrew adopts the name William Harris and takes a position teaching school. He courts and marries Peggy Undercliff, the daughter of the town doctor. After Andrew's marriage, Reb flees to the North, pursued by the Soulcatcher. Andrew and Peggy appear to be settling into a comfortable routine until Andrew finds Minty, a wreck of her former self, on the town's auction block. He takes her home, confesses some of his past, and tries to save her from her fatal case of pellagra. When she dies, Bannon reappears. Andrew thinks the Soulcatcher has finally come to claim him. Bannon has, in fact, come to tell him he is free. Unable to capture Reb, Bannon has given up slave catching. His more complete explanation of his soul-catching method includes an account of George's death; hearing a description of his father's end, Andrew finally fully understands the importance of reconciling the disparate elements of his identity. In a move that emphasizes Andrew's rebirth, the Soulcatcher "deliver[s]" him home to Peggy, with whom he takes up "the business of rebuilding . . . the world" (176).

• • •

Andrew's liminal position at Cripplegate exacerbates the double consciousness that drives his quest. Feeling unwelcome in his master's house, Andrew must also bear the brunt of George's ranting about the separation of white and black worlds. Once reluctant to criticize the Polkinghornes, the butler-turned-oxherd views his fall from grace as a sign: nothing in the white world is for him. Furthermore, George's change in position brings his racial militancy to the surface. He uses his separation from the Big House to solidify his dependence on a binary model of identity; as he proclaims to his son, "'If they say *hup,* Hawk, it's gotta be *down*'" (24).

George's pronouncements, which are among Johnson's most extreme examples of separatist rhetoric, represent the author's direct challenge to black cultural nationalism. They also demonstrate how such ideological stridency limits chances for new discovery. The oxherd's perspective on race keeps him from examining Andrew's complex position. As George argues his vision of blackness, he burdens his son with an enormous responsibility. "'Whatever you do, Hawk—it pushes the Race forward, or pulls us back. You know what I've always told you: If you fail, everything we been fightin' for fails with you. Be y'self'" (21). As George well knows, Andrew has both black and white ancestors; truly being himself means something different from what George has in mind.

What George really demands is that Andrew *divide* himself, placing primary importance on the elements of his identity that perpetuate George's idea of black manhood. For Andrew, the fallout from George's conviction that black men must collectively express who they *are* means he cannot yet articulate any sense of who he might *be* by looking at himself, his race, and the world differently from his father. Interestingly, Johnson uses this scene to introduce a key notion in his own exploration of black being. George's charge that Andrew be himself calls into question not only the issue of race but the entire concept of selfhood. In keeping with the Buddhist principles that inform the narrative, Johnson challenges the idea of essential selfhood as one of the fundamental forces creating interpersonal divisions. By embracing the idea that selfhood is constructed (which one sees reflected in the space between Andrew's reality and George's demand), one can overcome a divided consciousness and all of the suffering associated with it.

Andrew knows something of this Eastern idea, as he encounters it in his lessons with Ezekiel. The tutor's curriculum includes "lectures on . . . the 165 Considerations, Four Noble Truths, the Eight-Fold Path, the 3,000 good manners, and 80,000 Graceful conducts" (13). The Four Noble Truths and the Eight-Fold Path are central to Buddhist thought. The Four Noble Truths originate in India and flower in Zen Buddhism; their message is that one escapes earthly suffering by eschewing desire. The Eight-Fold Path of Zen, "the method or doctrine whereby self-frustration is brought to an end," is also the fourth Noble Truth (Watts 46–51). With the presentation of these doctrines, Johnson points to the problem of and the solution to Andrew's struggle.

The meditations on desire ground the belief that enlightenment comes by breaking the cycle of life and death, called *samsara,* that thoughtless individuals are doomed to repeat. One source of samsara is a belief that the self exists distinct from the rest of the universe. Desire, by definition, perpetuates this belief. For Andrew, the object of desire is a sense of himself, a quest that intensifies his separation on multiple levels. In the Buddhist teachings he provides, Ezekiel offers Andrew a means of rising above his chief difficulty. He can learn cessation of desire from the Four Noble Truths. To achieve this enlightenment he must open himself to the Eastern ideas, an effort best accomplished by revising his Western-defined perceptions.

Subsequent to composing the novel, Johnson published "A Sangha by Another Name," an article that identifies Buddhism as the ideal response for African Americans to the racial identity question. As he notes in that essay, "the life of a slave . . . was one of thinghood. It is, one might say, a frighteningly fertile ground for the growth of a deep appreciation of the First and Second Noble Truths" (43). The First Noble Truth, that frustration and pain characterize one's life, and the Second, that the suffering that generates those experiences has a cause, accurately describes African Americans' experiences in this country from the Middle Passage to the present. To this point, the vision resonates with George Hawkins's position; the crucial difference lies in how one responds to that awareness. Rather than fixate on that suffering, the Buddhist adopts the Eight-Fold Path to overcome it. Johnson argues that the "emphasis in Buddhist teachings on letting go of the fabricated, false sense of self positions issues of Race as foremost among samsaric illusions, along with all the essentialist conceptions of difference that have caused so much human suffering and mischief since the eighteenth century" (111).

Perhaps Buddhism does offer "the black American quest for 'freedom' its profoundest, truest, and most revolutionary meaning" (113). Still, one wonders about its ability to truly modify social realities; circumstances in the novel intensify that question. Reb might well be internally liberated, but he still faces the salt mines at Flo's whim. Furthermore, the Coffinmaker's resignation represents an extreme response. What of the seeker who, like Andrew, cannot achieve such levels of self-denial? Although he will raise such questions himself in *Middle Passage* and *Dreamer,* in *Oxherding Tale* Johnson embraces this idealistic notion of self-erasure completely. Racial questions dominate Andrew's quest for himself, and he must overcome the fragmentation that his father's demands on him represent. Turning to the East promises a chance of developing the new way of seeing that he needs in order to achieve liberation.

Ezekiel would seem an ideal guide for this process. His letter of reference from Noah Porter speaks of a "peculiar quirk of cognition that, like the Tibetan mystic, lets him perceive the interior of objects." It also states that Ezekiel is "perhaps the only man in North America who truly understands the *Mahabharata,*" the fable of India's origin that advances the idea of transcending desire (9). Ezekiel's visual trick illustrates how profoundly his perceptions differ from the norm. He has learned to look beneath conventional limitations such as external appearance. For someone on a quest to reconcile questions about racial identity, an ability to see through superficialities such as skin color would seem crucial. Similarly, Ezekiel has a grasp on the text that contains *The Bhagavad-Gita,* a work Johnson describes as "committed to transcending dualism" (Nash 51). Dualism is Andrew's problem, both literally in his ancestry and figuratively in his liminal position between racial and intellectual worlds. One might well think that learning his tutor's methods would enable Andrew to resolve his conflicts. However, Ezekiel's applications of his cognitive errata are much too ethereal. Alone with his books and the indecipherable articles he compulsively writes, the tutor cannot apply the abstract things he knows to any specific actions or experiences. He therefore becomes an example of wasted potential, one who could achieve enlightenment were he only to apply his gifts to living. One sees this in the account of Karl Marx's disastrous visit to Cripplegate and Ezekiel's actions after he leaves.

Marx demonstrates a vitality that Ezekiel cannot match, and his every action illustrates the weakness of Ezekiel's worldview. When Marx descends from the stagecoach, we learn he has another correspondent in Abbeville, one Jonathan Streitburgher, an abolitionist newspaper editor. After living close to Abbeville for seven years, Ezekiel has never once spoken with the newspaperman, though they would have at least abolitionism and a friendship with Marx in common. Marx's surprise at this shows Andrew his tutor in a different light. He sees for the first time that Ezekiel is "a lonely, unsocial creature unused to visitors, as awkward with people as a recluse . . . his rejection of society, his radicalism, was not, as he thought, due to some subtle rareness of the soul. It was stinginess. Resentment for the richness of things" (83). Comfortable only in the realm of the intellect, Ezekiel cannot connect meaningfully with anyone else. His perceptive abilities, therefore, are useless in Andrew's struggle to overcome his sense of separation.

Ezekiel's flaws become most painfully clear when he and Marx discuss his work on the self. Arguing that one exists only "*through* an Other," that one must have a sense of separation in every moment of perception to understand one's self as an individual, Ezekiel strikes at the heart of Andrew's identity crisis. Unfortunately, he overlooks the logical conclusion of his own argument. Marx spells it out for him: "'You argue that . . . *someone* must . . . be central to your existence. . . . Vhen two subjects come together, they realize . . . a common vorld. . . . The universal name for this final, ontological achievement . . . is *love*'" (86). Marx knows, as does Ezekiel, the difficulty of overcoming awareness of division. Not so fully versed in Eastern texts as Ezekiel, he does not have access to the meditation on transcending desire. Nevertheless, he offers a practical means of addressing the dilemma that proves itself daily in human existence. Unfortunately, loving another is beyond Ezekiel's ability. He tries to devote himself to Althea Moses, the crippled daughter of a corrupt hired hand, sacrificing everything he has to serve her needs. When he finally learns that Althea's father, Shem Moses, has deceived him, Ezekiel's heart literally breaks. His attempt at love fails because it remains an intellectual exercise for him. Marx's critique of Ezekiel points Andrew toward a solution; hope for him lies in finding the love that Ezekiel cannot.

Despite Flo Hatfield's priding herself on her knowledge of love, Leviathan proves rough ground for Andrew's search. Like some awful goddess, Flo sees her slaves as potential food for her appetites. Soon after Andrew arrives at Leviathan, she begins feeding on him, demanding service that intensifies his sense of bondage.[2] He soon sees that her version of love resembles Ezekiel's understanding of wisdom and, like the tutor's position, is flawed by its adherence to a dualistic perceptual model. Where he sacrificed the body for the mind, she privileges genital pleasure over cerebral stimulation. Flo further intensifies Andrew's identity crisis by fixing on his race as an important element of his being. As she explains, she takes slaves as lovers because she believes black men are most likely to understand her. "'People say a woman is *nothing* without a man! A kind of freak to be pitied. . . . Years ago I thought colored men were closer to seeing through this than anybody'" (59). Though she now doubts the accuracy of that view, Flo still needs black otherness in her world to define herself.

Flo's attitudes affect Andrew much as George's opinions did, despite an extreme variance in motivation. Both his father and his new master see essential differences between white and black manhood. The sympathy Flo believes she finds between white women and black men centers on their common victimization at the hands of white men. She, like George, asks Andrew to conform to a particular identity model grounded in fixed perceptions of black manhood. For the series of men who have been Flo's favorites before Andrew, her challenge to be black has been overwhelming; the corpses of her two most recent lovers demonstrate the lethal demands of her essentialist vision.

They also represent, ironically, the humor of Andrew's time at Leviathan. Her pursuit of him, from the moment of his first undressing to be measured for new clothes to his assertion of the simian characteristics of his love life with Flo, plays as a sex comedy. In this instance Johnson uses a light tone to counter the serious philosophical issues that inform Andrew's and Flo's relationship. One also sees humor elsewhere in the novel, from the description of George's and Anna's encounter to the Soulcatcher's parallel between masturbation and strangling hens that evokes a slang expression for autoeroticism. In fact, comedy marks Andrew's encounters with all of the narrowly focused teachers who would keep him in bondage. Even if, as Stanley Crouch notes, Johnson is "essentially a gallows humorist," the humor fulfills an essential function ("Charles Johnson" 137). Here, as throughout Johnson's corpus, the humor shocks the reader out of complacency and highlights the author's challenge to conventional modes of perception. It also emphasizes his primary response at this point to that legacy of African American suffering. By refusing to give in to that pain, Johnson strengthens his own case against that view of black life. He applied that tactic to treatments of slavery as early as *Black Humor* and continues it in his drawings for *Black Issues* magazine. In every case, he refuses to allow the record of African Americans' experiences of bondage to "fix" his ideas about racial identity. That resistance will be an ideal for Andrew, although none of his teachers to date has shown him how to achieve it.

From his first sighting of Andrew, Reb changes that. With one brief glance and a comment, Reb demonstrates an acute awareness of Andrew's liminality. He asks whether Andrew is "folks" (meaning African American) or white; when Andrew claims to be "'definitely folks,'" the Coffinmaker responds, "'You ain't folks or white. . . . You fresh meat, boy'" (36). Reb's assertion is harsh but accurate. So long as Andrew views himself in terms of essentialist racial designations, he is merely "meat," an object to be acted on by others' values and desires. In contrast, the Coffinmaker offers him a means of overcoming such definitions and freeing himself from the crisis of identity that plagues him. Reb provides Andrew with a fully articulated model of life beyond the parameters of dualism. Unlike Andrew, he is not plagued by the racial essentialism, the "epidermalized Being," that controls life at Leviathan (52). Reb's worldview also strikes at the foundations of Andrew's understanding of being itself. Johnson describes him as the novel's "resident Taoist," a man so far from desire and individuality that nothing he does bears the imprint of his identity (Nash 56). His explanation of coffin making, which includes a full week in seclusion attempting to shed his memories of previous jobs, illustrates this perfectly. "'After a day I can't remember none of 'em. . . . After five days, I forget the fact that I makes coffins. Seven days go by, and I forget all about myself, and that's when I start looking round for a tree that wants to be a coffin'" (47).

The Coffinmaker's worldview comes largely from his Allmuseri heritage. Building upon the tribal name he concocted for "The Education of Mingo" and "The Sorcerer's Apprentice," Johnson begins developing the tribe's fundamental features. By the time he composes *Dreamer,* he will refer to the Allmuseri as "the most spiritually evolved people on earth." At that point, he will also note that they "have transcended dualism, conquered that most ancient of objects—the self—and live lives of perfect peace, nonviolence, creativity and *ahimsa* ('harmlessness to all sentient beings.')" (Nash 56–57). One sees the roots of that position here. As Reb's shift in self-perception when he makes coffins indicates, the tribespeople understand identity as a constructed illusion that they can change as necessary to maintain harmony with their surroundings. This approach protects them from the sort of suffering Andrew experiences.

The Coffinmaker tries to explain this by telling Andrew the story of Rakhal, a shaman of the tribe, and Akbar, the Allmuseri king, who hates him for his adherence to the ancient tribal beliefs. When Rakhal tells the king he will call down rain that will drive the people mad, Akbar responds by collecting fresh water, avoiding the enchantment that takes over the rest of the tribe, including Rakhal. Unfortunately for him, though, Akbar finds no comfort in his sanity. As the rest of the tribe agrees that their new perceptions are reality, he becomes the isolate. He finally gives in, choosing harmony over separation and sacrificing a "right" view of the world in the process. The tale emphasizes the value of the Allmuseri's intellectual flexibility, which opens them to experiences beyond the realm of conventionality. This fluidity of perception, in turn, enables them to resist any sense of division from their environment.

Although Andrew sees the value of Reb's sense of harmony, he cannot yet access it for himself. This raises the question of utility. How effective can the

Allmuseri way of life be in the face of the outrages of the slave trade? The story of Akbar and Rakhal illuminates this; the historical record suggests that Africans refusing to embrace Islam more likely faced slavery than Rakhal's triumph of tricksterism. In this instance, Johnson suggests that Allmuseri-ness sufficiently counters the pressures of racialism; Reb's memories of the transatlantic voyage are abstract, indicating their inability to compromise his, and the tribe's, sense of self. This representation of such a signal horror of African American history demonstrates the author's unwillingness to submit to the negative vision that would threaten his aesthetic. In a significant move back toward social concerns, though, he will complicate this issue significantly by the time of *Middle Passage.*

But in the meantime, Andrew must undergo his own Middle Passage of sorts. His journey from the black to the white world causes an identity crisis not unlike what the human cargo must have faced during their journey to America. When he chooses passing for white and becomes William Harris, he betrays George Hawkins's values. That he sees his experiences in terms of separate black and white worlds illustrates how heavily his father's lessons weigh on him. Ironically, though, it is precisely the immersion in whiteness that he needs to unify his vision. Only by embracing the white world can he free himself from racial duality.

The other crucial element of his time in the white world is his relationship with Peggy Undercliff. Unlike Flo Hatfield in every way, she becomes for Andrew the salvation that Marx described to Ezekiel. After their wedding, they settle into a ramshackle cabin on the edge of town, and he takes up teaching. He finds, to his surprise, that his *dharma* "was that of the householder" (147). In this state, he does the work that he is given to do, aiming toward tranquillity and enlightenment. But such is not to be his fate, at least not initially. As Jonathan Little notes, "in the householder stage of life, in which one marries, works, has children, and pursues spiritual development, one must realize that one's duty, or *dharma,* is not only to oneself but also to the wider community" (*Charles Johnson's* 87). Andrew finds the limits of this social duty tested when Minty appears on the town's auction block.

Reaching back to the black world, he attempts to keep his long-ago promise. The former slave now becomes a slave master by buying her freedom. Though he means well by doing so, he nearly destroys his new world in the process, as he finds himself plunged anew into racial separation. As he feels himself othered from his own home, he must resist the desire and dissatisfaction that consumed George. He also finds himself back in the original dilemma that initiated his quest. Because he is not truly free in his fabricated life, he still cannot possess Minty. Even more than when he was young Andrew

Hawkins, his life is now an amalgamation of secondhand borrowings. Before he can escape this trap, Minty, as its representative in the new white world he has constructed, must die. And die she does, in a most horrific manner. This prepares him for the final interview with Bannon, which apparently fulfills the novel's promise and shows a way beyond essentialism.

But what of Minty, Flo, and Peggy, who remain trapped in their rigidly constrained gender identities? Johnson apparently does not fully extend his consciousness-transforming model to questions of gender. This is not to say that he does not try; as Jennifer Hayward notes, "Johnson makes a strong attempt to understand feminist issues and to inscribe them in his book." Nevertheless, in doing so he also glorifies women as representatives of a transcendent Whole, an "Eternal Feminine" whose presence in the text supports rather than subverts ideas of gender difference that run counter to his philosophical goals (690). Once again, the inevitable tension between ideal and application associated with the dialectic process of expanding the individual's consciousness complicates any assessment of Johnson's creative project. What are we to make of a system promising complete liberation that only succeeds by forcing some back into bondage?

In the world of the text, Bannon's reappearance saves Andrew from this fate by teaching him one final lesson about dualistic models of racial identity. His process of slave catching demands that he internalize elements of his victims' personalities; he cannot learn what they want without thinking like them. What he knows of each victim appears on his skin, giving him the appearance of being covered with tattoos. The images are in fact those beings, continually fusing and re-forming on Bannon's chest. While looking at Bannon's chest, Andrew has an Emersonian realization, an "Each and All" recognition that "the One and the Many gave me back my father . . . in every being . . . and, in the final face I saw . . . my own face. . . . I was my father's father, and he my child" (176). Confronted with this graphic representation of reunion with George, Andrew finally understands the possibilities for reconciling George's rigid model of black identity with his own more fluid sense of racial boundaries. Transcending that dualism brings a broader enlightenment that enables him to escape his illusions about individual and racial identity.

• • •

The integration and transcendence that Andrew experiences mirrors Johnson's literary accomplishment in *Oxherding Tale.* The novel combines a structure suggested by the *Ten Oxherding Pictures* with a pattern of Western philosophical references including Arthur Schopenhauer, Jeremy Bentham, Thomas Hobbes, and Martin Heidegger. Schopenhauer appears in the novel as Ezekiel's and Dr. Undercliff's favorite thinker, and Andrew explains how Ezekiel uses Eastern texts to unlock Schopenhauer's writings. Johnson weaves Bentham and Hobbes into the narrative when Andrew arrives at Leviathan. The plantation's name has much to do with Flo's adherence to Hobbes's principles. Her statement to Andrew about her role at the plantation is an almost direct quotation from *Leviathan,* Hobbes's treatise on the development of the state. Furthermore, her persistent misquotation of Bentham provokes a closer look at his ideas, which Johnson integrates, along with Hobbes's views, into his textual discussion of desire.

Johnson pays important tribute to Heidegger by referring to the concept of sein-zum-tod, or "being toward death." Building on an idea he explores in "Exchange Value," Johnson pushes a step farther in *Oxherding Tale* by showing a range of characters responding to death differently. For the Coffinmaker, who trades on death to some extent, it encourages detachment. For Andrew, it eventually motivates engagement, although he needs multiple exposures. Viewing Patrick's and Moon's corpses does not save him from making bad choices that prolong his suffering. To overcome his mental limitations, Andrew must directly confront mortality in his final interview with the Soulcatcher. He comes away from that experience more capable of transcending separation and finally free to rebuild the world with his wife and daughter. As these examples indicate, proper use of philosophy leads to enlightenment in *Oxherding Tale.* The individuals who struggle toward liberation commonly suffer from adhering too rigidly (or, in Flo's case at least, inaccurately) to a single thinker's ideals. To be free, Andrew must go beyond his teachers, synthesizing the strengths of their various lessons into a workable Whole.

Johnson makes a similar move in signifying on canonical works by white and black American authors and breaking them out of conventional interpretations and limitations. He poses the most obvious of these challenges to the slave narrative. In his efforts to demonstrate that race and a racialist conception of identity are illusions, he revises one of the pillars of the African American canon: Frederick Douglass's *Narrative of the Life of Frederick Douglass, an American Slave, Written by Himself.* According to Eric Sundquist, "no black American before Martin Luther King, Jr., more fully articulated the dream of self-determination . . . than Douglass" (85–86). In service of that dream, Douglass stresses three main themes: the slave's need to develop a sense of individuality that separates him from his master; the importance of literacy to his quest for freedom; and the difference between the slave holders' corrupt religion and the Christianity described in the Bible. Johnson makes use of each in *Oxherding Tale;* in every instance, he takes Douglass's liberating experiences and turns them into intensifiers of Andrew's bondage. As William L. Andrews notes, "it is neither inaccurate nor unfair . . . to suggest that the fundamental theme of Douglass' greatest writing was his own evolving sense of selfhood" (Introduction 4). In Johnson's invocation of fundamental Buddhist principles and his problematization of the very idea of the self, Douglass provides a useful starting point on which to build.

Parallels to Douglass's *Narrative* begin with the account of Andrew's origins. Like Douglass, Andrew is a mixed-race slave living on his white parent's plantation. His ancestry, however, is not shrouded in mystery as is Douglass's. In a bitterly ironic twist on literary and social traditions, Andrew cannot follow the lineage-of-the-mother rule. Douglass does, and that experience, combined with his lack of absolute certainty about his biological relationship to his master, exacerbates his identity crisis. Forced by law and social custom to define himself as black, his perception of whiteness, and especially his white father, seems entirely hostile. His account of white slaveholders' betrayal and abuse of their slave offspring becomes one of his most powerful condemnations of the institution. It also emphasizes the idea of otherness that drives his work. For Andrew, awareness of this racial divide in his ancestry weakens rather than empowers him. Liberation comes only with reconciliation of his black and white worlds, a direct challenge to the notion of racial identity that Douglass celebrates.

The description of Jonathan's and George's bed hopping shows that this signifying is not without humor; indeed, the lightness of Johnson's tone dispels any sense of tragedy that one might associate with the original. It also significantly changes the terms of heroic action, as one sees in his revision of Douglass's struggle with Edward Covey, the slave breaker he lives with in his sixteenth year. The event marks a turning point for the former bondsman. He says in prefacing his description of the episode, "You have seen how a man was made a slave; you shall see how a slave was made a man" (65). As the slave system denied African American males any sense of manhood, Douglass's ability to name himself thus indicates his resistance to that oppression. In making this statement, he articulates a powerful sense of his own identity. Furthermore, as he shows in the remainder of the *Narrative,* were he to have missed this opportunity to develop a strong sense of identity, he would never have gotten free.

In Andrew's case, the slave breaker would be Flo Hatfield; although the terms of the encounters differ significantly, one can see Johnson playing here with the idea of a slave being "made a man." Certainly Leviathan's master inspires the sort of terror and submission in Andrew that Covey evokes in Douglass. And, like his predecessor, Andrew strikes a literal blow for freedom that initiates the next phase of his individual development. But where Covey and his lessons are a scarring burden that Douglass would gladly leave behind, Flo's teachings prove useful to Andrew in a positive sense. When he and Peggy marry, he brings his experiences at Leviathan to bear, using the corrupted version of lovemaking he learned there as a tool to help him forge a real emotional connection with his new bride. In a move that anticipates his final statement, "(All is conserved; all)" (176), Andrew interweaves past and present, bridging one of the gaps between his black and white worlds and emphasizing unity over separation.

Although Johnson makes useful points by rewriting Douglass's origins and growing ability to assert himself, he saves his strongest signifying commentary for his revision of Douglass's education. Acquiring literacy is a turning point for Douglass. He describes his master's initial resistance to the project, which only made it more appealing; he recounts his tricking white children in his neighborhood into helping him learn to write; and he explains the value of literacy in his quest for freedom. He also, at one point, notes that learning to read gave him as much pain as joy before he got free, because he knew what he wanted but did not see how to get it. In these statements, Douglass equates literacy with desire and emphasizes how both help him achieve liberation and self-determination (Sekora 155–63).

In *Oxherding Tale,* Andrew's acquisition of literacy causes him a great deal of trouble. Paradoxically, although Ezekiel exposes Andrew to ideas that will ultimately help him be free, the process of gaining his formal education is a cause of his suffering. In the course of his study he learns a fragmented model of perception that divides head and heart and plunges him into the state of separation that he suffers until his final encounter with Bannon. As he grasps the message of Ezekiel's texts, he drifts farther from his father's world; the tension between his knowledge and the oxherd's emotional demands that he embrace a black identity is the primary source of his subsequent pain and confusion.

The problem in this instance is not simply Andrew's reading but rather his uncritical acceptance of others' ideas. The answer to his dilemma lies in learning to see differently what he has read. When Andrew views the world in terms of unity rather than separation, he can apply the fundamental ideas that Ezekiel exposes him to and reconcile his head-heart dichotomy. Similarly for Johnson, a too-strict adherence to the ideas about black identity presented in texts like Douglass's *Narrative* leads to a sense of racial division that contradicts his aesthetic. If one holds exclusively to texts that assert this separatist model of African American identity, the dichotomy Johnson seeks to overcome remains in place. His revision of this pivotal topos from Douglass's text revises what control of the word means in the African American tradition.

Johnson shares this concern over the impact of literacy on black identity with Black Aesthetic and New Breed writers, although his conclusions differ profoundly from theirs. For many Black Aestheticians and New Breed writers, the issue is not gaining control *of* the word but rather avoiding being controlled *by* the word, as African Americans submit to the intellectual domination of whites presenting a negative image of blackness. One sees this resistance to domination by the word in *Flight to Canada.* Like *Oxherding Tale,* Reed's neo-slave narrative challenges the form's sanctity and suggests that readers develop new understandings of the African American tradition. However, he makes a radically different claim about black identity than Johnson does. In *Flight to Canada,* Reed argues that African Americans have been controlled by white cultural values for too long. His purpose in the text is to establish a distinctively black sensibility that reverses the domination of white-defined perceptions.[3]

To achieve that, Reed adopts the disruptive strategies of postmodernism and challenges established notions about African American literature and history. In undercutting the foundation of national conceptions about the era of slavery, he hopes to raise questions about the process by which the historical record is constructed. He also demonstrates how blacks can use literature to free themselves from the intellectual bondage of the established historical record. By changing the terms of who determines the "truth," he undermines the racialized hierarchy that kept African Americans from this empowered, positive view of their heritage for decades.

Reed further demonstrates how African Americans can free themselves from mental bondage by mocking Harriet Beecher Stowe for exploiting Josiah Henson, the model for her character Uncle Tom. His treatment of the issue raises important questions about her co-opting of African American voices rather than allowing them to speak for themselves. *"She'd read Josiah Henson's book. That Harriet was alert.* The Life of Josiah Henson, Formerly a Slave. . . . *It was short, but it was his. . . . A man's story is his gris-gris, you know. Taking his story is like taking his gris-gris. The thing that is himself"* (8). Part of Reed's purpose is to suggest that blacks must reclaim their literary gris-gris, or magic, to gain power of the terms of their self-definition. In *Flight to Canada,* Uncle Robin, the crafty butler who redoes his master's will, is supposed to be one of Stowe's sources for a sort of sequel to *Uncle Tom's Cabin.*[4] At the end of the novel, he chooses Raven, a fellow black man, to write his story for him instead of entrusting it to the white author who so greatly misused Henson.

Reed makes another important point about continuity within the African American tradition when he has Quickskill encounter William Wells Brown onboard a steamer crossing from Buffalo to Canada. When he and Raven discuss Quickskill's poetry, Quickskill tells Brown, "'my poem "Flight to Canada" is going to be published in *Beulahland Review*. . . . I'm sure the critics are going to give me some kind of white master. . . . They'll say he gave me the inspiration and that I modeled it after him. But I had you in mind'" (121). Quickskill's comment illustrates Reed's belief that the literary establishment does not want black writers to prosper without legitimizing validation from some white author. It also shows Reed suggesting a separate flow of influence among black writers that white authors cannot access.

As *Oxherding Tale* indicates, Johnson does not share this view of the African American literary tradition. He values his predecessors, both black and white, and uses them freely in service of his artistic goal. Although he and Reed draw profoundly different conclusions, he acknowledges the significant debt that he owes his contemporary, whose work represents an important step in the evolution of African American literature. Johnson's subsequent efforts to reunite and reorganize elements of the national literary tradition depend to some extent on Reed's success. Only when one can see a shattered version of the conventional interpretive model can one consider alternative ways of reassembling its parts. With his articulation of an intersubjective plan, Johnson offers a new kind of challenge to established perceptions about African American life and literature.

One sees Johnson positioning himself in the national literary tradition most clearly through his signifying presentations of Melville and Emerson in the novel. He references Melville directly.[5] Soon after his arrival in Spartanburg, Andrew promises to discuss Melville's *Pierre* with Peggy Undercliff. Not only does he know the novel well, he tells her, but its author is "an old family acquaintance" (124). With its parallel light and dark women, a somewhat enigmatic father whose memory influences the son's actions, and, in that son, a protagonist seeking to resolve his internal conflicts about his personal and family identities, *Pierre* proves an apt reference text for *Oxherding Tale*. Indeed, Pierre and Andrew have so much in common that one might call them kindred spirits. These commonalities arise in part from their circumstances, but what motivates them at bottom are the authors' similar interests.

Melville provides a tremendously important example for Johnson's development. In fact, references to Melville permeate Johnson's work; in addition to the direct reference to *Pierre*, *Oxherding Tale* contains allusions to *Moby-Dick* (1851) and *The Confidence-Man* (1857). One might think of Flo as a monomaniacal Ahab or of Reb and Queequeg, whose coffins save the protagonists' lives in their respective texts. And one might also consider how Bannon's shape-shifting abilities and fluid racial identity, along with the Vet's offer to sell Andrew a "life-assurance" policy, evoke Melville's many-visaged swindler. Johnson describes his predecessor's work as "essential reading in . . . the 'epic conversation' of writers tackling perennial philosophical questions" (Nash 59). These questions, and the aesthetic impulses they inspire, shape both authors' works and provide the foundation for Johnson's signifying.

One of the most significant artistic values that Johnson and Melville share is the quest for "the liberation of perception" (Johnson, "Philosophy" 60). Melville's fascination with the pitfalls of unexamined perception manifests itself clearly in *Pierre.*[6] One could say that Pierre Glendinning's world falls apart largely because his way of being in it is too narrow. Were he able to consider interpretive options outside the realm of his early experience at Saddle Meadows, Pierre might resolve the problem of Isabel differently. Further, if he were less inclined to trust appearances, he might raise some of the questions about their relationship that come to him only when he sees the stranger portrait near the end of the novel. However, because he only encounters the world in one way, he cannot experience relief from his suffering.

Perhaps Pierre could see differently if he were not so obsessed with maintaining a strong sense of his individual and familial identities. He defines himself in relationship to his grandfather's famous exploits and his father's moral rectitude. Isabel threatens that identity, and everything he does subsequent to her revelation springs from his efforts to keep the family reputation intact. Ironically, Pierre sacrifices whatever personal identity he has in service of this illusion, destroying his sense of himself in an effort to preserve his father's honor. Furthermore, when he flees to the city and then takes Lucy in, he eventually crushes the family name as well. The message seems clear: the struggle to maintain a sense of identity is fruitless. As Peter J. Bellis notes, "*Pierre* marks an abandonment of Melville's earlier project, offering the first of a series of bleak and deeply ironic critiques of individual selfhood" (12).

Johnson addresses these twin issues of perception and identity in *Oxherding Tale,* though he shows a very different outcome from Melville's. Like Pierre, Andrew experiences an identity crisis after a conflict with his father. Bellis suggests that throughout his career Melville repeatedly shows his "fictional sons" experiencing an identity crisis related at least partially to the absence of their fathers. Furthermore, he notes, when Pierre flees Saddle Meadows he "finds that he has done away with the very ground of self-definition; he too must resurrect and internalize patriarchal authority, even if it means his own destruction" (7).

Andrew experiences something similar in his efforts to escape and then embrace George. As Andrew tries to situate himself between the house and the quarters, he must still weigh his individual needs and goals against those of the group. Unfortunately, Andrew's liminal position at Cripplegate makes absolute adherence to George's demands nearly impossible, and like Pierre he must strike out on his own in an attempt to quiet his inner turmoil.

Johnson critiques individuality through his description of his protagonist's quest, as Melville has before him. His critique, though, is neither "bleak" nor "ironic." One sees this most clearly perhaps by comparing the stories' endings; Pierre, Lucy, and Isabel all fall victim to his quest for self-determination. The image of Isabel's "ebon vines" shrouding Pierre's corpse and her final declaration—"'All's o'er, and ye know him not!'" (362)—further emphasize the failure of Glendinning's efforts and the author's deep sense of futility. By contrast, Andrew's end seems entirely hopeful and life-affirming. He looks on death, to be sure, but then Bannon throws his pistol into the weeds and Andrew need only die to his illusions about separation and individualism. As in his reading of Douglass, Johnson makes his predecessor's end the starting point in articulating his new social and literary vision.

Johnson balances his revision of Melville with a gentler critique of Emerson, another canonical figure whose work he finds particularly significant. As he says, "I've always read Emerson as my spiritual brother, and I'm deeply thankful for the presence of Transcendentalism in nineteenth-century literature. . . . In fact, I see myself . . . as writing in a latter day version of that literary tradition" (Nash 58). Though he mocks Ezekiel, the man representative of Emersonian ideals in the novel, for his overly abstract vision of the Over-Soul, he celebrates Emerson's vision by bringing Andrew to an enlightenment in which he applies transcendentalist concepts to his way of being in the world.

One finds in Ezekiel Sykes-Withers a parody of Emerson's extreme intellectualism and emotional sterility. From Johnson's first description of him, which includes details such as his "craglike face" and his membership in the Transcendental Club (11), Ezekiel resembles Emerson. The picture of him as "a figure who evolved in pieces from the snowdrifts" also suggests Emerson's "The Snow-Storm" (10). Even more compelling is Andrew's account of his evening journeys with Ezekiel to the banks of a nearby river, where his tutor lectures him "in language reshaped like soft wax, the power of his arguments vivid, their precise meaning veiled" (31). The gently mocking tone of this description suggests Melville's more pointed comment to Evert Duyckink that Emerson was full of "'transcendentalisms, myths, and oracular gibberish,'" a "'Plato who talks thro' his nose,'" and points with gentle humor to the difficulties one faces when reading Emerson (qtd. in Foster 335). Still, as Lawrence Buell explains, Emerson's complex style is a conscious choice that makes a significant contribution to the impact and success of the thinker's enterprise

(400). And Johnson seems intent on emphasizing that as well, even as he works to present a more accessible version of the examples and ideas.

In these moments, Andrew says, Ezekiel convinces him "that he and I, these frothy waves, this dust-seamed wind were somehow essential for the world to be, as if . . . the heart-shaped stones and scree . . . were full of some queer godstuff I could sense these nights in my blood but could never, never grasp" (31–32). Andrew's description of these walks parallels the transcendental experience Emerson describes in *Nature.* The comment about how Ezekiel leads him to see the "godstuff" in everything evokes Emerson's "transparent eyeball" passage, which describes how experience with nature makes one aware that he is "part or parcel of God" (11). In this instance, Ezekiel brings his student close to the transcendental experience by appealing to Andrew's intuition rather than to his reason. Unfortunately, the tutor does not provide any interpretive framework for the experience that would enable Andrew to grasp his true relationship to the universe. By the river, Ezekiel fails his student, as Richard Barrett fails Faith Cross, by not helping him grasp the meaning of his powerful lectures.

Of course, Ezekiel cannot change his shortcomings. Because he lives the life of the mind so completely, he is unable to mediate between his realm of knowledge and Andrew's. For the same reason, he cannot make enduring connections between intellect and emotion. This flaw in the tutor evokes Melville's marginal comments from his copy of Emerson's *Essays, Second Series:* "Mr. Emerson's . . . gross and astonishing errors & illusions spring from a self-conceit so intensely intellectual and calm that at first one hesitates to call it by its right name. Another species of Mr. Emerson's errors, or rather, blindness, proceeds from a defect in the region of the heart" (Leyda 649). Similarly, the etymological exercise Ezekiel gives Andrew perfectly exemplifies his intellectual and emotional imbalance. As Andrew learns more about the origins of the word "heart," he becomes increasingly detached from his emotions. He risks becoming like his tutor, whose heart trouble manifests in the killing tragedy of his failed attempt at love. In pursuit of his great Truth, Ezekiel acts according to his nature. Unfortunately, because of the way his mind works and his heart does not, Ezekiel can neither find nor lead his student to the human connection that grounds the experience of transcendence Johnson describes.

A similar popular image of Emerson persists. Certainly he experienced deep emotion; the deaths of his first wife and of his young son, Waldo, are well-documented sources of great personal anguish for him (Richardson 3–5, 358–60). However, his ability to "wrestle his horrors back under control at those moments when they erupt into full consciousness" gives much of his writing an austere quality (Doherty 425). This tension in his work gives rise to a mind-emotion dichotomy not unlike the one Ezekiel demonstrates through the clinical, intellectualized description of his father's gruesome internecine activities. By turning their emotions into abstract philosophical principles, Johnson suggests, the tutor and the transcendentalist risk extreme isolation and thereby weaken their message.

In his account of Andrew's tribulations, Johnson makes concepts that he and Emerson share more accessible. What Andrew grasps, and what Johnson offers the reader, is the insight that transcendentalism, like phenomenology and Buddhism, is something one *does*. More specifically, he demonstrates how Andrew's intuitive grasping toward reconciliation embodies key principles of Emerson's philosophy. One might think, in this instance, of "The Over-Soul," in which Emerson explains the relationship of the each to the all: "We live in succession, in division, in parts, in particles. Meantime within man is the soul of the whole; the wise silence; the universal beauty, to which every part and particle is equally related; the eternal One" (210–11). In his perfect union with the environment, a fusion so complete that his neck bruises when he passes a slaughterhouse, Reb overcomes this succession. And, through his experiences with the Coffinmaker and the Soulcatcher, Andrew gets a glimpse himself of the eternal One; that awareness, in fact, grounds his reunion with Peggy and their forging of a new world with Anna.

Similarly, the arc of Andrew's experiences evokes Emerson's view of life as process. In "Circles," he states that there "are no fixtures in nature. The universe is fluid and volatile. Permanence is but a word of degrees. . . . The life of man is a self-evolving circle, which, from a ring imperceptibly small, rushes on all sides outwards to new and larger circles, and that without end" (229–30). He goes on to note that the "only sin is limitation" (232). The most graphic illustration of this notion appears in Bannon's tattoos. Andrew's exposure to the "self-evolving circle" of his father's life opens him to the same quality in his own existence; and, in recognizing the fluidity of experience, he achieves communion with the eternal One. This enables him to embrace his dharma as a householder, which represents the best "doing" of transcendentalist-Buddhist-phenomenological values for Johnson at this point. Implicitly, the individual's recognition of how best to be in the world might lead to community improvement. He will push beyond that notion in *Middle Passage* and *Dreamer,* but here he embraces Emerson's early ideals as a major piece of his own response to social issues.

And one understands that attraction even better, perhaps, when one recalls Emerson's vision of the relationship between life and literature. In "Circles," Emerson notes that "literature is to afford us a platform whence we may command a view of our present life, a purchase by which we may move it. . . . We fill ourselves with ancient learning, install ourselves the best we can in Greek, in Punic, in Roman houses, only that we may wiselier see French, English, and American houses and modes of living" (234). One recognizes Johnson's application of this ideal in *Oxherding Tale.* The novel resonates with references to "ancient learning," as do all of Johnson's works, and here as elsewhere in his canon he seems to "wiselier see" contemporary experience. His signifying revisions of Douglass, Melville, and Emerson, all of which open new paths to the current debate over racial identity, demonstrates how this idea manifests itself in his work. Although Ezekiel might fail to make Andrew understand how transcendentalist ideals can be of use to him, Johnson makes these notions clearer to, and therefore more successful for, his reader.

With regard to "wiselier seeing" and the question of racial identity, one other literary source bears examination: the passing novel. Public recognition of the link between *Oxherding Tale* and the passing novel dates to Stanley Crouch's 1983 review, "Charles Johnson: Free at Last!" As I have suggested, Andrew's liminal status proves crucial to Johnson's effort to counter racial separatism. It also enables his signifying reading of this subgenre of African American fiction. The heart of the passing tradition is the racially mixed protagonist's crisis of identity and related attempt to negotiate the boundaries of the color line. Like the slave narrative, it occupies a prominent position in the history of black writers' attempts to define themselves. The form turns on the notion that race as a biological categorization is constructed—for how else to interpret the fact that a legally black hero(ine) has the opportunity to escape the societal oppression visited on "other African Americans" (the phrase must be set aside thus, as it privileges the ideology that the form challenges) by virtue of being phenotypically white? And yet, even as the form problematizes the whole notion of racial identity, many authors who write within it use the conventions of the passing narrative to *reassert* the very separatism that the protagonists of these texts overcome. For example, the protagonist of James Weldon Johnson's classic *The Autobiography of an Ex-Coloured Man* (1912) may well end in an ambivalent position, as John Sheehy notes (407), but I read the *character's* indecision, along with his numerous other foibles, as indicating the *author's* sense that passing means betrayal of the African American community.

As Vera Kutzinski has noted, *Ex-Coloured Man* proves important to Charles Johnson in his creation of *Oxherding Tale.* It clearly caught his interest well before he began writing fiction. In *Black Humor,* one finds an image of a "white" concert pianist performing Beethoven for an "all-white" audience. In the foreground of the cartoon, an audience member whispers to his companion: "Psst, he's a mulatto . . . pass it on" (figure 6). That early image mocks the idea that artists cannot or should not cross racial boundaries. In *Oxherding Tale,* Johnson presses even farther, revising the passing narrative's dialectic of racial dualism into his own vision of transcendence. If the passing novel functions at least partially to warn blacks about the dangers of betraying or denying the race, then in *Oxherding Tale* one sees its conventions revised to suggest that adherence to any model of dualistic racial identity leads to suffering. One can avoid this psychological trauma by embracing Johnson's vision of the One and the Many, his convictions that race and individuality are illusions.

One sees this clearly in the differing outcomes of *Ex-Coloured Man* and *Oxherding Tale.* Whereas Andrew ends up ready to rebuild the world with Anna and Peggy, the Ex-Coloured Man ruminates over his decision, feeling alternately glad for his children and dismayed with himself. Despite his assertion

Psst, he's a mulatto...pass it on.

Figure 6. Reprinted from *Black Humor,* © 1970 by Charles Johnson.

to the contrary (and he is a most unreliable narrator), he *does* wish to be other than he is. For if he were truly satisfied, why would he admit his sense that he has "chosen the lesser part" by rejecting his blackness (211)? In his case, unlike Andrew's, very little gets conserved. He suffers, in his liminality, from his inability to reconcile the dilemma of either/or. Andrew, by contrast, learns from passing to be both, to reconcile the fragments of his heritage in a manner that makes the question of race less divisive and less significant. "Passing" becomes for him not an act of deception about his "true" racial identity but rather a rite of pass*age,* as he learns to overcome the tendency to see distinctions that drives the passing narrative in general and *Ex-Coloured Man* in particular.

Johnson's revision of the passing narrative also addresses the notion that the passing individual likely faces a tragic end. This motif, most commonly inscribed in the myth of the tragic mulatto/a, usually leads to the death of the passer; such is the fate of Charles W. Chesnutt's Rena Walden, one of two passing siblings in *The House behind the Cedars* (1900). Driven into the swamp and nearly to madness by the concurrent pursuit of a white suitor and a black scoundrel, she eventually succumbs to a fever brought on by the incident. A neighbor's identification of her as "'a young cullud 'oman'" (195), in response to the white suitor's inquiry about who in her crepe-draped house has died, drives home the message that her race, or perhaps more accurately her sense of her racial identity, has helped destroy her.

In a text in which Chesnutt makes some bold statements about race, this reinforces fundamental ideas about racial essentialism. As Richard Brodhead notes, Chesnutt himself was ambivalent about the issue of race, particularly with regard to the limitations it placed on his future as an author (192–93). Some might interpret his publication of "The Goophered Grapevine" in 1887 without reference to his race as a form of *literary* passing. I hesitate to do so because it seems too condemnatory, especially given his subsequent self-identification as a black author. But what does seem clear is that Chesnutt experimented, in his life and his art, with fluidity of identity as a response to the problem of the color line. In both cases, though, it proved an unworkable option. However disturbed Chesnutt might have been about how blackness fixes an individual's position in American society, ultimately he could not breach the barrier. As Sheehy demonstrates, Rena's death "leaves the novel's simultaneous Signification on its own racial preoccupations spinning in space, unresolved and unresolvable" (413). This sense of "unresolved and unresolvable" dilemmas emphasizes the notion that the passer must ever labor under the shadow of this racial identity or be miserable, perhaps mortally so, in any effort to escape it. Clearly, this is not to be Andrew's end. This is where Johnson breaks with the tradition. His expansive perception of racial being suggests liberation for his characters and readers that diverges significantly from the double-consciousness that plagues most passers.

The grace and flair with which he handles the passing novel, like his revision of the grounding tropes of the slave narrative tradition, demonstrate the success of Johnson's literary project in *Oxherding Tale.* As he fuses philosophy and African American literature, he engages his predecessors' obsession with the quest for a sense of black identity. Through the example of Andrew's experience, he makes that historical fixation on racial selfhood the starting point for a new exploration of identity issues that transcends categories and, operating phenomenologically, eschews preconceptions. The novel presents his clearest and most intriguing articulation of his aesthetic goals. It also represents his most distanced examination of social issues. Although Andrew objects to the idea of "epidermalized Being" (52), a note that lightly suggests "*The Primevil Mitosis:* A Phenomenology of the Black Body," the tones sound differently in the novel than in the essay. The concerns are, at this point, more intellectual than political. As a result, *Oxherding Tale* lacks some of the tensions that mark Johnson's earlier and later work. He focuses more in this "platform novel" on his ideal vision, and that impulse bears significant creative fruit. As he moves forward from here, however, these social concerns reappear, especially in the expanded characterization of the Allmuseri. Given the tribe's nobility of spirit, as seen in Reb's bodhisattva life, what happens when such purity encounters anew the stain of racial identity? This intriguing question, which significantly problematizes possibilities for detachment and transcendence, becomes a driving issue in *Middle Passage.*

6 "Dualism Is a Bloody Structure of the Mind": *Middle Passage*

When *Middle Passage* won the 1990 National Book Award, Johnson became the first African American male to achieve that honor since Ralph Ellison won for *Invisible Man* in 1952. Aware of his spiritual and aesthetic debt to his predecessor, Johnson used the awards ceremony to honor Ellison and his monumental novel. Although less sweeping in scope than *Invisible Man, Middle Passage* shares some common ground with it, as do all of Johnson's novels. Once again, one finds a narrator seeking some understanding of his personal and racial identity, and, as in *Oxherding Tale,* he plunges into a whirlpool of experience at the heart of African American history. In this case, that means the transatlantic slave trade. Like *Oxherding Tale,* the novel presents a meditation on freedom and racial identity. But where *Oxherding Tale* ends by suggesting that one can overcome race and racialism, *Middle Passage* reasserts the tensions that characterize Johnson's earlier work. In exposing the Allmuseri tribe to the wrenching, fragmenting horrors of the Middle Passage, Johnson questions the sustainability of his ideal of unity. Although he brings his narrator, Rutherford Calhoun, to a resolution much like Andrew Hawkins's, the legacy of the ocean voyage remains, reminding the reader of the injustice that whites have systematically visited on African Americans and emphasizing Johnson's conflicted responses to the novel's social and artistic questions.

On the literary level, Johnson follows the patterns he established in *Faith and the Good Thing* and *Oxherding Tale,* although here he concerns himself less with philosophical allusion and more with treatment of specific literary texts. Once again committed to breaking down barriers within the American canon, he signifies on a range of authors, including Herman Melville, Saul Bellow,

Olaudah Equiano, and James Baldwin.[1] This amalgamation of influences affirms his creative program by reinforcing the notion that one can transform a legacy of suffering into a more hopeful and more unifying artistic vision.

Middle Passage began as a project for one of Johnson's graduate classes at Southern Illinois University; as in the final version, he used the form of entries in the ship's log to tell the story. The most significant difference between the two versions, and the thing that made the first version ultimately unsuccessful, has to do with his choice of narrative perspectives. In the first drafts, he "told it from the white captain's viewpoint and therefore could never get close to the slaves" (e-mail, 7 Nov. 1996). His creation of Rutherford Calhoun enabled him to overcome those initial difficulties. Calhoun's dual liminality, figured both in his role as mediator between the crew and cargo of the slave ship and in his racial identity, makes him sympathetic to both groups' perspectives. Although not a mulatto like Andrew Hawkins, he must also reconcile the tensions between the black and white worlds that fragment his sense of himself. But where Andrew acts out his reconciliation on a primarily individual level, Rutherford's development process demands that he engage more fully with the impact of slavery on the *group,* a difference that creates some of the novel's tension and complexity.

A manumitted slave and a petty thief, Rutherford drifts south from Makanda, Illinois, to New Orleans after the death of his former master, the Reverend Peleg Chandler, and a falling-out with his older brother, Jackson. Once in the Crescent City, Calhoun divides most of his time among stealing, gambling, drinking, and whoring; the remainder he devotes to the necessarily chaste pursuit of Isadora Bailey, a schoolteacher originally from Boston. Although he is fond of Isadora, Rutherford has no desire for a sustained connection. As he explains, he'd "always felt people fell in love as they fell in a hole; it was something . . . smart people avoided" (7). Not so Isadora, who loves and aspires to redeem Rutherford. Knowing that he owes money to numerous creditors, she goes to Philippe "Papa" Zeringue, the Creole gangster behind all the establishments where Calhoun has unpaid bills, and arranges to pay his debts in exchange for Papa's forcing Rutherford to marry her. Outraged at Isadora for what he sees as her betrayal, Rutherford flees, stowing away aboard the slave ship *Republic,* which is bound for Africa to claim a cargo of forty Allmuseri.

Once aboard, Calhoun must mediate among numerous groups that seek to control the ship's destiny. He falls under the spell of Captain Ebenezer Falcon, the monomaniacal dwarf who believes in the innate superiority of the white race and in the inevitability of human separation. As he tells Rutherford, "'dualism is a bloody structure of the mind'" that makes conflict and human bondage parts of the natural order (98). Although Falcon's ideas disturb Rutherford, he acts as the captain's spy among the crew. Simultaneously, perhaps partially because he regrets submitting to Falcon, Calhoun agrees to help Peter Cringle, the first mate, and a group of sailors who wish to seize the ship from Falcon. Finally, as the only black crewmember, Rutherford has a bond with the cargo. Early on the voyage home, he befriends Ngonyama, one of the Allmuseri men; he teaches the African some English and demonstrates the ship's steering and compass. In return, Ngonyama teaches Rutherford some of the Allmuseri language and explains their belief system.

Calhoun's attempts to balance the warring forces fail, as the Allmuseri rebel on the same day that Cringle and his cohorts had planned to mutiny. Once the Africans control the ship, Calhoun must plead with them for the lives of the remaining crew and officers. They agree reluctantly, offering to spare the captain contingent on Rutherford's ability to make Falcon serve them. He goes below to convey that message, only to see the captain commit suicide—but not before he first tells Calhoun that Papa Zeringue is part owner of the Allmuseri cargo.

Days of suffering, marked by sickness, starvation, and cannibalism (as Cringle sacrifices himself so that the others might eat), follow. Finally, Calhoun, Squibb, and three Allmuseri children escape the sinking *Republic* for the *Juno,* a pleasure craft bound for New Orleans. Rutherford spends his time aboard recording the *Republic*'s adventures in the ship's log, using the creative act to free himself from his haunting memories. He emerges from his cabin only when he learns that Zeringue is aboard and that on the following day he is planning to marry Isadora, for whom Rutherford has been pining ever since his transformation. He confronts the gangster, blackmails him into giving up Isadora, and reconciles with her. The novel closes with an image of their spiritual union as Rutherford explains who he has become during his voyage.

• • •

Rutherford's transformation during the Middle Passage moves him from a bitter obsession with racial difference to the unified way of being in the world that he finally shares with Isadora. His early attitudes manifest on shore, where he vents his outrage by picking pockets, breaking into homes, incurring bad debts, and taking advantage of anyone foolish enough to be nice to him. For every offense, he offers the same justification: "was I not, as a Negro in the New World, *born* to be a thief? Or, put less harshly, inheritor of two millennia of things I had not myself made?" (47). Ironically, although this statement is meant as a complaint, Rutherford would have happily inherited the vast wealth of his master, most of which he did not himself make. Barring that possibility of ascension from the status of property to the ranks of the propertied, Rutherford sees himself as entitled to exploit others because of his racially related suffering.

His rage at Jackson also affects his perceptions of black identity. As the elder of Chandler's servants, Jackson is the more trusted and valued. Burdened with the responsibility of raising Rutherford after their parents die, he devotes himself to pleasing his master, losing himself in the process. When the time comes for Chandler to pass on his inheritance, Jackson selflessly suggests that the land and property be divided among all of his master's former servants. This generosity illustrates Jackson's spiritual enlightenment and makes him, Rutherford eventually realizes, at least an honorary Allmuseri. Before he meets Ngonyama and learns the Allmuseri ways, though, Rutherford sees his brother as the worst sort of black man: a "gentleman of color," which to the angry young thief signifies subservience and weakness (9). His decision to continue victimizing others is in part a reaction to his brother's goodness, what one might call a selection of the "bad nigger" lifestyle as an antidote to the example of the "good nigger."[2] That rebellious anger also inspires his flight from Isadora. He notes his own enjoyment in her company and his accompanying sense of wonder at her goodness; he even reflects, at one point, on all that would be pleasant about life with Isadora. When she remarks to him that he is "not *common,*" though, he sees her trying to turn him into the sort of black man that he thinks Jackson is. His vision of that life, which embodies everything he does not want to be, drives him to sea.

Although Calhoun can escape the colored gentleman's life at sea, he cannot avoid the narrow perspective that undergirds his attitudes. Indeed, all of the major figures who appear prior to the *Republic*'s taking on its Allmuseri cargo live by restrictive notions that inform their perceptions; for most of them, racial essentialism proves especially troublesome. For example, just as Rutherford sees himself and Jackson in racial terms, Isadora sees herself and Calhoun in terms of blackness. When he confronts her about forcing him to the altar, Isadora tells him that she knows he would never marry her because she is blacker than he. Having accepted the socially constructed notion that black men always desire light-skinned wives, she sees Calhoun as shallow and herself as irrevocably stained. When she decides to save Calhoun by buying his debts, Isadora confirms her self-hatred and the racial essentialism from which it springs.

Her choice of co-conspirator in the plan to make Rutherford a gentleman of color could hardly be more ironic. Although Papa Zeringue has vast financial resources, he has no breeding; even more importantly, although he purports to love and support his race, he secretly despises the black community that he preys on for his income. As Rutherford notes, to many people Papa was "if not a hero, then a Race Man to be admired. . . . Aye, for many he was a patron of the race" (198). Zeringue has strong views about how African Americans could compete with whites and improve their lot in life. For all this good that he does, however, Papa also deals in slaves and runs the gambling dens, brothels, and bars that cause so much discontent and suffering in the black community.

Like Big Todd Cross and George Hawkins, Zeringue is both race man and father figure. As such, he conveys Johnson's reservations about dogmatic adherence to an essentialist perception of racial identity. In a striking reversal of George's charge to Andrew to be himself, though, Zeringue suggests to Rutherford that *his* self presents a problem for the community. "'If all cullud men was like you,'" he tells Calhoun, referring to the thief's lack of stable income or measurable assets, "'I 'spect the Race would be extinct by now'" (14). Setting aside the irony that Papa's operation and Rutherford's differ primarily in terms of scale, I see an important complication in this position. On the one hand, Zeringue's statement conveys tremendous pride in African Americans' potential: the Race deserves better than you. On the other hand, its adherence to a white-defined standard of success demonstrates the depth of Papa's antipathy for his community. His desire to elevate "the Race" necessitates a rigidly separatist consciousness, as his business methods indicate. "Once he bought a business, he never—absolutely never—sold it back to white men, because he feared if it left black hands it might never return" (198). As a result, his actions reinforce the very inequality between the races that he seeks to overcome. That Rutherford endures the Middle Passage only to find Papa figuratively aboard the *Republic* suggests the power and reach of Papa's attitudes. The link to the ship also makes Johnson's point: *mental* slavery starts in a world driven by this paradigm. Like his predecessors, Rutherford escapes. But the dramatic loss of virtually all the Allmuseri points to the real difficulties Johnson sees associated with any encounter with narrow racialist values.

Although it temporarily frees him from Zeringue, Rutherford's stowing away aboard the *Republic* casts him into the middle of another essentialist world. Like Zeringue, Ebenezer Falcon holds rigid opinions about race; his attitudes, however, rest on white supremacist convictions. For the captain, racial separation confirms his general assertions about dualism. Seeing this, Calhoun expects to use race to gain favor with the captain. As he cynically remarks, "a crafty Negro, a shrewd black strategist, can work a prospective white employer around, if he's smart, by playing poor mouth, or greasing his guilt with a hard-luck story." To that end, he complains to Falcon about the lack of opportunities available to him in a city "so bigoted a Negro couldn't even buy vanilla ice cream" (28). What Calhoun has not counted on is that

Falcon holds his beliefs about black inferiority so firmly that he does not care about Calhoun's excuses. To him, no blacks deserve an opportunity for advancement, because they are inherently ill-equipped for it.

Falcon's racial attitudes are not hostile; he genuinely pities Calhoun, assuming that the stowaway thought the *Republic* was a riverboat when he came aboard. He also speaks quite frankly about blacks' getting promotions based on race, only to find their new positions unsatisfactory because they lack the necessary skills. Some of these blacks, Falcon claims, even beg *not* to be offered opportunities because they understand their innate inferiority. This aside about blacks begging to avoid opportunity indicates some of the complexities of Johnson's position. Falcon advances a common argument against affirmative action. Given how deeply flawed the rest of Falcon's racial thinking seems, one might well conclude that his opposition to this programmatic response to racism indicates Johnson's support for it. Subsequent stories, such as "Executive Decision," bear that assumption out. Written while he was composing *Dreamer,* that short story takes a more explicit position on the question; in *Middle Passage,* Johnson continues to wrestle with a less clearly defined sense of his concerns. As a result, one sees a basic tension reassert itself. Though he argues ideally that race is an illusion, his presentation of African Americans' historical suffering keeps the need for redressing the community's social grievances present in the text.

A benevolent bigot of sorts, Falcon nevertheless perpetuates the rigid racial separation that plagues Rutherford and his peers ashore. For the captain, the dichotomy defines the natural and the economic orders; in his world, blacks are consumable commodities. One sees this in the story of the black cabin boy he and his crew ate on an earlier journey; when he looks at Rutherford, Falcon sees that cabin boy and thinks again of how he tasted. Even more horrific than his actual cannibalism, however, is his commodification of Africans and their cultures in the course of his business. As master of the *Republic,* Falcon controls the consuming maw of the slave hold. Through his actions aboard ship, he sacrifices the Africans and figuratively nourishes himself on their remains. In addition to forcing the Allmuseri into this mouth of hell, the captain also plunders their culture. The African god he has caged in the hold is only the most recent in a series of artifacts he brings back from his voyages at the behest of wealthy white patrons who want to decorate their homes with so-called primitive objects.

The sacred relics and works of art that betray Falcon's status as cultural predator also point to the fundamental irony of his attitudes. He believes without question that blacks are beneath him, as are all othered peoples; nevertheless, as a slave trader he depends economically on the dichotomy that sense of otherness indicates. The captain also relies on otherness for his sense of personal superiority, though his raiding of supposedly inferior cultures' temples yields ample evidence to the contrary. Like Horace Bannon, the Soulcatcher of *Oxherding Tale,* Falcon cannot exist without the blacks he preys upon. Bound by these fragmented perceptions, Falcon can never be more free than his human cargo.

Falcon is far from alone in his false-freedom position. Although Reverend Chandler manumitted Rutherford in his will, the former bondsman is not yet free; how could any African American crewing aboard a slaver be? There is also the matter of his shotgun betrothal to Isadora, which further limits his liberation. But even more than these, Rutherford must confront his invisible shackles: the attitudes about race that he brings to New Orleans and then to sea and the family history that moved him to flee Makanda in the first place. During his voyage, Rutherford learns that he cannot escape any of these things. Instead, he must develop a new mode of perception that will free him from the interconnected senses of suffering and entitlement that cause all of his troubles.

He learns that new way of seeing from the Allmuseri. One might predict that Calhoun would gain this from his encounter with the tribe in one of the first descriptions of them in the text. Expressing anxiety over the strangeness of the cargo, Cringle remarks to Calhoun that the Allmuseri are "'a whole tribe—men, women, and tykes—of devil-worshipping, spell-casting wizards'" (43). A wizard works by changing the audience's view of objects and events; this is the impact that the Allmuseri have on Rutherford. Although they do not cast spells on him, the tribespeople enable him to view his world differently. Johnson emphasizes the tribe's *collective* effect on Rutherford; he also provides him with individual guides whose lessons are especially useful. One of these is Baleka, the Allmuseri child who will teach Calhoun true selflessness. Effectively becoming her surrogate father, he achieves a sense of oneness with her much like Reb's fusion with the universe. In a statement that evokes Bannon's description of the Coffinmaker in *Oxherding Tale,* Rutherford tells Isadora, "'Whenever Baleka is out of my sight I am worried. If she bruises herself, *I* feel bruised'" (195). His experiences with the child enable his full application of lessons that he learns from his other teacher, Ngonyama.

In *The Signifying Monkey,* Henry Louis Gates Jr.'s explanation of the Esu-Elegbara myth includes a discussion of *ng'ang'ama,* a term that in Kiswahili "suggests one clutching a swinging branch of a tree . . . to escape torrential waters, only to lose one's grip" and drown "for the sake of *nganga.*" Gates suggests several meanings of *nganga,* including "interpreter" (18). These definitions make the aural resonances between *ng'ang'ama* and "Ngonyama" quite compelling. The Allmuseri *does* act as Rutherford's interpreter, after all, teaching him the tribe's cosmology, language, and aesthetic sensibility (163). Ngonyama also exposes Rutherford to the ideal of self-sacrifice that fully transforms the former thief into the man capable of returning to and connecting with the world ashore. When, in a last desperate act, Ngonyama sacrifices himself by holding the ship's wheel so that Calhoun, Squibb, Baleka, and the other Allmuseri children can escape, one sees him drowning for the sake of the interpretation he has taught Rutherford. In the face of such nobility, Rutherford can do nothing but fully embrace the tribal ideal, even though he has also seen how such noble aspirations can break down.

Prior to the rebellion, which significantly complicates the tribe's experience and Johnson's message, the tribespeople offer Calhoun numerous illustrations of their connection to all things. One of the most striking of these occurs in the passage where Ngonyama carves a pig that Squibb has cooked for Captain Falcon. With "his right hand gripping the cook's blade as if it had grown out of his wrist," the Allmuseri "slipped metal through meat . . . until the pig fell apart magically in his hands"; in the process, he "left no knife tracks" (75–76). This feat is not merely the parlor trick of an experienced carver. The Allmuseri are vegetarians, and Ngonyama has never done this before. What he does in the moments before he carves, though, is blend with both the knife and the meat. This ability to fuse with all things characterizes every Allmuseri action prior to the rebellion.

Admiring the tribe for their wholeness, Rutherford wishes that he might be one of them. Nevertheless, he recognizes that while he "might envy certain features of Allmuseri folkways, he could never claim something he had no hand in creating." To do so, he determines, would be to "insult" the tribe (78). This is quite a change from the image of the thief who revels in his ability to claim things to which he has no right; in his earlier life, Rutherford valued the insult to others he conveyed as much as he benefited financially from his activities. As he comes increasingly under the tribe's influence, he loses that sense of separation that made stealing so important to him. Though he does not yet recognize it, he is taking part in the Allmuseri culture as he gradually begins to adopt their worldview.

As he internalizes this outlook, Rutherford also begins to overcome his outrage at what he once viewed as Jackson's subservient betrayal. Throughout his early life in Makanda, Rutherford feels his outsider status; Jackson is Chandler's favorite, and nothing Rutherford does can earn him his master's approval. Recognizing that he will never be favored, Rutherford becomes a rebel, engaging in minor acts of vandalism that demonstrate his resistance to slavery. For each of Rutherford's rebellious actions, Jackson performs another act of submission. In effect, the brothers are diametric opposites, engaged in a conflict that springs from their warring conceptions of how to be black. During the Middle Passage, all of that changes. When Rutherford serves others aboard the *Republic* with no thought for himself, he gains insight into his brother's character. As he learns more about what motivated Jackson, Rutherford also finds a way to reconcile with the memory of his brother. When he sees the value in his brother's approach, which comes after exposure to Jackson's tribe, Rutherford can reject his divided model of blackness for one that celebrates and therefore reconciles different modes of racial being.

With the story of Rutherford's and Jackson's estrangement, Johnson makes his first reference to the biblical story of Cain and Abel, which he will treat more fully in *Dreamer.* In Bill Moyers's roundtable discussion of the book of Genesis (1996), Johnson says, "'Cain's problem is egotism. He's very much anchored in himself. Why do you want to kill somebody? Because there's *this* self and there's that *other* self. In each of us there's tension and conflict. It's all based on dualism'" (Moyers 103). In the biblical case, dualism is indeed "a bloody structure" of Cain's murderous mind; Johnson makes use of the motif in *Middle Passage.* The sense of fragmentation that causes Cain to kill his brother and that therefore indirectly dooms him to wander resembles the sense of separation that motivates Rutherford's travels. He does not literally kill Jackson, but he figuratively cuts him dead by stopping all communication with him. Even more importantly, he bears a murderous rage as a result of Jackson's betrayal; we know, for instance, that in the period between Chandler's death and Rutherford's departure for New Orleans he "felt angry at anything that moved" (118). This emotion, which resembles Cain's attitude, generates Rutherford's suffering and sense of isolation. After he comes to terms with his brother, he can overcome the obstacles that mark Cain's life.

By symbolically reconciling the first human conflict, Johnson offers a corrective to the fragmented worldview that is part of the first brothers' legacy to humanity. He also addresses an important source for much of the mythology of racialism. As Ruth Mellinkoff notes, the tradition of identifying the "mark of Cain" as blackness originated in ancient Jewish scholarly writings. That belief evolved into the popular mythology that Cain and his offspring, Ham, were the ancestors of the Africans brought to America as slaves. On the basis of that tradition, many American slaveholders justified their actions by saying that the slaves' bondage was the legitimate fruit of Cain's mark (76–80). In these terms, then, the "mark of Cain" evokes the idea of blackness as cursed. By choosing to retell Cain and Abel's story and to show the brothers reconnecting, Johnson makes a powerful statement against that racialist interpretation of the original story. In his vision, the "mark of Cain" represents the damaging dualistic worldview that plagues Rutherford until he encounters the Allmuseri. His "curse" is his *perception* of his physical blackness, his inability to see himself as other than victim or victimizer. As he evolves toward a more unified way of seeing, Rutherford can escape the fragmented worldview that plagues him.

If Johnson were to leave it at this, then one might reasonably read *Middle Passage* as an extension of his platform novel. But, as events aboard the *Republic* indicate, his views are not so clearly hopeful at this point as they were when he wrote *Oxherding Tale.* As Rutherford explains it, the Allmuseri vision of hell is "the failure to experience the unity of Being everywhere" (65). Their treatment aboard the slaver certainly qualifies. Forced to endure "tight packing" (the common practice of overloading the hold of a slave ship to compensate for those who would inevitably die during the journey) along with regular vicious beatings, nearly inedible food, and numerous other forms of systematic dehumanization, the tribe plunges fully into "the world of multiplicity, of *me* versus *thee,*" and rebels (140). Bringing their martial art into play and using their wooden pillows as weapons, the Allmuseri wreak a vengeance on their tormentors comparable to, and in fact based upon, the outcome of the uprising aboard the slave ship *Amistad.* Under the circumstances, their actions make perfect sense; and yet they hardly fit with the vision of the tribe as Johnson has created it up to this point. I find this among the most troubling and the most compelling of the novel's variations on Johnson's dominant themes. Certainly Mingo spills blood, but primarily the Allmuseri have represented transcendent harmony as a sustainable response to racialist separatism. And this raises an important interpretive question for students of Johnson's aesthetic: what to make of a scenario in which the former healers kill and, having killed, disintegrate under the weight of realizing the unsustainability of their worldview? This chain of events presents two conflicting messages, one having to do with choice and the other with circumstance.

The notion of choice plays a prominent role in this presentation of the tribe. As Rutherford comes to understand the Allmuseri more fully, he notices significant similarities between their prelapsarian mode of being in the world and his brother's. This leads him to the insight that they are "less a biological tribe than a clan held together by values" (109). On its own, this notion seems most hopeful; the idea that one can learn this new way of seeing and thereby achieve the liberation it promises reinforces the fundamental premises of Johnson's aesthetic. Rutherford's own transformation bears this hope out. Such a conception also has important extratextual implications, as it suggests that readers might adopt and apply the Allmuseri way themselves. This is not to say that they will be doing magic or speaking in a tongue like the tribe's. It does suggest, however, that perhaps individuals influenced by the tribe's prerebellion example might strive to embrace selflessness and to resist the temptation to privilege preconceptions over experience.

Despite that promise, Johnson introduces an element of doubt with the uprising. The Allmuseri come aboard the *Republic* with distinctive hands. Their "palms were blank, bearing no lines. No fingerprints" (61). In addition to emphasizing the tribe's rejection of Western conceptions of identity, the pristine nature of their hands suggests that the tribe has been as yet unmarked by history. That their first encounter with the Western world marks their palms not only with lines but with blood shows the difficulty of maintaining such innocence and idealism under any but the most isolated circumstances. Johnson notes in the novel that being in the tribe demands hard work. As Rutherford explains, the Allmuseri believe that "each man outpictured his world from deep within his own heart. . . . That meant an orthodox Allmuseri . . . had to watch himself twenty-five hours a day and police his heart. As within, so it was without" (164). On the *Republic,* though, the tribe encounters a world that they cannot control. Faced with that pressure, their mode of harmonious existence collapses.

Carl Pedersen describes the Middle Passage as "the defining moment of the African-American experience" (225). For many within the community, its legacy of suffering and strength does occupy a central position. Although Johnson rejects the notion of monolithic racial experience, I see suggestions in this rebellion that he recognizes the power of a claim like Pedersen's. And with that awareness comes the question: can one really *be* as the Allmuseri are in a world where forces are so clearly aligned against you? That doubt complicates Johnson's aesthetic position by pressing for acknowledgment of his social concerns.

Notably, Johnson entertains a much milder version of this possibility of failure in his representations of individually fallen Allmuseri. In *Oxherding Tale,* Reb's son Patrick operates on a theory of conflict that directly counters the tribal ideal. When Andrew suggests that they survive Leviathan by cooperating, Patrick replies, "'How people gonna work *together* heah? You tell me that!'" (42). Alone and fearful of the consequences when Flo loses interest in him, Patrick chooses self-destruction. In *Middle Passage,* readers meet a fallen Allmuseri well before the voyage begins, although neither they nor the characters know it yet. In Rutherford's final confrontation with Papa, however, the gangster's henchman, Santos, suddenly recalls that one of his ancestors "'use to call hisself'" an Allmuseri (201). One could hardly imagine an individual more antithetical to the tribal ideal. Nevertheless, Santos has no meaningful awareness of his heritage beyond the limits of his personal experience. Given who life has conditioned him to be, his actions make sense.

What seems more complicated, though, is Santos's reaction to Rutherford's description of the journey, Papa's involvement in it, and his own relationship to the remaining cargo. Throwing his allegiance to Calhoun as the former thief outlines his expectations of Zeringue, Santos exacts his own revenge. As Rutherford exits the gangster's cabin, he hears "ever so softly, the former dirt-pit wrestler say, *Papa, I'ma kick yo' natural ass*" (204). This perfectly justifiable outrage conflicts with the tribal standard, just as the rebellion itself does. One might argue that Santos cannot be expected to immediately adopt a mode of perception he has not been exposed to or trained in. In Rutherford's explanation, the henchman must *choose* to be an Allmuseri to successfully step away from his violent past. With this, Johnson reminds the reader again of how difficult it would be to live Allmuseri-style in the postlapsarian, racialist world. The focus seems more on what Santos has to overcome than on whether or not he will succeed. His status as one of several individually fallen Allmuseri in Johnson's work suggests some enduring reservations on the author's part about the tribe's aesthetic. The account of the whole tribe's rebellion undeniably foregrounds the issue and requires the reader both to confront the legacy of slavery and to fully weigh its impact on any attempts at transcending racialism.

That idea of complete engagement with the Middle Passage raises another pertinent issue: Johnson's other treatments of the transatlantic voyage. As with many of his recurrent themes, his interest in the impact of the Middle Passage on African Americans dates to the period of his cartooning. An image from *Black Humor* portrays the hold of a slaver where the cargo is in conversation (figure 7). The shockingly light-hearted suggestion of a sing-along certainly conflicts with the horrors he describes in *Middle Passage.* Although the expressions on some of the other faces suggest terror and sadness and the arrangement of bodies denotes physical discomfort, humor dominates the image. On one level, this might jolt the viewer out of complacency or rigid ideas about the Middle Passage. In an era of racial militancy, this suggestion of something besides suffering for the transported Africans might be a needle intended to deflate collective outrage.

Read another way, the image suggests how various members of different tribes begin the process of cultural amalgamation that occurred during the Middle Passage, the transformation that made a group of people with diverse tribal identities into African Americans. Such a reading, which emphasizes the idea of cultural retention, positively counters racist notions that African Americans came to America without heritage. In either interpretation, the emphasis is on links forged rather than bonds broken. That has been the characteristic tone of Johnson's descriptions of the slave trade. Only in a passing allusion

Say, why don't we have a sing-along?

Figure 7. Reprinted from *Black Humor,* © 1970 by Charles Johnson.

in *Faith and the Good Thing* does he note any of the journey's horrors, and even there he downplays it as a stage in a more primal return. In *Oxherding Tale,* by contrast, Reb recalls "squatting to sing still vivid Allmuseri melodies . . . on the deck of *The Fortunata* . . . because now he was not rainmaker and magician but the shaper of gentle songs" (50).

Johnson keeps that notion of song shaping alive in "The Transmission," one of the twelve stories in *Soulcatcher.* An account of a young Allmuseri, Malawi's, tribulations aboard the slave ship *Providence,* the story illustrates the captives' intermingling of African tribal traditions and the interplay between European and African cultures aboard ship. Malawi loses all of his family except for his brother, Oboto, on the trek to the coast, when they are captured by Asante warriors and sold into slavery; miraculously, they are allowed to remain together in the hold of the *Providence.* Oboto shares his *griot* training with

Malawi, singing him the history of the Allmuseri tribe so that at least one other will know it and help carry it on. When Oboto dies, Malawi must preserve all that he has learned. Significantly, as a new griot, he must also make new songs that tell the story of his horrible journey. Those songs catch the ear of a young white sailor, who encourages Malawi to sing and listens respectfully.

For Malawi, knowing the tribal history gives way to making art describing his new experiences. As he begins "weaving the events since his and Oboto's capture onto the last threads" of the tradition Oboto has passed on, he demonstrates the impact of European culture on his tribe's sense of itself (11). At the same time, his ability to reach even one sailor suggests the power of Allmuseri traditions to affect a Westerner. Initially drawn to Malawi because he sees the young man suffering, and then entranced with his beautiful singing, the young sailor finds his perceptions of the Africans transformed and his aesthetic sensibility modified. In his analysis of Middle Passage narratives, Carl Pedersen identifies two significant camps in the tradition: a view that sees the journey as the end of African cultural influence on black American life, and an Afrocentric view that argues the persistence of unaltered African traditions in African American culture (226). Recognizing the inadequacy of both views, Pedersen posits a third strain, which he calls "cultural syncretism." This view, which he sees in Olaudah Equiano, Robert Hayden, George Lamming, and Charles Johnson, holds that the transatlantic slave trade is "the beginning of a distinct New World multicultural system" in which cultural impact flows back and forth between Europeans and Africans (226–27).

Such an interpretation reflects Johnson's aesthetic goals, although he might object to the "multiculturalism" label as divisive. His effort in "The Transmission" to emphasize that connection process makes the rift in *Middle Passage* all the more striking. One could argue that the Allmuseri are feeling the impact of the West and, through the change they work on Rutherford, making their own mark. But if that is the case, the extreme imbalance of that interplay bears noting, as it reinforces negative conceptions that Johnson has battled elsewhere. I am not suggesting that Johnson *should* show the Middle Passage as anything less than horrible; indeed, this representation makes more sense on first examination than his cartoon. Still, given the tone that he has frequently adopted, the description in the novel stands out, particularly in its emphasis on the social repercussions arising from such exploitation.

To complicate things further, this indictment of social injustice comes in the midst of a strong argument *against* racial separatism. Johnson's account of the tribe's postrebellion actions contains a pointed condemnation of contemporary anti-integrationism. After Ngonyama and his peers take control of the *Republic,* one of the Allmuseri, Diamelo, begins emphasizing the superiority of Allmuseri culture over the crew's. Arguing that "the master's house must be dismantled," he orders that only Allmuseri may be spoken, that Allmuseri maps must be used for steering the ship, that only Allmuseri dishes may be prepared, and that the crew may neither address nor look at the Allmuseri women who remain. What Diamelo advocates represents a return to slavery, with the power dynamic reversed, and an extreme version of the fundamental principles of black cultural nationalism.[3]

That the tribespeople who survive ultimately reject Diamelo's ideology, and that he finally destroys himself and all standing near him with a botched cannon shot, privileges Ngonyama's, and Rutherford's, more harmonious alternative. Despite that pointed avowal of a more inclusive, universalizing approach, the legacy of suffering remains. This represents perhaps the strongest example of the tension between ideal and application that occurs throughout Johnson's work. Although he cannot overlook the suffering of the slaves aboard ship and its legacy for the African American community, he hopes for the sort of transformation that Rutherford experiences. Significantly, in support of that aspiration, Rutherford continues learning from the tribe even *after* they fall.

A crucial moment in his evolution occurs when he encounters the Allmuseri deity face to face. Like Tommy O'Toole, the *Republic*'s cabin boy before him, Rutherford comes away from the experience forever changed. Johnson shows us the god's ability to transform people when young Tommy goes down into the hold to see it, only to crawl "back on deck with half his mind—or maybe it was twice the mind he had had before" (68). He undergoes, Johnson tells us, a "sea change," a shift in perception that shows him how he and the god, along with the rest of the universe, are one (69).

Rutherford has a similar experience, emerging from the hold, as Tommy does, with enhanced perceptual abilities. Even more significantly, he comes up from the depths with a new understanding of black being. The god appears to Rutherford in the shape of Riley Calhoun, the absentee father he has missed and resented his entire life. It then spins out Riley Calhoun's history, which includes a facility with women, the ability to beat any of those women's husbands in a fistfight, a well-nurtured racial grievance that he uses to justify the womanizing and the violence, and an ignominious death in the swamps during a futile attempt at flight. As he learns the details of his father's life and death, Rutherford overcomes his lifelong anger and sense of loss, which have been primary sources of his own separation. When the god shows Rutherford how Riley and he fit into the universal scheme of things, Rutherford can finally overcome the isolation that has driven him away from Jackson and Isadora. He has a reunifying moment as he becomes the god, who is also his father; in recognizing this pattern of connections, Rutherford realizes that "the (black) self was the greatest of fictions" (171). When, in the aftermath of his trip to the hold, he vomits up "black clumps" that he "can only liken to an afterbirth or a living thing aborted from the body," the transformation is complete. The purging of this "homunculus" marks the loss of Rutherford's black self. The victimization mentality that has driven him to his negative actions dies from him in this process, and he emerges from the ordeal free from that internal conflict. Ironically, earlier in his description of the suffering after the mutiny, Rutherford says that the worst affliction the survivors experienced was "Black Vomit" (156). In his case, vomiting the poison of his narrow view of blackness saves him.[4]

When the crew of the *Juno* pulls Rutherford, Squibb, and the remaining Allmuseri children from the ocean, an act that emphasizes Calhoun's rebirth, circumstances soon test Rutherford's new resolve. Papa's presence aboard the boat, and his guilt for illegally trafficking in slaves, gives Calhoun an ideal opportunity to do something selfish. Indeed, Zeringue helps him a great deal, offering him a substantial bribe in exchange for his silence. The old Rutherford would have taken the money and run; the new Rutherford exists above Papa's exploitation. He *does* blackmail Papa, but his demands are less self-serving now. Eschewing his own material gain, he seeks instead reparations for the Allmuseri children and liberation for Isadora. It happens that both benefit him, but his manner in the encounter suggests that his altruism is sincere. With this, Johnson offers at least one possibility for reconciling ideals and actions. Rutherford uses negative methods, but only to achieve a noble purpose; this ability to overcome his earlier selfish impulses suggests that, for the individual at least, some chance of liberation exists.

He extends that glimpse of freedom, and brings the focus firmly back on the ideal, through his treatment of Rutherford's obsessive efforts to fill the logbook of the *Republic.* At first primarily cathartic, the writing becomes a way for him to "transcribe and therefore transfigure" the events of the Middle Passage; his goal is not to fix them but instead to "make [his] peace with the recent past by turning it into Word" (190). As Daniel M. Scott demonstrates, this passage illustrates Johnson's ideas about "the role writing plays in the reconfiguration of the self" (645–47). When Rutherford uses the ship's log as a bargaining chip in his final discussion with Papa, he demonstrates how far he has come and how important his telling the story of the journey is to achieving his last liberation.

Rutherford's writing also symbolizes Johnson's quest for unity through his own creative process. More than any of his other works, *Middle Passage* is a story about writing. As the former bondsman tells his story of the Middle Passage, he weaves in elements of his early, eclectic education, a detail that reinforces the link between his and Andrew's experiences. In one sentence, for instance, Rutherford mentions Teresa of Avila, Bishop Berkeley, Aristippus, and Sir Francis Bacon. Elsewhere he refers to the Vedas of Indian culture, and in another place he mentions Heraclitus. His ability to interject these allusions into his logbook demonstrates Johnson's quest to find the universal in the particular and his own tactics as author.

Rutherford's mix of references reflects a subtler blend of influences that Johnson draws on to create his narrator's voice. As Scott notes, "like Rutherford, the novel pilfers this and that. All writing is this appropriation, this reiteration of writing that has come before it, this reproduction and recirculation of the written and the play of new writing in reference, response, and reaction to the Tradition—one's re-integration of the individual past, present, and future with that of the collective. These things mark the textual aporia by way of which *Middle Passage* opens up Rutherford's experience beyond the limits of fiction, beyond the specificity of African-American writing, without taking fiction and race out of play" (650). Among the sources Johnson avails himself of in opening up Rutherford's, and the reader's, experience are the American writers, black and white, on whom he signifies. Here, as in his other works, especially *Oxherding Tale,* the pattern of literary references supports the best intentions of his creative project. Despite his own concern over the social issues I have outlined, he finds in the literary realm at least some respite from "the madness of multiplicity" (65). By revis(it)ing Melville, Bellow, Equiano, and Baldwin, he makes the best possible case for his intersubjective aesthetic.

Although Johnson does not refer to him by name, as he does in *Oxherding Tale,* Melville is a presence in *Middle Passage.* The novel contains many allusions to both "Benito Cereno" (1856) and *Moby-Dick;* once again, Johnson concerns himself with his predecessor's views on perception and freedom, creating interesting situational similarities and bringing them to different ends. In many ways, Rutherford and Ishmael are soul mates. Each flees to sea to escape dissatisfaction and misanthropy ashore, only to labor under the command of a monomaniacal captain in pursuit of an elusive ideal. Furthermore, each forms strong bonds with an enigmatic "other" who exposes him to a different belief system and who somehow ultimately saves the narrator's life. Finally, each returns from his ocean voyage profoundly affected by the experience and creates an account of the journey as a means of making peace with the past. Where the two narrators differ is in their positions at the end of the novel.

Ishmael describes himself finally as *"another orphan,"* a statement that indicates the sense of isolation that he brings back from his voyage (573). As

Kerry McSweeney notes, Ishmael's end "recalls the earlier experience of Pip . . . as a result of which his finite body survived but the infinite in his soul drowned" (112). This grim conclusion illuminates Melville's famous comment to his neighbor, Nathaniel Hawthorne: "I have written a wicked book and feel spotless as the lamb" (*Correspondence* 212). In these terms, one sees in *Moby-Dick* the loomings of the negative view of self that festers in *Pierre* and erupts in *The Confidence-Man*. This seems to have been a difficult position for the author. As Hawthorne notes in his reflection on Melville's struggles with the novel, "'he can neither believe, nor be comfortable in his unbelief'" (qtd. in McSweeney 114). In the end, that ambivalence manifests in the narrator's endless effort to make sense of what he has seen. With the "infinite in his soul" destroyed, Ishmael can only reflect obsessively on his experiences, searching for their meaning but convinced that they convey no larger single truth.

By contrast, Rutherford returns with a strong awareness of his connection to others, a fact nicely symbolized in his creating a family with Isadora and Baleka. His ability to forge such a bond suggests that he *has* found a truth in his experiences. As he and Isadora meet in her cabin at the story's end, he describes "a vast stillness that felt remarkably full, a feeling that, just now, I wanted our futures blended . . . our histories perfectly twined for all time" (208). And in that connection one sees that community building, that act at which Ishmael ultimately fails, becomes the concrete manifestation of that truth in Rutherford's, and Johnson's, world.

Although Johnson takes issue with Melville over community, he agrees with him on the value of transforming perception as the means to mental liberation. Perhaps the most famous illustration of Melville's commentary on perception appears in "The Doubloon," where various members of the crew interpret Ahab's proposed reward according to their particular desires or biases. The last of the perceivers, the cabin boy, Pip, does not read the doubloon in these terms. Instead, as he stands before the doubloon, he conjugates the verb "to look," pronouncing the different forms as he gazes on the coin. His ability to see the process of seeing (which his statement represents) rather than to look only at the object comes from his having been immersed in the ocean.

Pip's time as a castaway echoes in Tommy O'Toole's deep dive into the *Republic*'s hold, where he encounters the Allmuseri god. Like Pip's before him, Tommy's experience changes his ability to see. He comes forth from the hold, "his skin all one bluish color as if he had been baptized in the Deep" and speaking a "slabber of Bantu patois, Bushman, Cushitic, and Sudanic tongues." Furthermore, his eyes have changed; they glow like "splinters of luciferin indigo that, like an emulsion, had caught the camphor of a blaze once before them" (68). Tommy's eyes suggest that his experience with the Allmuseri god has opened him to a new way of seeing; similarly, his ability to speak new languages suggests that his immersion has opened and enriched his mind. What I find striking with regard to Johnson's signifying on Melville is the difference in the result of the perceptual shift. When Pip comes up from the deep, he expresses the richness of being by breaking objects into discrete parts. Tommy, in contrast, comes up from the hold with the ability to *synthesize* experiences. Here, as with the contrast between Ishmael and Rutherford, Johnson uses Melville to reinforce his counterpoint about the possibility for universal human connection.

Johnson's rewriting of Pip's deep dive also has implications for his argument about racial identity formation. Melville makes much of Pip's blackness, using it frequently to emphasize his separation from the rest of the crew. That he makes this young Other the voice of multiplicity suggests his conviction that the black American has a special role to play in the nation's evolution. As Carolyn L. Karcher notes, "in his role as a prophet, Pip acts both as a harbinger of doom and as a potential savior" (88). Although the position demonstrates Melville's generally positive predisposition toward "the Race," it also reinforces a strict construction of racial identity that Johnson rejects. Like Flo Hatfield in *Oxherding Tale,* Melville needs Pip's blackness to make his meaning. Johnson counters this idea by immersing Tommy, the archetypal white youth, in blackness. His transformation when he emerges from the hold proves that connection, as it suggests his transcendence of racial boundaries and equips him to embody unity rather than division.

The description of his immersion also calls to mind the experience of the slaves who endured the actual Middle Passage. As members of various tribes commingled in the slave holds, the need for a common language became apparent. And certainly these transported people must have emerged from the ships with a new way of seeing the world. My impulse is to see Johnson's subjecting a white male to a version of this experience and showing how radically it transforms him as another attempt to break down rigid views about race and racial experience. If that is the case, though, it somewhat undermines his position, as he then needs Tommy's whiteness just as Melville needs Pip's blackness. At the very least, it reinforces the difficulty one faces in trying to break down limitations to perceptions of racial identity. Because discussions of race and racialism are necessarily dialectical, illustrating the conflict and people's means of transcending it threatens to reestablish the power of the very ideas one seeks to dismantle.

Melville confronts the difficulties of racialism even more directly in "Benito Cereno," which Johnson references overtly and extensively, especially in his account of the slave's shipboard revolt. For instance, he notes that Falcon had given several of the Allmuseri the task of picking oakum, pulling old ropes apart for the fiber. In "Benito Cereno," the oakum-pickers are a constant, ominous presence looming above the deck as Delano tours the ship. He makes the pattern even more clear in listing the names of Ngonyama's fellow rebels: Babo, Atufal, Diamelo, Ghofan, and Akim. All of these rebels bear names that Melville uses in his story, which is undoubtedly important to Johnson for what it has to say about perception. The tension of "Benito Cereno" arises from the disconnect between actual events aboard the *San Dominick* and Captain Delano's persistent misinterpretation of them. It reads, therefore, as a cautionary tale about the dangers of adhering too firmly to fixed impressions, a message that echoes in Johnson's artistic attempts to liberate perception.

The struggle for freedom that makes up the substance of Melville's story also illuminates its significance to *Middle Passage.* Although blackness means more to Melville than mere skin color—as his remarking on the "mystical blackness" in Hawthorne ("Hawthorne" 540) or the image of the tortoise in "The Encantadas" illustrates—in "Benito Cereno" the dichotomy between light and dark turns on the question of race. Delano's limited perceptions have everything to do with his fixed notions about racial identity. He cannot see Babo's nefarious power over Don Benito because of his "weakness" for blacks playing the servant role. The utter horror of the shaving scene, in which Babo terrorizes Don Benito with a razor and simultaneously humiliates him by using his national flag as a towel, does not register with Delano. He sits, "amused with an odd instance of the African love of bright colors and fine shows," never grasping the import of the play he witnesses (84). His crude grasp of black being in this instance is of a piece with Ebenezer Falcon's assumption that Rutherford could not discern a sailing ship from a riverboat.

Delano's racial essentialism makes him rather pitiful, as he revels in what he thinks is the sight of good old-fashioned black servitude. Clearly Melville's view of race in this story is much more sophisticated than any of the attitudes he assigns his characters. For him, race is not a defining mark. This illustrates a striking shift for him away from the limiting need for Pip's blackness that shapes *Moby-Dick.* In her discussion of "Benito Cereno" as an antislavery story, Joyce Sparer Adler notes, "Melville knew that the master-slave relationship does not depend on color, that no race is naturally fit to be either master or slave, that both whites and nonwhites have been slaves at some time in human history" (81). Part of the purpose in showing the flaw in Delano's worldview, therefore, is to educate readers about the dangers inherent in a narrow conception of racial identity. The captain's near fatal errors also offer an object lesson in how not to approach an encounter with an "other." This emphasis on open-mindedness in "Benito Cereno" reflects Melville's larger philosophical plan.

Just as he posits limitless meanings for whiteness in *Moby-Dick,* Melville suggests a broad, rich range of interpretations of blackness in "Benito Cereno." Captain Delano's final exchange with Don Benito—his exclamation, "'you are saved; what has cast such a shadow upon you?'" prompts the Spanish captain's fateful reply, "'the negro'"—demonstrates precisely the model of narrow definition that Melville seeks to counter (116).

I see Johnson using "Benito Cereno" to examine a shadow that racialism has cast over African Americans. The rebels who lead the Allmuseri uprising at least temporarily adhere to Diamelo's strident nationalism after they gain control of the *Republic.* Their counterhegemonic impulse, although initially liberating, ultimately proves destructive, especially when Diamelo forbids the use of the captain's maps and charts. In the wake of that decree, the tribe finds itself literally and figuratively directionless, unable to sustain the harmony on which it has long thrived. The shadow of Diamelo's ideology lifts only with the survivors' rejection of his divisive identity politics. Taking Melville's argument for a more complete understanding of blackness an important step further, Johnson shows the pitfalls inherent in any narrow attempt at definition from *within* the community, at least on the level of aesthetics.

Even as he advocates for a liberating vision of blackness, though, Johnson also makes a case for a black writer's right to control the word and to complete the story. By getting close to the rebels in a way that Melville does not, Johnson claims the literary version of the "'place at the table'" that he wants African Americans to have (Nash 52). His assertion of this side of the slave rebels' story, like his appropriation of Melville's meditation on freedom—"Who ain't a slave?" (*Moby-Dick* 6)—by making it the heart of an ex-slave's quest, proves that race is *not* an illusion to him, at least not one that he is willing to set aside in favor of completely abstract exploration of ideals. This tension, which in some ways drives Johnson's use of African American literary forms, demonstrates why one must understand his work as *black, philosophical* fiction. He aspires to a literature by writers who "happen to be black" (*Being* 123); however, his work privileges the examination of racial being in a manner that suggests that an incidental recognition of black identity cannot sufficiently explain his position.

Johnson's use of white American writers' quest stories as a component of his black philosophical fiction extends beyond his interest in Melville. One sees this in *Middle Passage* in Johnson's reference to Saul Bellow's *Henderson the Rain King* (1959). Bellow participates, like Ralph Ellison, in what M. Gilbert Porter calls the "neotranscendental," or optimistic, tradition in twentieth-century American literature. As Ellen Pifer notes, Bellow's heroes all "set out in search of an authentic self—hoping to discover the freedom of real being."

Liberation comes only with a new way of seeing the world. "Only after he has delved through all the 'cultural superstructures,' sifted through and discarded them one by one, may the Bellovian hero awaken, as Henderson says, from 'unreality' to reality and discover his authentic bond with creation" (6). This quest, which parallels the phenomenological bracketing of preconceptions to achieve intersubjectivity, strongly resembles the process that Johnson's protagonists experience. The primary difference lies in the ultimate resolution of the selfhood question. Like Bellow, Johnson seeks reconciliation of the individual and the communal. Given his Buddhist beliefs, though, he sees that reunion coming with his protagonist's recognizing, as Rutherford does with the Allmuseri god, that the self is an illusion.

What Rutherford gets from his experience with one African tribe parallels the lessons Henderson synthesizes from his encounters with the Arnewi and the Wariri. Robert F. Kiernan sees the two tribes as diametrically opposed. He notes that the "Arnewi live in a prototypical Golden Age," characterized by their harmonious relationship with their cattle and their unwillingness to harm the frogs, even though they threaten the tribe's existence. By contrast, the Wariri occupy a "fallen world" and believe that "a primal wrongdoing has somehow cursed man's existence. Phonetically, their names suggest that the Arnewi are new men, eternally Adamic; the Wariri are war weary, experienced in life's battles" (82–83). Taken individually, neither tribe can meet Henderson's needs and still the voice crying, *"I want, I want!"* (Bellow 24).

Significantly, each tribe resembles the Allmuseri in some detail of their worldview or their appearance. The Arnewi's connection to their environment and their unwillingness to disturb it suggests the harmonious sensibility that best describes Johnson's wizards. Henderson's observation that the Arnewi village "must be older than the city of Ur" (47) evokes Rutherford's comment that the Allmuseri "might have been the Ur-tribe of humanity itself" (61). Furthermore, the Arnewi have distinctive hands, the palms of which are "the color of freshly washed granite. As if, you know, they had played catch with the light and some of it had come off" (Bellow 51). Unlike the Allmuseri, though, nothing stains their palms and wrenches them out of their pre-Hendersonian existence. His wrecking their cistern does not fundamentally change the tribe's identity. Among the Wariri, Henderson meets Dahfu, who believes that "almost everything in man's experience originates in his own mind" (Kiernan 92). His attitude, which arises from the teachings of Wilhelm Reich, resembles the Allmuseri belief that each member of the tribe "outpictures" his or her own world. And, in a note of concern that recurs throughout each author's work, that ability to conjure experience leads eventually to the ultimate act of symbolic alienation: murder.

That Johnson's tribe embodies so many diverse elements of Bellow's two societies indicates the authors' differing views of the possibilities for reconciliation. Kiernan suggests that when Henderson leaves Africa, the "voice that has said, 'I want!' for so long now says, '*She* wants, *he* wants, *they* want!'" (78). One hears echoes of Pip's "reading" of the doubloon; and yet Bellow is not so pessimistic as Melville. Instead of surrendering to multiplicity, he "learns to live with" the divisions he has encountered and to make the best of an imperfect world (Newman 81). In *Middle Passage,* Johnson pushes a step beyond that, at least in his attempt to enact the ideal. Rutherford quiets his internal voice. In his final encounter with Isadora, he remarks that desire is "'too much of a wound, a rip of insufficiency and incompleteness'" that keeps people "'constantly apart'" (208). Reflecting the Allmuseri ideal that Johnson first embodies in Reb's perfect resignation, Rutherford finds the means of making the journey back across "the Flood, and countless seas of suffering" (209).

Apart from this question of degree, Bellow and Johnson share two other important beliefs. Each sees love, both romantic and paternal, as the means of overcoming human isolation. Rutherford brings Baleka home with him to Isadora, explaining that he needs her help to make a family for the Allmuseri child. Henderson, on his way home to Lily, figuratively adopts a young orphaned boy whose American parents had raised him in Persia. The men's ability to love in multiple ways suggests the depth of their healing. As each man has felt abandoned by his own father, his ability to *be* a father affords him the chance to overcome the psychological wounds of his childhood. Building on that, each can finally engage in a sustained relationship with a loving spouse, thereby creating within their own homes the harmony they have been seeking.

Both Rutherford and Henderson ascend to this liberating vision of love because of their encounters with death. For Henderson, an obsession with death—his brother's death, his desire for and fear of his own demise, and the jarring expiration of his housekeeper—inspires his initial quest. Among the Arnewi, who are surrounded by death as they watch their cattle perish from dehydration, he gets no help. Indeed, he exacerbates his suffering as his fixation moves him to become the frogs' executioner. Henderson's time among the Wariri enables him to see death differently. His conversations with Dahfu expose him to a new viewpoint; visiting Atti, Dahfu's pet lion, in her den also helps him conquer his own fears of physical death. Finally, he sees Dahfu die in the tribe's ritual lion-battle and learns that the tribe expects him to follow the king. He refuses but still adheres to the king's teachings. As he says to Romilayu, "'the king lived under threat of death himself, and what he lived with I could live with. He was my friend'" (317). Recognizing his bond to Dahfu, Henderson comes to see how emotional connections sustain beyond death.

This frees him from his fear and enables him to understand his father's suffering when Dick died. Building on that, he begins his journey home. Aware now and unafraid of death, Henderson finally begins to live.

For Rutherford, the exposure to death has a similar impact. Aboard the *Republic,* in the course of the Middle Passage, he has ample opportunity to look on death. The turning point comes when he helps throw the now-rotting Allmuseri boy over the side on the morning of the slave rebellion and the attempted mutiny. After his fingers puncture the corpse's skin and he feels the stain of Allmuseri blood on his right hand, Rutherford prepares to cut off the offending limb. This action, also the Allmuseri punishment for thieves, suggests his awareness that he is stealing the tribe's way of life. Fortunately, Ngonyama saves him from this self-mutilation. Subsequent to that, in the course of the rebellion, Rutherford has yet another chance to look on death. In this case, the deaths are both physical and symbolic, as the tribe does violence to its way of life by attacking their captors.

Out of this series of deaths Rutherford develops his own Allmuseri-ness, forgetting himself in his efforts to meet others' needs. He chooses unity over division, achieving the ultimate connection in his encounter with the god, when he loses even the sense of death as distinct event: "Then I fainted. Or died. Whatever" (171). This confrontation frees him to a new sense of harmony with his environment, an attitude he will act out in forging his final bond with Isadora. Like Andrew in *Oxherding Tale,* Rutherford also comes to terms with his father's death as a part of reconciling himself to and overcoming his racial legacy. He understands the tragedy of Riley's life and the damage his victimization mentality brings. Equipped with that knowledge, he can more easily choose to embrace a different way of being in the world. And in that mode, which emphasizes reconciliation, one can see a compelling metaphor for Johnson's signifying on Melville and Bellow. Challenging any notion that racial boundaries can separate authors, Johnson emphasizes the shared values that make all of these authors in some way members of the same tribe.

Just as Rutherford comes to terms with his father as a stage in his developing a new way of seeing, Johnson engages with literary forefathers from the African American tradition in *Middle Passage,* as he has in all of his novels to date. His efforts in this case to, in bell hooks's words, "see darkness differently" (113), include signifying on works by Olaudah Equiano and James Baldwin. In many ways, Johnson's debt to Equiano is as overt as his use of Melville. Indeed, one could hardly expect to read a narrative including references to black participation in the slave trade without thinking of *The Interesting Narrative of the Life of Olaudah Equiano, or Gustavas Vassa, the African* (1789). Equiano's autobiography begins with a description of his life among the "Eboe" tribe in what is now called Nigeria and an account of his capture and transport aboard a slave ship bound for Barbados. His account of shipboard suffering, although presented in more reserved language, resonates with Johnson's description in *Middle Passage,* demonstrating the latter's interest in historical accuracy. What seems most striking, though, is the progression of events. Equiano describes the Middle Passage and numerous other voyages he made as a slave, buying his freedom, and his continued travels as a free man. Transformed by his experiences at sea and brought into Western culture more fully by his conversion to Christianity, Equiano seeks freedom within the parameters of a strong Protestant work ethic. In a sense, his acceptance of a new way of seeing enables his liberation; the source and the terms differ greatly, but something similar happens to Rutherford. Although physically free, he suffers under the burden of a *spiritual* bondage that ceases only with his embracing of Allmuseri values. It might be too much to say that he completely reverses Equiano's position, but the tribe's rejection of material desire shows Johnson challenging the foundations of a system that has contributed in many ways to the physical and mental bondage of African Americans.

I do not mean to suggest that Equiano is fully complicit in the actions of his oppressors, though I find the descriptions of his crewing aboard slave ships, especially after his manumission, troubling. Although he was certainly not the only black seaman to serve on a slaver, within two decades of his publishing his *Narrative,* African American sailors were formally resolving not to participate in the slave trade despite the relative difficulty they generally had in obtaining berths (Bolster 160). This detail only emphasizes the complexity of Equiano's position. He advocates abolishing the slave trade; and yet, his participation in it puts him in a difficult, or at least a liminal, position. One might argue a resemblance between his liminality and Rutherford's. After all, as Elizabeth Muther notes, Rutherford knows he is stowing away aboard a slave ship before he even boards the *Republic;* in the moment, though, his concerns for himself outweigh any objections he might have (652). Once he comes to know the Allmuseri, of course, his attitudes change. One might note something similar in Equiano's experience, as he becomes an increasingly ardent abolitionist after repeated exposure to the horrors of the slave trade.

Despite all that, I see compelling differences in how the authors use this liminality. Unlike Rutherford, Equiano never describes the slaves he meets aboard ship in any detail; rather than getting "close to" the cargo, as Johnson describes his major concern in rewriting the apprentice manuscript, Equiano keeps the slaves perpetually at a distance. Instead, he relies on himself, and a detailed description of the tribe from which he originates, to make a compelling case for emancipation. When he does describe other cultures, as in his encounter with the Musquito Indians, he does so in terms of his hope of converting individuals to Christianity. His hierarchy of values keeps white dominance operant, as does his suggestion that leaving blacks in Africa and going there to convert them will be the best solution to the moral quandary caused by the slave trade.

Johnson signifies on these notions by having Rutherford realize a radically different version of self-reliance, especially after the rebellion. He describes the demands that circumstances place on him and notes learning that "the 'I' that I was, was a mosaic of many countries, a patchwork of others and objects stretching backward to perhaps the beginning of time" (162–63). Rather than championing his own rugged individualism, as Equiano does, he shows how losing that sense of separation affords him a different, and to Johnson a more significant, type of freedom. I also think that Johnson desires the fusion of cultural systems, although he complicates that by enumerating the phases of the tribe's decline. The counter to that, which one might call his aspiration to the ideal, comes in his description of how the surviving crew, especially Squibb and Cringle, change after the rebellion.

Most notably, Squibb, who has previously been so selfish as to eat food reserved for the slave children, forgets himself entirely in his service to others. This goes so far that he eventually resembles the prelapsarian Ngonyama. As Squibb bends over Rutherford's arm to bleed him, the former thief remarks, "I felt perfectly balanced crosscurrents of culture in him, each a pool of possibilities from which he was drawing, moment by moment, to solve whatever problem was at hand" (176). Similarly, there is Rutherford himself, whose balancing of African and American modes of being promises great transformation and complete liberation for him. Without losing sight of Johnson's own ambivalence about its possibility, one does well to note the impact of this idealized hope for the cross-cultural blending that can occur on an equal footing with the emancipation of one's point of view.

Of course, as in all slave narratives, Equiano concerns himself with the liberation of perception, although the terms of his discussion differ from Johnson's. This accounts, at least in part, for an important stylistic commonality between the works. As William L. Andrews notes, Equiano's narrative "is an elaborate spiritual autobiography that exploits the ideas common to evangelicals and romantics that all of life's incidents become meaningful and valuable when viewed from an enlightened perspective." Enlightenment for him comprises both his own enrichment of experience through his travels and his efforts to convince his readers of the need to abolish the British slave trade. In order to educate his audience, Andrews explains, Equiano posits an implied reader for his autobiography who "was to be converted from his monocultural errors by experiencing repeatedly the gap between Western materialism and Western idealism." The reader experiences this disconnect when he or she undergoes "a de-culturation process through which he divests himself of his insider's cultural myopia and accepts the complementary value of the African outsider's perspective" (*To Tell* 57). Part of this comes from his detailed account of Eboe culture, which challenges received notions about the brutality and savagery of so-called primitive Africans. Another key piece evolves from his parallel associations of the brutality and inhumane treatment that he sees whites inflict on blacks. By establishing this contrast, he helps develop a pattern that recurs throughout many slave narratives, as the implied white reader must see both groups, slaves and masters, differently. This forced confrontation enables, perhaps even requires, the reader to overcome preconceptions about race that have previously restricted experience.

Johnson employs a similar technique in *Middle Passage,* as he uses Rutherford's asides in the log book to create his own implied reader. As Calhoun experiences cultural enlightenment and personal transformation, he guides the implied reader through the same process, one that undercuts established Western racialist attitudes about identity. In these terms, *Middle Passage* becomes an abolitionist document in its own right, although the systems of bondage under attack differ dramatically. Where Equiano sought freedom for his fellows from physical bondage, Johnson seeks liberation from the divisiveness that rigid views of racial identity perpetuate.

As I have suggested, a key moment for Rutherford in achieving this resolution comes in his encounter with the Allmuseri god. That experience also resonates with an important moment in *Go Tell It on the Mountain,* James Baldwin's first novel. Baldwin's influence on Johnson during his apprentice period, and Johnson's subsequent repudiation of his predecessor's work as he strove to articulate his own aesthetic, make his return to this literary ancestor in such a reconciliation scene especially provocative. Like Baldwin's protagonist, young John Grimes, Johnson must struggle against the example of his (creative) father in an effort to achieve (aesthetic) salvation.

"The Threshing Floor," part three of *Go Tell It on the Mountain,* describes John's conversion experience in Harlem's Pentecostal Temple of the Fire Baptized. This event marks the culmination of the fourteen-year-old's struggle with himself, especially his ambivalence about the church and his confusion about his sexuality, and with his stepfather, Gabriel. An amazingly unrepentant, hypocritical minister, Gabriel Grimes hates his stepson and reserves what little affection he can express for his biological child, John's half-brother, Roy. To further complicate matters, John does not know that Gabriel is not his biological father, as his mother, Elizabeth, has been compelled to conceal his origins from him. In "The Threshing Floor," while he lies "astonished beneath the power of the Lord," John must confront his three fathers—Gabriel, God, and Richard, about whom he has never heard—and make peace for himself (189).

His Middle Passage, from loss to salvation, holds mental terrors akin to the physical suffering the slaves endure. Cast down, like them, into a dark place, he must come to terms with his sense of sinfulness in order to gain the "liberation" of God's grace. Like Rutherford, John suffers under the burden of paternal rejection. And, as in Calhoun's case, that conflict with his father inhibits his progress toward freedom. Long before God strikes John down, the reader learns of the youth's determination to resist his earthly father's domination, despite the spiritual consequences. The difficulty he faces on the morning of his conversion, which also marks his birthday, is his queer awakening, which he conceives of as an abomination and which tests his resolve, as Baldwin notes. "His father was God's minister, the ambassador of the King of Heaven, and John could not bow before the throne of grace without first kneeling to his father. On his refusal to do this had his life depended, and John's secret heart had flourished in its wickedness until the day his sin first overtook him" (21).

Having defined himself by his hatred of Gabriel, John now must choose between that position and the consequences of what he has been taught to view as a mortal transgression. As he lies on the threshing floor, he realizes that he fears death more than he resents Gabriel. And, learning in his vision that he cannot rely on any of his earthly family for support or enlightenment, he surrenders to the terror and beauty of Gabriel's religion, losing himself in an effort to resolve his identity crisis. Although his attraction to Elisha remains, he can now at least temporarily sublimate it under the guise of brotherly love; and despite his earlier aspirations to flee, he now finds a way to reenter his father's house, at least for the moment.

John's confusion also affects his sense of racial selfhood. Gabriel's faith rigidly separates the races. As John walks through the streets of Manhattan on his birthday, marveling at the white crowds all around him, he recalls that Gabriel "said that all white people were wicked, and that God was going to bring them low." And yet, as he has seen in his encounters with teachers who encourage him in ways that Gabriel cannot or will not, not all whites are bad. Despite that conflicting experience, he must face the message of his father's world: "He, John, was a nigger, and he would find out, as soon as he got a little older, how evil white people could be" (36). Gabriel's marking of his stepson with this epithet represents the potential harmfulness of his position. Baldwin reinforces the point by showing the reader that John has looked on Gabriel's naked body much as Ham looked on Noah in the tent on Mount Ararat. Feeling himself cursed for this action, he recalls the biblical injunction against Ham that slaveholders used to justify their actions: *"A servant of servants shall he be unto his brethren"* (197). In essence, part of what John wants is salvation from his blackness, which he perceives in this moment as a *stain.* Ironically, though, as Baldwin notes, participation in the Temple of the Fire Baptized does not mean liberation from a negative view of his blackness. The ironic voice in John's head, which represents Richard, insists that John "rise from that filthy floor if he did not want to become like all the other niggers" (194). John is figuratively damned to racial suffering and otherness no matter which father's way he follows.

Richard's emergence in the threshing-floor scene presents a powerful counter to Gabriel's ideology. After all, he is the one who, when Elizabeth "timidly mentioned the love of Jesus, said: 'You can tell that puking bastard to kiss my big black ass'" (163). Still, although he represents the voice of a radical individualism that challenges almost everything that Gabriel clings to, Richard cannot overcome his own despairing sense of racial oppression. Having suffered unjust imprisonment and unwarranted brutality because of his blackness, he kills himself. His selfish act propels Elizabeth, who had elected not to tell him of her pregnancy, on the path that ends in submission to Gabriel. And, like his mother, John also ultimately chooses this Way. Moved by a fear of death, he calls on God to "bring him through" to eternal life (202).

Of course, one must note that Baldwin raises real questions about the *quality* of life that John will find among the saints. The streets that the saints tread together on the morning of John's conversion, for instance, remind the reader that John and his fellows still face a grim, hostile, and spiritually dangerous world. And, in John's case at least, it raises the question of whether or not his new gospel armor provides adequate protection. Ambiguity surrounds John's conversion, and his final discussion with Elisha, in which John already speaks of his newly won salvation in the past tense, suggests that he will not remain among the chosen. Whether or not John is destined to backslide, it seems clear that the novel promises that suffering will inform his continuing quest for himself. None of the fathers he encounters offer him a means of reconciling his conflicting impulses about race, sexuality, and salvation; like Pip after his immersion, John comes up doomed to the sadness of multiplicity.

Johnson's signifying response to Baldwin embraces many elements of John's situation. Rutherford's youth in the house of Reverend Peleg Chandler, a slaveholding minister who values Rutherford's brother, Jackson, but cares little for him suggests the basic dynamic of the Grimes household. While Reverend Chandler is not violent, as Gabriel is, his constant criticism of Rutherford alienates the young slave much as Gabriel estranges John. Interestingly, if one pursues this analogy completely, Rutherford more closely resembles

Roy at this point in terms of his behavior, and at the start Jackson seems possessed of the spiritual nobility that marks the former thief's conversion. Jackson's example proves useful later, because it suggests to Rutherford that biology does not determine Allmuseri-ness. But before he comes to know the tribe, Calhoun's active resentment of his brother's betrayal and his former master's rigidity blocks his ascension as surely as John's anger at Gabriel impedes his.

Rutherford also bears the burden of knowing that his father, Riley, abandoned him. Although John suffers from Richard's absence, he has no idea of it. That Rutherford does only intensifies his pain. Indeed, when describing the Allmuseri god's transmogrification into a replica of the fugitive slave, Rutherford notes that it "had chosen to present itself to me in the form of the one man with whom I had bloody, unfinished business" (167). Having long hated his father for deserting him, Rutherford drifts into a hostile sense of disconnection that leads him first into thievery and then to the conviction that as a black man in America he is marked for suffering. Not actually a bastard child, as John is, Rutherford nevertheless sees himself as illegitimate in a cultural sense. This feeling of alienation, and the accompanying antisocial behavior it inspires, are the sins that Rutherford carries with him into the *Republic*'s hold.

Although there are powerful similarities between the terms of John's and Rutherford's physical experiences, the character of the latter's time on his figurative threshing floor differs dramatically. First of all, he can *see* the god and, more importantly, his absentee father. John can hear Richard's voice, but he knows not who he is. And the people he does recognize do not speak to him, for "there was no speech in the grave" (Baldwin 200). Because of what he *cannot* learn from his predecessors, John cannot choose the path out of the Temple, the way that might save him from salvation. Rutherford's ability to understand that Riley's separatist way, which has been his own, will not sustain him finally frees him from it. Also, as he can achieve sympathy with his father and thereby more fully understand both his reasons for running and why it was not a viable choice, Rutherford can forgive Riley's actions. With that forgiveness comes the step toward recognizing that his father's suffering need not be his own. More important, though, than his first sight of his father is Rutherford's experience of losing him again. As he watches Riley's failed escape attempt, the Allmuseri god blends Riley "back into the broader, shifting field" of all experience; Rutherford says that "his breathing blurred in a dissolution of sounds and I could only feel that identity was imagined." This leads him to the realization that "the (black) self was the greatest of all fictions" (171).

Here is the heart of Johnson's signifying on Baldwin. He has said of his apprentice period that he turned away from Baldwin as a literary model because he realized that too strict loyalty to his predecessor's style and vision inhibited his own creative expression. Especially repugnant to him were the notions that art must be political (an assertion Baldwin apparently made in a private critique of *Faith and the Good Thing*) and, as that political orientation suggests, that race is some sort of fixed or fixing entity that should motivate or demand certain kinds of responses (e-mail, 7 Nov. 1996). Whichever way John Grimes goes, his future will be racially determined. What Johnson tries to show with Rutherford's conversion is that such a consciousness can be overcome. In service of that aim, part of what Johnson gives Rutherford that Baldwin keeps from John is the ability to see his personal past, and the collective African American past, differently. This change in his vision enables his liberation just as John's sense of himself as bearing the curse of Ham ensures his bondage.

In addition to knowing the past differently, Rutherford experiences death profoundly differently. His recognition that death and fainting are almost interchangeable strongly counters the fear that motivates John's entry into fellowship with the saints. Indeed, one might extend this recognition to include all sorts of fears; because while anxiety motivates all of John's actions, Rutherford's ability to overcome his fright leads him toward a more sustainable pattern of beliefs and actions. That assertion of fear might be said to arise from this loss of selfhood as well. John seeks to save himself, though of course he must sacrifice his individuality to do so. Rutherford's salvation, by contrast, comes from his recognition that his selfhood is an illusion. Continuing the pattern he begins in *Oxherding Tale,* Johnson advocates a Buddhist/Allmuseri way of seeing that, by denying or transcending the idea of individuality, leads one to liberation from all fear or uncertainty.

One can see this in the seekers' respective responses to their environments after the encounters with their gods. As John walks the streets of Harlem, his recognition that the environment has not changed motivates his fear that his feet will slide in due time. Rutherford, by contrast, knows that he returns to an America corrupted by all the forces that previously tortured him; nevertheless, he finds that he still wants it anyway. Furthermore, in his declaration of patriotism, one sees a thoroughgoing change in his sense of values that will carry him through from division to harmony. "If this . . . caricature of a country called America . . . this cauldron of mongrels from all points on the compass—was all I could rightly call *home,* then aye: I was of it. Do I sound like a patriot? . . . What Negro, in his heart (if he's not a hypocrite), is not?" (179). In this view of America, Rutherford recognizes both the multiplicity of individuals and the unity of the national framework that holds them. In these terms, even an Other could love a system that allows for some inclusion. As the *Republic* goes down, Rutherford hopes to have replaced it with a new nation, a group to which he by definition *does* belong. With this conception of the national and his personal identity, Johnson rewrites Baldwin's despair and suggests that perhaps there is room for hope instead.

Or at least that is the claim he makes on one level. His *own* concerns about the sustainability of this vision surface (or sink?) in the aftermath of the Allmuseri rebellion; and that complication indicates that the true patriotism that Johnson celebrates is that which affirms the good in the nation without hesitating to critique the evil. Perhaps Baldwin would find this novel more appealing, as it at least hints at the political issues the nation must face if African Americans are to sustain the sort of liberation that Rutherford finds during the Middle Passage. It might not be enough for him, however.

It turns out not to be enough for Johnson, either. Between *Middle Passage* and *Dreamer,* the author takes up the social questions again and pushes harder for their resolution. At the forefront of that discussion, one finds one of Baleka Calhoun's lineal descendants, Chaym Smith. His status as the most fallen Allmuseri raises further questions about the viability of their moral vision. It also enables Johnson to look to the American historical record for an ideal positive role model to replace the tribe: Martin Luther King Jr. By focusing on the minister's life work and intellectual endeavors, and by tracing the impact of his life and ideas on this fallen Allmuseri, he finds a new means of addressing the tensions that characterize *Middle Passage.*

7 "Just Possibly I Was Composing a Gospel": *Dreamer*

The aesthetic tensions between ideal and implementation in *Middle Passage* coalesce in *Dreamer* (1998). This is hardly surprising, as this novel treats the last two years of Martin Luther King Jr.'s life. Few subjects more clearly illustrate both the horrors African Americans have faced and the possibility of transcendence contained in a morality of resistance. And yet one must also note the bitterness persisting in the wake of King's assassination. In "The King We Left Behind," Johnson describes what the nation has become: "almost weekly we are bombarded by news articles detailing public incivility, new depths of vulgarity in popular culture, worsening poverty in the inner cities, and the new status of young black men as 'an endangered species'" (8). His hope in *Dreamer* is to counter these trends by bringing the minister's values back into Americans' collective consciousness so that King's response to racialism might regain ascendancy.

In undertaking such an effort, Johnson faces the same dialectical dilemma that plagues his earlier work. Any effort to talk about who King became demands that one address what he overcame. Rather than sidestepping this issue in *Dreamer* (as he does elsewhere in his corpus), however, he foregrounds it. One might well conclude that he would have to, given the end of his historical subject's struggle. That is not to say that the fiction writer cannot take liberties with the historical record. Indeed, the main premise of the novel, the education of Chaym Smith as King's body double, proves that Johnson does challenge the sanctity of the actual.

Strikingly, his plan for the novel included more additions to the record designed to extend King's vision even farther. In *King,* David Levering Lewis notes that "to imagine a Martin King surviving the electoral summer of 1968 raises plausible speculations whose promise and pain are stupefying" (397). Johnson appears to have had such a project in mind when he began *Dreamer.* In an article published in the *Seattle Times* some months prior to his completing the novel, he describes the ultimate function of the minister's fictional body double. "The realization of Martin right down to his smallest tics and social gestures will be so complete by April of 1968 that when the fateful gunshot is fired from the high-powered rifle we shall not know—nor will our narrator—which man was killed in Memphis." Johnson goes on to note that because one of the twins survives, "the question that King asked Rustin, 'Where can I go from here?' can be pursued if not on the pages of recent history then in the theater of a novel that will test . . . the possibilities of this life as it is projected . . . into our own time" ("Searching" B5). Ultimately, this proves too bold a step. In the novel, Chaym disappears before the assassination, and Johnson offers no sustained speculation on what his life might be after that fateful day.

Interestingly, right before Smith disappears, Johnson reveals that he is "'pretty much the last'" of the Allmuseri (205). In a brief span, then, both his ideal tribe and their historical counterpart, King, are gone, leaving behind a bereft narrator and a broken world. Although this is admittedly the grimmest scenario he constructs, Johnson does not leave the reader to despair. Rather, he extends a pattern of intertextual allusion that provides a more effective, if still qualifiedly hopeful, resolution.

In a 1998 interview conducted as he was finishing *Dreamer,* Johnson asserts his affinities with Ralph Waldo Emerson, which manifest clearly in *Oxherding Tale* and *Middle Passage.* The Emersonian ideal that resonates in the earlier novels is the more idealistic vision of human perfectability that one finds in *Nature* and "Self-Reliance." In *Dreamer,* which effectively denies the idea of sustained individual perfectability, Johnson turns to Emerson's later works and alludes to essays such as "Experience" and "Fate." "Fate," which was composed not long after the passage of the 1850 Fugitive Slave Act, shifts from the bold claim in *Nature,* "Undoubtedly we have no questions to ask which are unanswerable," to a recognition of uncontrollable social and environmental forces marshaled against humanity (22). Rather than simply denying or submitting to them, however, Emerson advocates confrontation, keeping always in mind this question: "How shall I live?" ("Fate" 330).

In *Dreamer,* Johnson adopts a similar position. Recognizing the difficulty of living out his aesthetic ideal in the face of powerful social pressures, he turns from a transcendence model to advocate more active engagement with these oppressive forces. In chronicling the efforts of his three primary male characters—King, Chaym, and the narrator, Matthew Bishop—to achieve perfection, he offers both the impossibility of the ideal and the hope of an actual response, which he calls "doing well." He defines "doing well" as making a contribution to King's vision of "the beloved community," a unified understanding of humanity unhampered by divisive definitions such as racial identity. In these terms, a new way of seeing the world is not sufficient; one must also behave differently. This focus on the actual makes *Dreamer* his most socially engaged, activist work. It also, therefore, marks an important shift in his aesthetic direction. *Dreamer* still qualifies under Johnson's description of "black philosophical fiction." But here, more than anywhere else in his body of work, he emphasizes the application of philosophical principles in pursuit of a socially defined life well-lived.

When King brings his campaign to end slums to Chicago in 1966, Matthew Bishop signs on. An aspiring philosopher, deeply convinced of his own insignificance, he exists on the periphery of the movement until Chaym Smith arrives. This disillusioned drifter appears at King's Lawndale apartment bearing a hard-luck story and a striking physical resemblance to the minister. Although it takes some effort, he convinces King to take him on as a body double; the minister in turn assigns Matthew, and his co-worker Amy Griffith, to teach Smith how to play his new role.

For that purpose, the three go into seclusion in southern Illinois, near Makanda, at Amy's ancestral home. Once away from Chicago, Smith reveals himself to be much more complex than his interview with King suggests. A modern-day Ishmael, Smith has wandered the East, studying for a year in a Japanese monastery; he also has developed an encyclopedic knowledge of Western philosophy. Nevertheless, despite all he knows, Smith remains convinced that hopefulness and philanthropy are merely illusion. As he tells Matthew and Amy, "'there's two kinds of people in this world. Predators and prey. Lions and *lunch.* You see it any other way, buddy, and people will chump you off'" (55). Although Amy rejects this assertion out of hand, Matthew soon finds himself torn between the minister's and the misanthrope's visions of humanity.

All of that changes when Smith, in Chicago to stand in for King, takes a bullet intended for his twin. Back at their hideout, Smith undergoes a profound philosophical change. No longer bemoaning his fate as a victim of circumstance, the body double focuses on trying to bring forth King's spiritual ideal through his daily actions. Once a sharp critic of Christianity, Smith volunteers his services as gardener and carpenter at a small church near their hiding place. His example proves useful also to Bishop, who serves as his assistant in these endeavors. In addition to some rough carpentry, Chaym teaches Bishop how he might also better contribute to creating the "beloved community" despite his personal imperfections. Unfortunately, all of Smith's efforts to gain enlightenment fail when government agents appear and force him to participate in their plot against King.

Before the government can use Smith, it is April 4, 1968. With the body double gone, only questions about his and the minister's legacy remain. For Bishop, one inheritance is a heightened awareness of accountability for the civil rights leader's death. As he tells Amy, they all killed him, "black and white—because we didn't listen when he was alive" (235). Despite that recognition, he does not despair, because his encounter with the body double has shown him the possibility of redemption. Reflecting on Chaym as he follows behind King's casket, Bishop realizes that "Chaym had in his covert passage through our lives let us know that, if one missed the Galilean mark, even the pariahs, the fatherless exiles, might sometimes—and occasionally—doeth well" (236).

Johnson takes this notion of doing well from the story of Cain and Abel, which appears in the fourth chapter of Genesis. His comments to Bill Moyers demonstrate that he sees this as the generating point for dualistic thinking and obsession with the self. Here, however, Johnson looks past that notion, focusing instead on God's gentle challenge to Cain: "'Why are you angry, and why has your countenance fallen? If you do well, will you not be accepted?'" (Gen. 4:6–7) That emphasis leads necessarily to a reassessment of Cain's mark. Although generations of interpreters have viewed it as a curse, the Old Testament account pointedly suggests it is more protection than stigma. "Then the Lord said to him, 'Not so! If anyone slays Cain, vengeance shall be taken on him sevenfold.' And the Lord put a mark on Cain, lest any who came upon him should kill him" (4:15). This rethinking of what became a powerful tool of racist oppression sounds a dominant note in *Dreamer,* one that resonates through King's, Chaym's, and Matthew's experiences in the struggle for individual and community freedom.

One might call the historical King's battle for racial equality an effort to erase the mark of Cain as it has been popularly understood. This seems a reasonable interpretation of his actions up until the Chicago campaign. From the Montgomery bus boycott to the March on Washington, the minister's efforts to bridge the gap between the races repudiate the power of this image of blacks as cursed. And indeed, every victory in the struggle weakened the power of this notion. But near the end of his life the minister's vision changed. As David Levering Lewis notes, as a result of his time in Chicago, "Martin began to emphasize the economic enfranchisement of the poor far more sedulously than in the past" (354). That shift in his consciousness was an important step toward the sentiments he expressed on the eve of his first trip to Memphis in early 1968: "'There is a need to unite beyond class lines. Negro haves must join hands with Negro have-nots'" (qtd. in Lewis 380).

That claim shifts the emphasis of the Cain and Abel paradigm from Cain's actions to Abel's filial responsibility. Traditionally, Cain's resentment of God's favoring Abel has been read as a sign of weakness, an interpretation with striking implications in the push to associate him with blackness. This outrage takes on a different character when one looks at it through the lens of inequity, which reveals that the injustice exists *before* Cain strikes. Why is one brother better than the other? Following the implications of this scenario to their logical end, one can reasonably conclude that inequality is inherent in the human condition, something that one must learn to accommodate or at least address. If one extends the racial-reconciliation reading of the Cain and Abel story through this interpretation, the post-Chicago shift in King's message takes on new significance. The call for "haves" to help "have-nots" signals the minister's recognition that total equality is not the first achievable goal, because of the inherent inequities existing between individuals. Notably, though, it is also *not* an admission of defeat; instead, it represents a refinement of the Emersonian question: "How shall I live?"

In *Dreamer,* Johnson dramatizes King's conversion process. Chaym's story illustrates the depth of inequality within the black community. At the end of Chaym's account of a life that "was a nightmare, a ghastly joke on everything he'd once dreamed of becoming," the minister says, "'If we can achieve our goals for equality here, I think things will be better for you.'" Smith's reply—"'What if you don't?'"—pulls the minister up short (38–39). After his physical twin leaves, he broods on the implications of Smith's story and its biblical analogue, finally concluding that his responsibility to help Chaym emblematizes a whole course of actions for the movement. Ruminating over Smith's visit, King realizes that the *"least advantaged had every right to break the social contract that had so miserably failed to meet their needs. They would rebel, riot as they were doing now in Chicago. For their own sake and survival, God's favored had to lift those on whom He'd turned his back"* (50). The minister's realization also becomes part of the foundation of *Dreamer's* social program.

Their first interview, in that Lawndale kitchen, makes it clear that King is Abel to Smith's Cain. Favored by God in all things over his twin, King exemplifies all that Smith has ever sought. Furthermore, Smith knows he is Cain before he approaches the minister; indeed, that knowledge proves to be one of his primary motivations for making the trip. Johnson reinforces the parallel in his character's name. "Chaym," he tells us, derives etymologically from "Cain." Furthermore, "Cain" means "Smith" in Hebrew. The body double arrives, therefore, both symbolically and actually doubly marked. The actual marks, his poverty and his consciousness, prove most compelling. Still reeling from years of disappointment and despair, Smith believes that God has cursed him. His expression of that attitude, and more particularly his efforts to convert Matthew Bishop, counter King's assertions and provide the dramatic tension that propels the first half of the novel.

That tension also represents a significant evolution of Johnson's creative enterprise. While Chaym speaks in terms reminiscent of Johnson's other fictional mouthpieces for the victimization model of black identity, none in the author's corpus have ever spoken more forcefully than the body double does. Perhaps even more importantly, none come to the victim position with the breadth of experience that Chaym possesses; his wide reading in Western philosophical texts and direct experience of Eastern religious practice shape his running commentary to Matthew Bishop. Certainly his is a radically different voice from Big Todd Cross's, George Hawkins's, or Riley Calhoun's. In some respects, with this expansive education and his artistic abilities, Smith resembles Johnson himself. This change in approach indicates his willingness to address the argument for "Cain-ism" more fully than he ever has before. That willingness comes from his more complete acceptance of this view in light of the current social realities that African Americans face.

Chaym begins his assault as they head south to seclusion at the Nest, the Makanda farmhouse where Bishop and Amy plan to teach King's body double his new role. While Amy sleeps, Smith lectures Bishop about blacks' inability to build community because of their ingrained sense of rejection. As he makes these points, he brings it all back to the Cain and Abel story. "'What you got to face, Bishop . . . is the possibility that we are . . . descended from the first of two brothers whose best just couldn't hack it . . . the world . . . kicked off with killing and righteous hatred. . . . Envy . . . is the Negro disease . . . the mark. Nothing else really explains our situation'" (66). Although he argues against Chaym's reasoning, Bishop does not miss the lesson. He demonstrates the quick hold Smith gets on him when he destroys the small, horrifically backward and unbelievably dirty diner where he and his companions stop on their way downstate.

Strikingly, just before he snaps, Matthew recalls his mother's humiliating attempts to procure food and clothing for him throughout his youth. The terms of her degradation almost exactly match those that Faith Cross remembers of Big Todd in the wake of her being raped. This moment becomes, then, Bishop's parallel descent into hell. Unlike Faith, however, he has in Smith a Mephistopheles who explains his outrage in nearly irresistible terms. When Amy rejects Bishop's advances because he is not enough like King, he gives in to Smith, albeit warily, embracing the body double's sense of isolation as his own.

At first glance, it seems as if the author cannot resist the call either. Two elements of Smith's early experience suggest Johnson's own exploration of questions about dualism, isolation, and raciality. Smith's incomplete sketchbook renderings of the Ten Oxherding pictures and his failed attempt at liberation in the Japanese *zendo* point to Johnson's Buddhist practice, which has been for him a powerful counter to racialist conceptions of identity. Ideally, one would expect that a system that rejects the notion of the self would erase the mark of Chaym. And yet even the zendo cannot escape this dualistic consciousness. This proves especially tragic because the body double is almost free. As he tells Matthew, his time at the zendo enables him to not think about the world or his racially defined suffering in it.

Unfortunately, his gradual awakening does not meet the expectations of the *roshi,* or master, who sends Smith away because only the Japanese can become truly enlightened. The failure of his guide's own quest effectively ends Smith's, as he sees that even meditation and withdrawal from the world cannot protect him from racialist ignorance. Although the roshi calls him *"gaijin,"* Smith hears "nigger," the signifier that he associates with his Cainite mark. When this, his best hope for liberation, fails him, he surrenders to his "lions and *lunch*" attitude.

With this turn of events, one must wonder whether or not, or to what extent, Johnson withdraws his commitment to Buddhism. If this account represents any cooling of his ardor for a mode of thought that rejects racial and personal identity, then that signals a reversal of his position. One sees evidence for this notion in Smith's claim to Bishop about the difficulties he found in his meditation practice, which demands a focus only on the moment. "'And the hardest thing a man can do, especially a colored man whose ass has been kicked in every corner of the world, is live completely in *now*'" (97). This seems a far cry from what we have seen in Johnson's earlier work, images of black characters who slip easily into meditation and happily lose the negatives of their racial heritage (such as Rudolph Jackson in "China").

In my view, these details represent instead a careful consideration of the responsibility that accompanies enlightenment. Stopping with the eighth Oxherding picture, or deciding that gaijin cannot ever achieve enlightenment, emblematizes a blind embracing of teachings, something more along the lines of the failed philosophers in Johnson's early works. As a counter to that, the author returns to the idea of social engagement that Little sees in *Oxherding Tale*'s model of the householder (*Charles Johnson's* 105). In this version, however, the stakes are considerably higher; the answer is "doing well." Although Chaym cannot or will not embrace them until after his near-fatal encounter with another Cainite, the text presents several models of doing well that illustrate how one might achieve the reconciliation promised in King's vision of the "beloved community."

Significantly, all of these people are Abelites in some sense. If money is not their endowment, and in several cases it is not, then they possess a wholeness of *spirit* that enables them to do well for themselves and for others. The minister himself is, of course, chief among these figures. But Johnson also includes portraits of an entire generation of African Americans who rose above racist oppression without ever losing sight of, or pride in, their black identity. Their example becomes, in the end, a powerful inspiration to both Bishop and the reader. Taken together, they provide a compelling answer to the novel's basic question: "How shall I live?"

Although Matthew does not understand it, his mother provides him a model of the spiritual Abelite lifestyle. Her unwillingness to submit, either to oppression or to bitterness, embodies the resilience that all of the chosen in the novel share. Matthew sees her spiritual nobility but cannot easily follow her example himself. He tries; his whole involvement with the movement is, in fact, such an effort. But a growing sense of his own Cainite nature keeps him from fully grasping his ancestral example. Only exposure to a community of African Americans who typify the Abelite ideal even more fully than his mother does can bring him to her enlightenment. He and Chaym have one shining example in Dr. King. Even more compellingly, though, Johnson presents Amy's family and community, all of whom belie Chaym's notions about blackness as stain. The body double's reactions to the stories prove instructive for Matthew and the reader. His movement from outrage to despair marks an important stage in his progress toward embracing, however fleetingly, the minister's ideals.

Amy's love for her family becomes apparent with the appearance of Mama Pearl, the grandmother who has raised her since her father murdered her mother. That detail, although mentioned only in passing, proves significant. Given what we learn of Amy's family, her mother's tolerance of an abusive mate is quite surprising. Perhaps it signals some qualification of the general message that the Abelite Griffithses convey; maybe it serves as a reminder of the difficulty of sustaining such a vision. Nevertheless, despite this setback, the Griffithses' worldview clearly represents, for Amy and possibly for Johnson, the best hope of countering the notion of blackness as curse. Mama Pearl demonstrates this, teaching Amy the confidence and selflessness that make her so powerful and so appealing to Matthew. Her self-reliance is striking on its own; things become even more compelling when Amy, Matthew, and Chaym arrive at the Nest, where she describes Mama Pearl's family.

As Amy spins the story of her great-grandfather and his children, Matthew notes, "it was like being gently led into the past, a distant, better time when black people were the moral fiber of a nation" (88). The Griffithses, who into the 1950s make their clothes and furniture, grow their own food, and educate their children, represent an ideal of self-reliance largely absent from contemporary American society. Furthermore, they are part of a network of African Americans in the area who practice this lifestyle and barter among themselves for what they cannot make. At the center of this self-contained empire was the family patriarch, Amy's great-grandfather, James. Amy describes his leading by example: demonstrating devotion to his family, conditioning himself to deny his desires, and believing that after being pampered long enough to develop a strong sense of self-worth, his offspring should devote themselves unceasingly to serving others.

In many ways, the Griffithses resemble the prelapsarian Allmuseri of *Middle Passage*. James Griffiths's belief that the family "was far more than a group bonded by blood" (90) evokes Rutherford's realization that more than biology holds the tribe together. The tone of Matthew's narration in this passage suggests the tragedy of the family's decline; in this, they most greatly resemble the Africans. The dilapidation of the house and the overgrowth of weeds suggests a kingdom in ruins; Amy confirms that the pressures of modern American life made the self-sufficient enterprise unsustainable in the 1950s. With James deceased and his children migrated to Chicago in search of a better life, the Griffithses' way of life seems merely a relic. Despite Mama Pearl's strength of character and Amy's devotion to what was, the family's values cannot last in the urban world any more than the Allmuseri can escape intact from the "madness of multiplicity" that they encounter aboard the *Republic*.

Johnson's elegiac presentation of this lifestyle affirms the need for positive social engagement. The ideal that the Griffithses represent, especially James's calm, self-assured refusal to be ruled either by the world or by material desire, is something to strive for; however, the novel offers no suggestions as to how one might achieve it. In this spirit, the realistic description of the Griffithses as "self-reliant" bears further mention (90). This is, of course, the Emersonian ideal as advanced in the early essays; but as I have suggested, Johnson's particular sympathies with the transcendentalist lie elsewhere in this novel. His account of what keeps the Griffithses from succeeding offers some insight into his and Emerson's shift in perception.

How striking, given the significance of the Griffithses' disappearance, that

Chaym, the fallen Allmuseri, reacts with outrage to Amy's story. It rattles him so greatly that he must retreat into meditation, a process that naturally evokes his year at the zendo. As he spins his own narrative of that transformative year, one sees strong parallels between the monastic existence Smith finds in the Japanese forest and the Griffithses' independent lifestyle. Both promise empowerment and liberation; and, tragically, neither proves sustainable. Part of the threat to each lies in the Cainite anger that Chaym vents in his descriptions of both. As he draws Bishop into the sphere of his divisive influence, Smith demonstrates the mentality that jeopardizes harmonious existence. In light of this, it is appropriate that Johnson reminds readers that the biblical Cain was the first builder of cities—because it is the urban world, with its roiling mass of resentments alienating the haves from the have-nots, that challenges the Griffithses' model of independence. Furthermore, as Johnson takes his reader back to that world with a further look at events in Chicago in 1966, he provides a more viable model of response to the recurrent question of how one might best negotiate the pitfalls of modern life.

Chaym's first assignment as King's stand-in comes on August 5, 1966, the day of King's march to Halvorsen's Realty to protest unfair housing policies. With this detail, Johnson turns the historical record to a particular purpose. The actual march to Halvorsen's was especially tense and hostile, featuring (as does Johnson's version of events) an enormous, violently angry white crowd and the minister being injured by a thrown brick (Ralph 123). In the novel, Smith acts as a decoy so that the minister can secretly escape. Encouraged by the body double's performance, King sends him out that night to Calvary A.M.E. Church in Evanston to accept an award. As this is Mama Pearl's church, Amy has insight into the congregation, which she discusses with Matthew and Smith on the ride north. What one sees in her description is the urban alternative to the Griffithses, a group of Abelites "so toughened by prejudice, by the rule of having to do twice as much to get half as far, that they regarded no problem as insurmountable" (127).

Chief among the parishioners of Calvary A.M.E. is Robert Jackson, a successful entrepreneur, who built first a milk delivery business and then a construction firm, both to serve the needs of Evanston's black community and to escape the dominance of a white-controlled marketplace. Utterly confident in his success, Jackson shares his wealth. His construction company, for example, employs members of his extended family, offering them a ticket north and a means of sustaining themselves upon their arrival. In a sense, his approach proves the logical extension of the Griffithses' rural self-reliant lifestyle. As such, it suggests that not even the call of the urban environment need destroy the independent spirit that Johnson admires in Amy's, and indeed his own, rural ancestors. The significant wrinkle in the discussion at this point concerns the responsibility that such an Abelite as Jackson has to address the much more pressing needs of his unequally blessed community. His active financial and personal support of Calvary A.M.E. demonstrates his sense that he must give a great deal to his fellows. In this, he resembles other of his Calvary peers, such as Dr. Jennifer Hale, a physician who dreams, then realizes, a hospital for African Americans in Evanston. In their example, which Johnson clearly admires, one sees a sustainable response to the harsh realities of American racism.

Johnson's warmth in describing these people comes largely from the fact that he is telling his personal history in doing so. Robert Jackson closely resembles Johnson's great-uncle William, whose construction company provided the author's father, Benny Lee, the impetus to come to Chicago. He pays tribute to "Uncle Will" in "The Second Front," the essay he contributed to *Black Men Speaking* (1997). This collection of commentaries on the meaning of African American manhood, which Johnson coedited, demonstrates his increasing emphasis on racial matters during the period he was composing *Dreamer.* Furthermore, his own contribution, the final essay in the volume, reaffirms the fundamental equation that drives Johnson's work at this stage. With his expression of anger over racial injustice and shame at what he sees as the decline of the black man in contemporary American society and his articulation of a thoughtful response to both, one sees how completely Johnson has achieved a balance between his social and philosophical concerns.

In this amalgamation of thought and action, he strongly resembles his great-uncle, who provides Johnson's practical model, a complement to King's ideal example, for the life well-lived. He says in "The Second Front" that "black men today can do no less" for their children than his Uncle Will did for the Johnson family. His other charge to his readers, one that William Johnson also embodied in his every action, is to battle "the enemy within," that negative conception of blackness that keeps African Americans confined by received models of racial identity (183). In short, the "enemy within" might be called the Cainite consciousness that makes people see their blackness as stain. William Johnson's Abelite reaction, in contrast, is to "do well," to transform that sense of cursedness into the fuel of opportunity.

In the novel, where Robert Jackson offers the same response, Johnson demonstrates the power of this position to dominate the Cainite view. As Chaym hears Amy's account of Jackson, Hale, and their peers at Calvary, his composure begins to dissolve. He exclaims to his escorts, "'everything here seems so . . . *finished.* God loves these Negroes. What do I *say* to them?'" Matthew's vehement response—"'Nothing!'"—proves absolutely right. Completely undone by his sense of inadequacy, Smith can only watch from the shadows as King, who arrives at the last moment, gives a speech proclaiming the unity of all things and the notion that "'every man and woman is a speculum, our mirror. Our twin'" (140). In that moment of seeing *his* twin receive accolades for things that he would say himself if he were able, Smith experiences "a kind of living death" (142). This, as much as the assassination attempt that follows it, functions as the Heideggerian moment of sein-zum-tod in this novel. In this formulation, the brush with death is a crucial push toward liberation. *Dreamer* follows the pattern exactly, as this marks the turning point of Chaym's quest for relief from his pain. Indeed, in listening to the woeful tale of his would-be killer minutes before the old man pulls the trigger, Chaym makes his first, painful step toward being like King. The pistol shots merely accelerate the process.

That Smith's encounter with this community, and with King in the context of it, so profoundly affects him signals Johnson's view of its power and value. Unlike the Griffithses' model, which demands for its success an untenable isolation, Robert Jackson's example functions within the urban landscape. It even sustains that landscape, as Jackson is himself the builder of the city. This represents an Abelite assumption of Cain's historical role, or perhaps more clearly the means of "doing well" that made an Abelite out of one bearing Cain's mark. And, the novel implicitly asks, if Jackson can achieve this transformation, why not anyone else?

That question becomes explicit in the description of Chaym's healing period, during which he partially purifies himself of the poisonous hostility that characterizes his existence before the shooting. Significantly, Smith temporarily loses his physical resemblance to King during this evolution period, growing hair and a beard that mark him for one observer as LeRoi Jones. This rounds out a complex portrait of a man who first appears with a beard "as rubicund in tint as Malcolm Little's" (33). Perhaps this representation of such a triumvirate in Chaym's appearance supports Johnson's notion of interconnectedness, as it offers a graphic re-formation of bonds among three activists who have come to be popularly regarded as almost antithetical. Alternately, that figurative fragmenting of his physical self might play on his spiritual sense of division, indicating the depth of confusion that remains unresolved for Chaym at this point. Either way, his spiritual self-reformation gains a particular focus on the day that he and Matthew take Amy to catch her return train to Chicago.

Driving back from the station, they stop at Bethel A.M.E. Church, the Griffithses' erstwhile home parish and the site of their family cemetery. Arriving as the minister, Allan Littlewood, ascends to the pulpit, they hear a pertinent sermon that takes the Cain and Abel story as its text. Strikingly, though, Littlewood emphasizes not Cain's exclusion but what redemption he might achieve. This vignette provides the most direct statement of the novel's solution to the dualism riving American society in the cultural moment Johnson describes. Noting that God marks Cain for protection, not as a curse, the minister also foregrounds the possible redemption that God offers Cain. He asks, "'does not God say to the elder brother . . . *if thou does well, shalt thou not be accepted*? . . . His deliverance—and surely ours—is wrapped in the perennial mystery of what that divine counsel . . . means. . . . As a question, it is cast best . . . in the quality of sacrifice and sentience itself'" (157). Although Chaym rejects Reverend Littlewood's overtures about membership after the service, the minister's words clearly strike a chord in him. His offer to do landscaping and carpentry for the church signals his effort to enact that sermon's message. Littlewood's not insisting on the body double's faith as a prerequisite for service reinforces the point, proving to Smith that there can be a place for him where actions matter more than labels.

That crucial distinction separates the Bethel A.M.E. experience from his time at the zendo; in most other respects, the two phases of existence prove quite similar. His recuperation time at the Nest has a monastic quality, an element of further withdrawal from the world and its battles. Then, with his volunteering himself and Bishop to serve at Bethel A.M.E., he puts his newly formed self into action. As during his other time of retreat, Smith finds every action to be holy, all of a piece in his sacrifice of self. When Matthew returns from a visit to Chicago, during which he finally fully connects with Amy, he finds the body double possessed of an inner peace that seems to counter all the rage that he once felt. One has the sense that if he were called on to make a speech for King at this point he might well be able to; this suggests that doing well might be enough to mend the rift in his Cainite consciousness. If that were truly the case, though, the novel would come to a more hopeful conclusion than it does. Two interrelated difficulties (in addition to the historical record) preclude that, however. First of all, there is the nature of Chaym's personal transformation; second, it takes place in isolation, at a remove from the urban world that threatened the Griffithses initially. Together, these circumstances undermine Chaym's newfound hope and jeopardize his progress and the minister's larger vision.

Chaym's realization that he is being watched makes him summon Matthew back quickly from Chicago; Amy insists that he go. Bishop arrives in Makanda to find Smith working at Bethel A.M.E. When the narrator asks if he "got religion" while healing from his gunshot wounds, Chaym replies, "'I don't believe in a blessed thing, including me. I'll never be one of the faithful. It's just that I figure work is all I got to offer. . . . I ain't worried 'bout it bein' fair'" (182). Although it leads to positive action, this position remains grounded in the same sensibility that characterizes his time at the zendo. Given what else the novel has to say about resolutions reached in isolation, one can hardly expect this conviction to be sustainable. Furthermore, that Chaym believes in nothing also suggests potential problems. Perhaps the obverse of his narcissistic hopes for immortality, this position cannot protect him from external forces that would turn his work to nefarious purposes. When such pressures arise, in the form of agents Groat and Withersby, Smith cannot resist their influence. While he agonizes over agreeing to participate in their plot to "save" King from himself, in the end he does agree. His transformation is not so complete as to allow this final, total sacrifice of himself; it is as if the ideal he momentarily touches cannot survive the presence or power of the real.

How fitting, then, that we learn of his Allmuseri heritage at this moment in the narrative. The FBI agents who pressure Chaym to participate in the plot against King mention in passing that he is a lineal descendant of Baleka Calhoun, who appeared in *Middle Passage* as the child that Rutherford saves and takes back to Makanda. In the former novel, she represents the hope that some modicum of the Allmuseri Way might survive the horrors of the Middle Passage. By bringing her lineage to this conclusion, Johnson asserts his strengthened conviction that the tribal ideal cannot survive in modern American society.

Ironically, Chaym is living Allmuseri more fully in the days before this interview that he ever has before. But that self-sacrifice will not sustain. Faced with the choice of complicity or imprisonment, Smith submits to the government's demands. Significantly, as they lead him away, they begin playing on his old egotism, calling him a "genius" (206). And, sadly, Chaym is not immune to such manipulation. This sounds what seems to be one of the novel's most tragic notes: to have seen the body double come so close to healing only to miss the mark. After all, he even signs the commitment form, the pledge of submission to the movement's ideals that he rejected so forcefully when Amy first offered it to him. However, that commitment strikes me as specious at best. Even as a merely symbolic act it proves painfully inconsistent; with that inconsistency, all of the difficulties of the tribe's position in *Middle Passage* resurface. But in that novel Johnson offers some glimmer of a chance for the tribe to survive. *Dreamer* diminishes that faint light—first in Chaym's submission and then with reference to the assassination. Since participation in the tribe can occur on the basis of shared values, none could be called an "honorary Allmuseri" more easily than King. Neither could any other present a less attainable ideal of self-sacrifice than the minister. Smith understands this, first bitterly and then with something more like resignation. Knowing what he cannot do, he does what he believes he must, even though that action probably leads to the minister's doom.

Ultimately, then, Chaym lives out the double marking of his name. Despite all his efforts to the contrary, he cannot do well enough to save himself or the minister. This resolution challenges the Cainite-Abelite balance that Johnson sustains throughout the novel. Early on, in his first reflection on Chaym's situation, King decides that assisting the Cainites is imperative, or else *"rancor and bloodshed might never cease"* (50). Unfortunately, all efforts to assist Chaym still lead inevitably to bloodshed—King's own—and to the groundswell of accompanying rancor that exists extratextually for the three decades (and beyond) between the events and Johnson's fictionalizing of them. In short, this does not appear to be a situation that the minister's ideals can fix. Furthermore, if two so gifted as this pair of Cainite-Abelite twins (and surely Chaym is blessed as well as cursed) cannot achieve this goal, what hope is there for anyone who brings less to the process? Furthermore, given that certainty of failure, especially in a world fragmented by the forces one sees in Johnson's Chicago, what benefits lie in even engaging the struggle? The novel raises all of these questions, creating in the process a potentially much darker vision than one sees elsewhere in Johnson's corpus.

What light he casts against that shadow comes from Matthew's account of his own transformation. In many ways the relative of Johnson's irreverent earlier narrators (as in the description of his sexual encounter with Amy), he also provides an assessment of King, Chaym, and the events of the narrative that proves more systematic and introspective than anything else one finds in Johnson's work. The tendency to examine comes from the deep sense of personal inadequacy that also makes him a prime target for Chaym's "lions and *lunch*" philosophy (55). Struggling with his awareness that he cannot live up to King's ideal and stung especially by Amy's citing that as her reason for initially rejecting him, he falls under Smith's spell. Because of his training in philosophy, though, Bishop does not go quietly into nihilism. He evaluates Smith's and King's arguments, trying to determine how best to confront his own personal demons and what position best serves the larger aspiration for racial justice.

Matthew's problem is not only uncertainty about to whom he should listen; at bottom, he does not know what to believe, either about himself or society. As I have noted, he joins the movement for his mother, aware for himself only that he cannot "breathe life . . . into any system of meaning" (54). His is a terrible dilemma, as he is simultaneously aware of all the terrors that he and other blacks face and unwilling to surrender to them if he can avoid doing so. In this, he strongly resembles the Emerson who wrote "Fate." For both, the recognition of the pitfalls arrayed against them results in the query, "How shall I live?" As Matthew struggles to find his answer, he guides the reader through the moral and philosophical path that Johnson advocates. He also advances the author's social-activist response to the question.

One sees the philosophical undercurrent most clearly in his efforts to come to terms with the Cainite-Abelite dilemma. Increasingly aware of his affinities with Chaym, he does what any good philosophy student would: reads a book about Cain and Abel. His reflections on that tome, the title of which is not given, provide Johnson with the vehicle for his assessment of Cainite consciousness and its prevalence throughout history. He cites a range of texts in which the paradigm appears, from *Beowulf* to *Billy Budd,* and notes the prominence of the image in such popular-cultural artifacts as *Shane, The Time Machine,* and *The Magnificent Seven.* All of this rumination leads to a sweeping assertion: "It was said that Western man himself was Cain, cursed with the burden of restlessness and the endless quest for selfhood" (161–62). I see in this Johnson's effort to universalize the dilemma, a technique that would counter the sense of racialized victimization that Chaym expresses.

Still, even as he does so, he inserts reminders of those specifically targeted elements of this dilemma. In his ruminations on the labeling of Jews by the Nazis, Matthew notes, "the color black, of course, was its own mark" (161). This aside keeps the reader from forgetting what for Johnson is the primary issue at hand. He reinforces the point by moving Matthew from this reading on the train to a series of reflections on the racialized economic injustice that he sees running rampant throughout Chicago. Not matter how much he might intellectualize the problem when he leaves the city, Matthew lapses back into resentment over what whites are keeping from him. This suggests the author's conviction that although one can abstract the issue, such an approach does not yield meaningful results. This, after all, has been Matthew's problem all along: even though he knows the problem is larger than his particular circumstance, he still must determine what to *do* about it. That leads to his next function, as an evaluator of the various modes of being black that appear in the novel.

The positive assessment in this goes, as we have seen, to the Griffiths clan and the Abelite parishioners at Calvary A.M.E. Johnson reinforces that orientation through Matthew's reflections on the spirit of his age. Just after that galling bus ride across Chicago, Matthew confronts the inadequacy of both his old apartment and himself. The latter has much to do with his conception of his context. "American culture in the mid-60's was becoming so fluid, so polymorphous you could change your identity—reinvent yourself—as easily as you restyled your hair. It was the first truly *theatrical* decade. A moment when role-playing and how things appeared took primacy over reality" (164). As a product of an earlier era, Matthew feels no comfort in this landscape. His perception is that this makes him a Cainite; clearly, however, in Johnson's vision, this disconnect represents Matthew's most Abelite attributes. The author's description of the era's histrionic raciality indicates his lack of patience with it as a meaningful response to the real socioeconomic pressures that surface in his character's bus ride through the Loop. Much better to be philosopher and critic, as Matthew, Chaym, and King all are, than to be caught in the whirlwind of other people's drama. The comment about hairstyles and self-making especially emphasizes this point. It also evokes an image from *Black Humor* (see figure 8) which demonstrates Johnson's doubts about appearance-driven identity politics.[1] One sees something similar in the novel's description of the "dashiki-clad radicals" who drive Matthew from the black student union for not being "black enough" (174).

What Matthew knows, and what the novel advocates, is that the only productive results of his quest for personal and communal liberation arise from actions, not appearances. Ideally, this is not to say that revolutionary hairstyles and clothing cannot be part of a life well-lived; in all fairness, though, the novel does equate such clothing with a certain kind of narrow-mindedness, a move that indicates the author's own biases. My sense is that Johnson's main objection is not to the appearance itself but to the substitution of appurtenances for substance. After all, this decision about loyalties based on appearance is, at bottom, a recreation of the difficulties driving the racialist paradigm. So long as African Americans view each other in these terms, then any hope for effective community building is at best incomplete.

In addition to the insights he provides into the problem of community on the larger scale, Matthew also illuminates the challenges facing the African American family. Given how strongly Johnson affirms the Griffithses' response to their racist environment, one can reasonably conclude that this emphasis on family is a crucial element of the best-case response to the challenge of doing well. We know from Matthew's descriptions of his mother that he was a devoted son; nevertheless, with her passing, he is alone in the world, as are Johnson's other narrators. The focus of his meditation on this subject, then, primarily rests on the challenges African Americans face in trying to build family in a broken world. This shapes much of Matthew's interaction with Amy, who despairs of ever finding a black man with whom she can truly connect. Her early refusal of Matthew shows that she only wants an Abelite, "'somebody a little more like the men I knew growing up. Or like Dr. King'" (94). Profoundly convinced that the minister's is an example he cannot live up to, Bishop re-

Cut it all off. I'm changing my philosophy.

Figure 8. Reprinted from *Black Humor,* © 1970 by Charles Johnson.

cedes into the detachment of his Cainite consciousness; he emerges, however, willing to try again when she eventually offers encouragement.

The hope of finally connecting with her brings him temporarily back to Chicago and sets up the context for his reentry into the world of envy and racialism that proves so troubling. As a part of this, he also reflects on the challenges facing them as they attempt to build a relationship. This passage is especially revealing of the conflicts inherent in Johnson's view of women and his sense of what racism has done to the black family. The first element appears more subtly in the flaws in Amy's character; she is every inch the "typical" shrinking fainthearted female for most of the novel. But here the critique takes on a new edge, as Matthew notes that he feels compared to all of Amy's former boyfriends and judged guilty of their failings until he can prove himself innocent. This awareness yields a comment striking for its bitterness: "only a black American woman could place that burden on a man" (170). One sees a version of this dynamic in each of Johnson's earlier novels, but nowhere has he more bitterly or more pointedly critiqued black women than he does here. On its own, I find this assertion most troubling, as it points to a still-unresolved conflict between Johnson's theory and practice.

Yet he does not leave it entirely on its own but quickly notes that the problems that Matthew and Amy face are not unique to them. As Bishop says, they are of a piece with the "centuries of black men and women hurting and betraying and possibly hating each other . . . the damage wrought by centuries of discrimination" that makes forging meaningful connections difficult, if not impossible (170). This, again, takes the reader to the heart of *Dreamer's* social agenda by recognizing the pressures threatening the community and challenging readers to dream viable responses to them. Matthew and Amy forge such a bond by mutually recognizing the futility of racialist outrage. They remain committed to the push for social equality but see doing well, adhering to King's values, as the only viable means of achieving that end. As they and Mama Pearl march together in the minister's funeral cortege, they reaffirm this commitment; they also symbolize another fusion of the past values of the Griffiths clan with the activism of their age. This, Johnson clearly believes, is the best hope for the black community.

If the discipline of romantic love is difficult in this world, then the challenge of parental love is even harder. The novel extends the Emersonian question about being in the world to a subject that Johnson treats throughout his corpus: the dilemma of the African American father. From Big Todd Cross to Riley Calhoun, Johnson's previous father figures all represent basically the same resentments over racialist oppression and similar nonviable victim responses to it. In essence, these black males cannot be fathers because they do not believe American society will let them be men. This position reflects much common mythology about African American fatherhood and resonates with many scholars' takes on the relationship between race and parenting.[2]

For Johnson, in his earlier work, this position is not a fact to live with but a state of being to revise. In every case, the children must overcome this sense of racialized suffering on the way to their eventual liberation. *Dreamer* presents an interesting variation on this pattern, as Chaym and Matthew never know their fathers. Indeed, much of the Cainite bitterness that each experiences arises from the sense of spiritual and social illegitimacy accompanying their actual family circumstance. This emotion represents on one level Johnson's real concern about a challenge facing the black community. In "The Second

Front," he discusses his experiences as both son and father to illustrate the role that black men can, and in his opinion should, play in saving the community from further pain and self-destruction. He acts that out in the novel through a parallel series of attempts at parenting that demonstrate first the difficulties and then the benefits of doing well as a black father.

The first tragic attempt at parenting appears in the novel only as an element of Chaym's history. When he meets the three young sons of a prostitute living in his tenement building, Smith informally adopts them. He makes a good-faith effort at nurturance, taking the boys places, feeding them, and trying to be a positive presence in their lives. He even marries their mother, whom he does not love, to save the youngsters. Ultimately, though, he cannot sustain even the dream. The economic and social pressures of his situation destroy him; he and his wife descend into a round of substance abuse and domestic violence that ends only with the murders of the woman and her sons. Chaym has no knowledge of who committed the crimes, as he was wandering the city in an alcoholic daze the night they happened; nevertheless, he becomes the prime suspect and ends up confined to a mental institution. Whether or not he committed the murders, Chaym believes that by surrendering to the external pressures that he had hoped to save the youngsters from, he committed a crime before the boys and their mother died. He cannot parent effectively, at least partially because he has neither a role model to draw on nor a belief that he can make emotional connections with others.

Although the twist of the murders elevates Smith's tale beyond the mundane, Johnson conveys a sense that such stories are all too common an element of twentieth-century African American urban life. He also, through the example of Chaym's well-intentioned failure, shows how *wanting* to save these young black men is insufficient without a deep commitment to some sort of salvific belief system. Though one might not be a James Griffith, a Robert Jackson, or a "Daddy" King (the novel's trinity of strong black patriarchs), one must constantly struggle to do well if one is to survive the horrific and real dangers that kill Chaym's foster family and almost destroy him, psychologically and spiritually.

The second example of parenting in the text proves more viable, as both Smith and King effectively become father figures for Matthew. This also repeats a pattern from Johnson's earlier work, but in this instance we see the protagonist work through the lessons of his surrogate parents to develop a more viable engagement with the racialist realities of his environment. As Bishop realizes the deeper similarities between his fathers' examples, he loses his sense of illegitimacy. Or, perhaps more precisely, he recognizes that even the mark of such physical bastardy need not define him. Walking behind the mule-drawn wagon bearing the minister's body, Matthew sees "that if the prophet King had shown . . . the depths of living possible for those who love unconditionally in a less than just universe engraved with inequality . . . then Chaym . . . let us know that, if one missed the Galilean mark, even the pariahs, the fatherless exiles, might sometimes—and occasionally—doeth well" (236). With this final note, Johnson reaffirms the twin poles of his agenda in *Dreamer,* reminding the reader of the suffering the community faces and the potential that lies in meaningful engagement against it. He also notes how such an approach honors and extends the work of previous generations of strong father figures who transform the racialist pain inflicted on the black community into a source of power.

• • •

In addition to exploring transformative social expressions of black life, Johnson also considers the examples of his literary ancestors. In *Dreamer* he continues the practice of drawing on literary sources across racial boundaries. Here, as elsewhere in his corpus, that technique creates a sense of unity in the face of divisive forces. However, as Johnson's project in the novel includes meaningful engagement with those forces, he does not simply rest on previous accomplishments. Instead, he minimizes emphasis on allusions to white writers in order to focus on the works of African American authors who have engaged the dilemma that drives *Dreamer:* can one balance racial outrage and a meaningful hope for social and spiritual improvement? His signifying revisions of Richard Wright, John A. Williams, and Eldridge Cleaver suggest that the primary answer is "no," or at least "not very easily." In countering those authors' individual negativities, though, he does make fleeting reference to two predecessors, Ralph Ellison and W. E. B. Du Bois, who ground his efforts to move beyond the portrayal of suffering to achieve greater harmony.

Dreamer's Chicago ghetto is Bigger Thomas's territory; Johnson makes the allusion more specific by having Smith rent a room from Vera Thomas and her mother at 3721 Indiana Avenue. The two women clearly represent Bigger's mother and sister; Johnson takes care to make Vera the right age, and his description of the elder Mrs. Thomas's wish that Smith had been her son echoes Wright's portrayal of the first Mrs. Thomas's bitterness toward Bigger. Furthermore, in affirmation of the idea that absence and presence share equal significance, Buddy Thomas does not appear; this leaves one to imagine his fate, which Wright himself had suggested would be not unlike Bigger's. By leaving the tattered remnants of the Thomas family in the same location and situation where Wright placed them, Johnson affirms the horror of the social forces pressing down on them. Even in doing so, he still resists the notion that such a fate is inevitable, as the experiences of the Griffithses and of Robert Jackson amply prove.

To make space for his vision, however, Johnson must acknowledge Wright and (at least symbolically) dismantle his agenda. Smith's burning of the apartment building represents the second stage of that process. By destroying the master's house, Johnson makes different conclusions possible. He does not deny the power of Wright's work or ideas; in an odd way, this allusion honors one of the primary influences of his apprentice period. Nevertheless, Wright's Chicago is a world where "doing well" is impossible, where the environment provides a single, immutable answer to the "How shall I live?" question. To promote his social and philosophical agenda, Johnson must transform this particular urban landscape. Smith's arson is the crucial first step in freeing literary Chicago, and the reader, from domination by Wright's perceptions of the city.

In addition to challenging Wright's determinism, Johnson also signifies on two writers who sought to undermine the minister's reputation with their divisive responses to his assassination. He lists John A. Williams's *The King God Didn't Save* (1970) among the texts he acknowledges in *Dreamer*. Williams's work portrays the activist as a failure whose outmoded, nonviolent approach to integration necessarily gave way to the greater force of Black Power. In his introduction, he baldly states his position: "So now the man is dead, and time is already proving that his philosophy began to die before he did" (23). Williams's assertion jars when one compares it to the iconographic image of the minister that dominates current perceptions of him. Nevertheless, this view is consistent with much of the criticism of King that arose within the younger ranks of the black community in the late 1960s and that has persisted into the present. Stokely Carmichael's call for Black Power was a major step toward the eventual break between the Student Nonviolent Coordinating Committee and the Southern Christian Leadership Conference (Lewis 327–28). As that schism deepened, the young revolutionaries took a large percentage of their generation with them, away from King and toward the vision that Williams promulgates.

In his effort to privilege King's views in the ongoing liberation struggle and to defuse criticism of King—the purpose he announces explicitly in "The King We Left Behind"—Johnson painstakingly counters Williams's view of the civil rights leader. Throughout *Dreamer,* he takes issue with Williams's characterization of King's actions and attitudes. In *The King God Didn't Save,* Williams claims that "Martin King was a part-time Chicagoan. . . . While in Chicago, King actually lived in a slum tenement in order to draw even closer attention to the work of the Union to End Slums (but the apartment had been painted and refurbished for him by UES people)" (92). The historical record supports

Williams's assertions: King did travel repeatedly during the Chicago campaign, and workers did repairs to his Lawndale apartment before he moved in.[3] Nevertheless, one can take issue with Williams's implication, in this statement and throughout his description of the campaign, that King was unwilling to suffer the afflictions of the people he was representing.

Johnson challenges such notions by presenting a different picture of the minister's apartment and the time he spends away from it. In his vision, King's participation in the Chicago campaign is neither incomplete nor "soft"; it is, instead, the struggle of a leader who sees his power base slipping but who remains convinced that his is the most morally sound means of pursuing liberation. First of all, he imagines King's temporary home without mention of any improvements. The wretched flat is an unbearably hot hovel in a building reeking of urine and surrounded by the urban war zone of the West Side, where riots are raging when the novel begins. In one striking moment from the narrative, *"a cataract of black and brown cockroaches. . . . some dragging translucent lunular eggs behind them,"* tempts King to violence, as he struggles with and resists the impulse to crush these filthy *"constant companion[s] of the poor"* (46). With this image, Johnson demonstrates not only King's commitment to staying in the apartment but also how it becomes a test of his most basic principles. In not killing the roaches, King meets the challenge of ahimsa that he raises for participants in the movement. This vignette counters the notion of King as "part-time" anything. It also suggests that whatever time King spent in such squalor merits recognition rather than mockery, as it indicates another sacrifice the leader made for his followers.

Johnson takes the same approach to King's travels during the Chicago campaign, focusing not on any of King's potentially glamorous journeys but on his weekly commute to Atlanta to meet his responsibilities at Ebenezer Baptist Church. As he portrays it, King's weekly trip is more duty than any sort of escape. Although he leaves Chicago behind briefly, he cannot elude the pressures of the larger work he has taken on with his efforts to create the "beloved community." In *Dreamer,* even the plane ride brings demands, as King must sign forty copies of one of his books for the flight attendant. His selfless acceptance of this task further demonstrates Johnson's belief in King as completely devoted to his cause. By consistently presenting this view of King's actions, Johnson counters the harsh cynicism of Williams's portrayal.

In the same spirit, Johnson modifies Williams's assessment of the inevitability of racial struggle. In *The King God Didn't Save,* Williams repeatedly asserts that racial strife is the natural outcome of white America's historical abuse of blacks. In telling the story of King's being hit by a brick during the Marquette Park march, Williams reminds his audience that the victim of this attack had won the Nobel Peace Prize, an award that elsewhere in the world would afford him some measure of protection. Not so in America, Williams notes, as he outlines the results of such blindness. "That Martin King won the award augured well for the American possibility of gaining racial peace; that Americans failed to recognize this has damned them to a restless racial future—which they well deserve and, in fact, have long deserved" (97).

Dreamer admits that America's racial history has been restless, but Johnson holds out hope for some coming calm. In his view, a return to King's principles might save the nation from the damnation that Williams describes. He makes the point by adding fictional elements to his narrative around the brick-throwing incident. Later that same day, only hours after he has faced this physical assault, King makes the speech at Calvary A.M.E. Church that resoundingly demonstrates the futility of separatism. As he puts it, "'the segregationists lost even before they began. Nothing stands alone. . . . After a time, I tell you, a man comes to see only a We . . . a universe of interrelatedness'" (139–40). Although he does not deny that struggle will still occur, with these words Johnson asserts the possibility for harmony. In these examples, King's vision of the "beloved community" seems something reasonable to strive for, a legitimate response to the novel's Emersonian query.

As Johnson counters Williams's negative example and offers a more hopeful resolution to American racial conflict, he also takes a stand against the third of the three authors whom he describes as influential in his development. To find his voice, Johnson had to step away from each of these predecessors' views on race. Much as he figuratively burns down Wright's house, he undermines Williams's position through his deliberate contradiction of the views in *The King God Didn't Save.* Note, in that light, the title of the essay he wrote asserting the values he would present in *Dreamer:* "The King We Left Behind." With this title, and in his portrayal of the minister and the movement in his novel, Johnson shifts blame from the leader to those who mistakenly chose not to follow him. His assertion of this position marks his coming to terms with his literary forefathers and his celebration of "doing well" as an alternative to an alienating, narrow vision of black identity.

In addition to resonating with his fatherhood theme, Johnson's treatment of Wright's and Williams's work evokes his personal creative evolution. Long before *Dreamer* appeared, Johnson began discussing the personal journey that the novel represented to him. He says in "Searching for the Hidden Martin Luther King, Jr." that King's ideal "was replaced in me by black cultural nationalism before I fully had the chance to subject the black American goal of integration to philosophical examination." He also notes that he felt the need to address King's life and legacy in order to be leading "an examined life" himself

(4). In *Dreamer,* he presents a version of his examined artistic life. Although, by his own admission, Johnson had lost sight of King during the first two decades of his career, he recognizes important commonalities between his ideas and the minister's. As a tribute to King's influence, therefore, he revises key moments in his aesthetic development to reflect the civil rights leader's values. He also makes Matthew Bishop a vehicle for this self-exploration process.

In his review of the novel, Richard Bernstein remarks, "one suspects that Matthew is modeled on Johnson's youthful self" (C8). Johnson does, in fact, invest Matthew's character with elements of his own experience, such as a passion for philosophy, to illustrate how he grew toward the articulation of his aesthetic. This intellectual orientation enables Matthew's assessment of King and Smith; it also equips him to deal with other more vocal proponents of particular models of black identity. In the latter stages of the narrative, this results in one of the novel's most pointed commentaries on Johnson's personal experience and the racial climate of late-1960s America.

When Matthew returns to Chicago, he and Amy attend a lecture by an activist, Yahya Zubena, at the Black People's Liberation Library. This fictional establishment closely resembles the Black People's Topographical Institute, a revolutionary enclave that existed on Chicago's South Side in the late 1960s and early 1970s. As Johnson demonstrates in *Dreamer,* the institute argued that urban blacks were ghettoized so that the state might better contain them in the event of any insurrection. It also, in his version at least, challenged African Americans to prepare for "'the coming race war'" (172). Matthew and Amy have no idea about the library's politics when they decide to attend a lecture there; they go out of curiosity, hoping to find others who share their interest in ending oppression. What they find instead is a group of people who wish to become the oppressor, to use violence to overthrow the white majority.

In this vignette, Johnson captures some of the fundamental political tensions dividing the black community in the late 1960s. He also addresses a specific conflict of that era by incorporating details from historical figures into his portrayal of Zubena, the library's director, whom Amy and Matthew hear speaking when they visit. The ex-convict poet and revolutionary strongly resembles Eldridge Cleaver, the black radical author of *Soul on Ice* (1968). Both Zubena and Cleaver, for example, brag about raping black women in order to perfect their technique for white women. Like Cleaver, Zubena was a violent criminal who underwent a political conversion while in prison. And, most importantly, like Cleaver, Zubena is a militant separatist with no respect for King or for his values.

Zubena calls Amy and Matthew "'Uncle Tom nigguhs'" for working with King (173). Two days after King's murder, Cleaver remarked that "Dr. King represented a stubborn and persistent stumbling block in the path of the methods that had to be implemented" to end white oppression ("Death" 73). He also noted that King had the "role of one who was hated and held in contempt, both by the whites in America who did not want to free black people, and by black people who recognized the attitude of white America." Furthermore, as Williams would do two years later, Cleaver claimed that in the wake of King's death, "the only way for black people in this country to get the things that they want—and the things that they have a right to and that they deserve—is to meet fire with fire" (74).

Johnson's choice of Cleaver as a model for Zubena is an important part of his effort to advance the minister's quest for the "beloved community." In "The King We Left Behind," he notes that when King and his peers fell out of favor for their "hopelessly assimilationist" views, "our preferred black spokesmen . . . became streetwise ex-rapists like Eldridge Cleaver, or Huey Newton . . . or severe critics of the entire Eurocentric enterprise of Judeo-Christian civilization such as Malcolm X." He decries this trend, saying that these separatist militants "are the true spiritual fathers of today's Crips and Bloods" (8). In *Dreamer,* however, Zubena does not carry the day, at least not with Amy and Matthew. Johnson uses this encounter to deflate the separatist position and to show why, in his opinion, King's is the better approach. Consistent with his quest to apply his aesthetic principles, he offers a new way of seeing a crucial developmental moment in the history of African American identity politics. In the process, he also suggests that the Way (in the Buddhist sense) largely abandoned in that era holds effective answers to still-pressing questions.

He places Cleaver's militant separatist rhetoric into Zubena's mouth, offering a clear picture of the opposition to King's ideal. At the same time, he makes that mouthpiece morally repugnant and intellectually limited. Zubena's virulent misogyny frightens and repels Amy; he sees this and uses his presence to bully her into submission. By contrast, Bishop is not so tractable. As they wait the revolutionary out, enduring his diatribe, Matthew (ever the philosopher) analyzes his logic and quickly discovers the weakness in it. "The way he reasoned, with racial politics as every syllogism's major premise, led all his thoughts to the same terminus. (Of course, if the only tool you have is a hammer, it's likely you'll treat every problem—and person—as a nail.)" (174). By showing these deep flaws in the representative of blind militancy, Johnson undermines that position. He further intensifies the distinction between the separatist ideology and the ideal of the "beloved community" by showing how much more firmly Zubena's rantings entrench Matthew and Amy in King's camp.

The incident also emphasizes the author's reconsideration of his own experiences. This event resonates profoundly with Amiri Baraka's 1969 speech at SIU, which was also characterized by a divisive ethos. Although his rhetoric was perhaps slightly less confrontational, Baraka's refusal to speak with whites in the audience and his insistence on black art for black people conveys much the same message as Zubena's speech. By advocating cultural separatism, Baraka declares creative war on white society; similarly, like Zubena, he adheres to a notion that African Americans must be "black enough" to meet his standards. In the moment, Johnson accepted Baraka's message; the elder statesman of black cultural nationalism was in some ways a mentor to him at a crucial point in his artistic development. As he continued his philosophy studies, he became less enchanted with Baraka's narrow attitudes—positions that, Johnson is quick to note, Baraka himself abandoned in the mid-1970s. In *Dreamer,* Matthew's studies save him from the trap of Zubena's agitprop rantings, thereby keeping him from some version of the struggle that his creator endures.

This juxtaposition of Cleaveresque mouthpiece and Johnsonian narrator also evokes Johnson's first published aesthetic statement, his critique of Cleaver's "Primevil Mitosis." As I have noted, Johnson's 1976 encounter with Cleaver's writing indicates the ambivalence that recurs throughout his early work. His reimagining of the experience in *Dreamer* reflects the spirit of his 1993 postscript to the revised essay, which enriches perceptions of black male identity. In the novel as in the essay, Johnson notes that racialism and racist oppression present dangerous challenges to the African American community. Nevertheless, he clearly believes that Cleaver's violence, Williams's bitterness, and Wright's determinism are not the most viable responses to these forces. As he evokes and signifies on these ancestors, he also affirms the ideas of two other literary predecessors: Ellison and Du Bois.

One sees the tribute to Ellison in the Optic White paint that Bishop notices on Smith's face during their turning-point conversation at Bethel A.M.E. Church. This mark, which symbolizes Ellison's unifying aesthetic, shows Chaym's evolution away from his Cainite bitterness toward his moment, however fleeting, of intersubjective hopefulness. As I have suggested, this enlightenment does not appear viable in its purest form. Johnson does not emphasize it, therefore, only offering it to the reader as an example of what one might hope for. By contrast, his reference to Du Bois's classic, *The Souls of Black Folk,* which Matthew finds in the false front of the Black People's Liberation Library, suggests a more sustainable response to the social and psychological pressures that the novel chronicles.

Few books hold stature comparable with that of Du Bois's *Souls of Black Folk* in the African American canon. Published in 1903, this genre-crossing amalgamation of essay and fiction crystallizes important terms of the debate over black identity that has continued into the present. Du Bois's formulation of the notion of double consciousness is sufficiently well known not to require another explication. What does bear consideration, however, is the positioning of that idea in this debate. Strikingly, Du Bois is a figure whose work receives positive attention from proponents of both integrationist and separatist ideologies. This apparent inconsistency arises not from the willful appropriation or misinterpretation of his ideas but from the complexities inherent in the text itself. As Ross Posnock notes, *The Souls of Black Folk* represents a "double project" for Du Bois. "He works both within and beyond the veil, celebrating the 'Negro Soul' in the former, while preparing black Americans for the 'chance to soar'" beyond that barrier, to the realm "where the 'sovereign human soul' expands, protected by the 'centres of culture,' which have no racial designation" (89).

Du Bois's paradoxical synthesis of attitudes about black identity grounds Posnock's articulation of his antirace race man paradigm. It also explains why such a text would be of interest to Johnson, whom Posnock mentions fleetingly as building on Du Bois's foundation. The tension appears implicitly throughout his pre-*Dreamer* body of work. In Matthew's encounter with Zubena, he finds a more effective means of reconciling the conflict and of figuring it into his literary efforts to "do well."

That both the revolutionary and the narrator deem Du Bois's book worthy of notice suggests again the conflict of antirace race ideology at work. The "fervent nationalism" of his strong condemnations of American racism echoes in Zubena's claims. At the same time, his interest in "championing the ideal of human brotherhood" suggests King's ideal of the beloved community (Baker 98). In the context of Johnson's own increased commitment to activism, however, I see the inclusion of *The Souls of Black Folk* at this point in the text as potentially resolving the conflict, or at least affirming an effective means of negotiating it. Du Bois supplies a practical response to the "How shall I live?" query: in addition to working for economic and social amelioration of unjust conditions, one must also always recall the importance of soul or spirit work. For Johnson, whose interest prior to *Dreamer* has apparently rested in the latter realm, King provides an ideal example of how best to balance these potentially conflicting aims on a social level. Du Bois, and his successors in the "antirace race" tradition (especially Ellison), provide the author with a similarly inspirational literary example that enables him to achieve a new level of activism without eschewing the philosophical foundations of his aesthetic.

And yet one fact remains to complicate this reading: the extra "s" appended to Du Bois's original title in Johnson's text (where it appears as *The Souls of Black Folks*). As William Gleason notes, that single letter suggests a number of intriguing possibilities ("'Go There'" 8). I am inclined to read this additional "s" as Johnson's final, fleeting rejection of Du Bois's looming essentialism, a signifying revision of the original that allows the author to claim his own space within this intellectual-activist camp.[4] In *The Art and Imagination of W. E. B. Du Bois,* Arnold Rampersad claims, "in using the term 'folk' to describe this most oppressed and despised group in America" Du Bois "was making a strong claim for the recognition of its dignity and separate identity" (75). Similarly, Bernard Bell claims that Du Bois's title "racially and culturally connotes a distinctive group of persons bound together by common experiences, memories, and aspirations" ("W. E. B. Du Bois's" 111). At the heart of Johnson's vision in *Dreamer* is the multiplicity rather than commonality of experience among the black community. His recognition of the Cainite-Abelite dichotomy demonstrates this division and suggests the means of overcoming it.

Although Chaym, Matthew, and King have all experienced racist oppression at the hands of the white majority, each brings different perspectives, and therefore different responses, to these encounters. Rather than contradicting Du Bois's view, however, this approach enriches his original vision. What Johnson offers, ultimately, is a vision of multiple roads that lead from the val(l)e(y) of the veil to the mountain top of the "kingdom of culture" (Du Bois, *Souls* 46). There are, in this view, many ways to address this tension around identity that plagues Du Bois. The responsibility of adherents to the various ways is to pursue them toward the ultimate end of the beloved community.

With the recognition of that multiplicity comes liberation from the need for perfection; as Matthew notes finally, the "Galilean mark" is not the ultimate end, and there is no single correct path toward it. What matters more is the challenge resonating through the comment Matthew and Amy hear as they pause during the march: "'Excuse me, keep moving forward. If we stop, we'll fall and be trampled'" (236). This becomes the heart of Johnson's newly awakened activist impulse, the command for progress in the name of love. In many ways, this position resembles the emphasis on love that one finds in the earlier novels. The difference lies in the more frank admission of the need for action, which points to a more effective reconciliation of the political and artistic attitudes that exist in tension throughout Johnson's pre-*Dreamer* corpus. In achieving this reconciliation, he completes his own cycle of Oxherding Pictures, molding his enlightenment to serve his community through this process of social and aesthetic engagement.

CONCLUSION: "The 'On-going Experiment' Continues"

Late in *Dreamer,* after his first failure in Memphis, the fictitious King asks Ralph Abernathy, "'Where can I go from here?'" As Johnson shows, the only option is back to Memphis, where *"a fuller, deeper and more perfectly broken heart"* awaits him (225). Having completed his story of the minister's struggle, Johnson might well ask the same of himself. Fortunately, in his case the answer is strong and hopeful. The shift toward activism embodied in the idea of "doing well" manifests itself throughout the projects that immediately follow *Dreamer;* it also points a direction for Johnson's thought and writing about race in the early years of the twenty-first century. Although the tensions that inform his earlier work reappear, the lessons that he learns in writing *Dreamer* provide a model for negotiating them. In doing so, he affirms the social and intellectual missions of his philosophical black fiction.

Immediately after Johnson completed *Dreamer,* he set about composing the twelve stories for the *Africans in America* companion volume. These short pieces, which were subsequently republished as *Soulcatcher and Other Stories* (2001), together provide an account of American slavery that demonstrates anew the tensions between ideal and application that characterize the author's corpus. As Johnson explains in his preface, one of the major goals that he achieves in the collection is to employ a variety of forms in telling these stories. And yet, even as he ranges across a number of styles to accomplish that purpose, he also creates a confusing thematic picture. The first story of the collection, "The Transmission," imagines a cross-cultural fusion of slave and free that begins in the Middle Passage and implicitly continues into the present. Another, "Poetry and Politics," explicitly rejects the notion of a black artist, in this case Phillis Wheatley, making political art that protests the injustices of slavery. A third, "The People Speak," affirms the unwillingness of Philadelphia's black population to embrace expatriation. Each of these stories suggests a possibility for real, meaningful human connection. One sees in them the continuation of Johnson's aspirations toward intersubjectivity and his claims that the black artist's proper role eschews any social demands that weaken his or her artistry. These notions evoke his earlier work, especially the treatment of slavery in *Oxherding Tale.*

Johnson balances this intersubjective argument with stories that emphasize the gross abuses of slavery and that, at their most extreme, call for a black solidarity that leans toward separatism. The most militant of these, the title story, explicitly challenges *Oxherding Tale's* ideal. I see the creation of this "Soulcatcher," in which a profoundly different set of values reigns, as an important qualifier to, if not a reversal of, his earlier position. In this case, the "Hunter," Clement Walker, has none of the sense of holy mission that Horace Bannon bears; furthermore, the "Hunted," Frank, is not a spiritual seeker like Andrew but rather a simple man, perhaps an alcoholic, who arrives in Boston after fleeing his master's farm (75). What meditation Frank does engage in centers on his regret at the loneliness of the fugitive life.

The answer to that isolation, the story tells us, is black community. Although Frank does note that there were whites who helped him get north, it is his life among free blacks that gives him the courage to stand his ground. This call for racial solidarity would not, on its own, complicate Johnson's earlier position; what does, however, is the fact that among the citizens of Frank's new community are "members of Boston's chapter of the Liberty Association, devoted to killing bounty hunters on sight" (81). Their execution of Walker guarantees Frank's freedom and enables him to rest.

While I neither dispute the historical validity of this story nor object to its ending, I am struck by what this conclusion means for Johnson. To present such a resolution as a viable response is to significantly shift the momentum from the direction one sees in the collection's earlier pieces. It also, by extension, affirms a modification in his larger creative program. Johnson follows "Soulcatcher" with a series of stories that further validate its claims. In "A Lion at Pendleton," he fictionally occupies Frederick Douglass's consciousness and pays tribute to that great leader's unceasing service to abolitionism. In doing so, he also notes Douglass's negative reactions to white abolitionists' attempts to control his labor for the cause. To be sure, Douglass had reason for such emotions, as his relationship with William Lloyd Garrison demonstrates. By privileging that element of his experience, though, Johnson emphasizes the conflict in his own position. He ends his tale with Douglass reflecting that "he did not have a spare moment. . . . to wait for white men—even the good ones—to catch up to him" (92). The terms of this critique, which emphasizes racial division over intersubjective commitment to the liberation struggle, show Johnson at something of a distance from the claims he makes in "Poetry and Politics."

The same is true of "The Mayor's Tale," a fairy tale that imagines the consequences of the Fugitive Slave Act of 1850 for a northern city whose "free" blacks flee en masse for Canada. The story's message is twofold: first, blacks could not count themselves safe anywhere in the United States as 1851 began, and second, the country that treated them so harshly was simultaneously dependent on them. One might read in this a version of Ralph Ellison's argument about African Americans' integral role in the national history ("What America Would Be Like without Blacks"). And yet in Johnson's story one gets a sense of outrage that is absent in Ellison's work. The final image of the white mayor weeping in the snow reads as justice for him and his kind. As such, it only reinforces the tension operating in the collection.

What resolution Johnson offers to this tension appears in "Murderous Thoughts," the last story in the collection, which takes the form of a series of man-on-the-street interviews conducted in Boston in 1854, the day after fugitive slave Anthony Burns was returned to his master. This action touched off a storm of abolitionist protests across the nation; one participant was Henry David Thoreau, who composed "Slavery in Massachusetts" and delivered it from the lecture platform at an antislavery rally in July of that year. In Johnson's story, Thoreau appears, unnamed, as the last speaker. His comments combine actual language from that essay with a broader affirmation of the doctrine of civil disobedience. Through Thoreau, Johnson holds out the hope that action to depose the corrupt state might clear the way so that "men and women of God, blacks and whites, can rebuild America with wood less crooked than that used by the Founders" (110). This statement and the story's final line ("'One of the most important things we can do, young man, is never forget . . .'" [110]) affirm the social program of *Dreamer.* Furthermore, although the author emphasizes his considerable aesthetic accomplishments in describing the stories, these social claims are the volume's most important contribution to Johnson's ongoing project. He leaves the call to "never forget" open-ended, thereby challenging the reader to keep both problem and solution present and active in mind. In Thoreau's hope of rebuilding the nation, Johnson also takes his "rebuilding the world" image from *Oxherding Tale* and gives it a specific twist that makes the dream more focused and more attainable. In that case, the thrust was primarily personal and spiritual; in *Soulcatcher,* he makes it an integral element of what he calls "the on-going adventure of democracy" (xv).

He builds on those notions in "Accepting the Invitation," an article written for *Tricycle* magazine that considers whether or not Buddhists should vote.

At first glance, this seems antithetical to the foundations of the religion. Indeed, as Johnson notes, "the sphere of politics . . . especially racial politics" is "the perfect illustration of samsara" (63), the realm of desire that Buddhists aspire to transcend. And yet, even as he claims this, he recites a litany of abuses perpetrated on African Americans in the effort to deny them the franchise. This is not a history to be denied or compromised. What then is the racially aware Buddhist to do? How shall he or she live?

In Johnson's view, one resolves this dilemma by engaging in the struggle while remaining faithful to the basic tenets of the religion. As he explains, "one way to read the injunction for Right Conduct, an essential part of the Eightfold Path, is to see it as calling us . . . to translate the dharma into specific acts of social responsibility . . . that surely means voting for . . . initiatives that . . . reduce suffering and violence, ignorance and hatred" (64). Cast in these terms, Right Conduct clearly resonates with *Dreamer*'s ideal of "doing well." Here, as in the novel, Johnson holds up King as a model to emulate. He notes, in the final paragraph of the essay, that the minister's example of spiritually informed political action offers the best hope that enlightened individuals have for achieving personal and political freedom.

In addition to honoring King's ideals in his fiction and essays, Johnson also provided the text for *King: The Photobiography of Martin Luther King, Jr.* (2001). In the preface to this collection of haunting images, he notes that "each and every photo" in the book offers a way into "a watershed life produced by America's ongoing, unfinished experiment with democracy." He goes on to invite readers to "Enter, enjoy, and be enlightened," which he has defined as the goal of political Right Conduct (6). His addition of "unfinished" to his description of the national experiment with democracy emphasizes the need for struggle. Such enlightenment comprises both the horror and the wonder that Bob Adelman's photographs convey; it also reflects, as do the images themselves, the tensions inherent in Johnson's literary corpus and his growing conviction that King's example might be the one that affords him some resolution.

But at this stage of his career, the minister is not Johnson's only inspiration. In the midst of these other projects, Johnson has also undertaken a volume of philosophy, the first he has written since *Being and Race.* Tentatively titled *The New Souls of Black Folks: A Phenomenology of Race for the Twenty-first Century,* the project promises much and will likely be a landmark work. Certainly Johnson aims at such an impact; why else would he deliberately evoke so seminal a text as Du Bois's?

At some point, serious writers must address the question of legacy. In 1998, Johnson stated his hope that his work might add "even a little" to efforts to move American fiction "toward a greater appreciation of the life of the spirit" (Nash 61). Throughout his career, he has worked to this end; one cannot read any of his fiction without considering spiritual questions. In the closing years of his third decade as a professional artist, though, one sees him shifting his awareness of spiritual responsibility more toward Du Bois's socially informed way of being in the world. This change allowed Du Bois a means of negotiating conflicts around questions of racial identity that even today seem firmly, perhaps immovably, rooted in the American mind. That modification allows Johnson similar opportunities for addressing these recurrent issues and therefore enables him to fulfill his aspirations to write philosophical black fiction. That he will carry this ever-refining sense of himself and his political-aesthetic project forward into the fourth decade of his career and the early years of the new century promises further challenges to and inspiration for subsequent generations of readers and authors alike.

NOTES

Chapter 1: Origins and Influences

1. I am indebted to William Gleason for suggesting the resonances between Johnson's work and Posnock's view of the black intellectual in an essay entitled "'Go There': The Critical Pragmatism of Charles Johnson." Gleason argues that Johnson's essays and reviews qualify him for inclusion within this tradition. I agree with this assessment and also see strains of this antirace race attitude throughout Johnson's fiction as well.

2. At a conference at the State University of New York at Stony Brook in May 2000, Johnson stated that he prefers the term "intersubjectivity," which connotes a sense of meaning shared among individuals, to "universalism" as a more precise description of his aesthetic approach. In *Being and Race,* however, he notes that he "stump[s] endlessly for the importance of 'universality' in black fiction" (114). My sense is that the terms are effectively interchangeable, at least in reference to this discussion of the African American literary tradition.

Chapter 2: The Aesthetic Articulated

1. For a detailed articulation of Husserl's philosophical program, see *Ideas Pertaining to a Pure Phenomenology and to a Phenomenological Philosophy.*

2. SUNY–Stony Brook awarded Johnson his Ph.D. in philosophy in May 1999, when he returned to deliver the commencement address. Citing the publication of *Being and Race* in 1988 as evidence of his significant accomplishment as a philosopher, members of the philosophy department recommended that the degree be dated 1988, the year *Being and Race* appeared.

3. This will prove important in Johnson's discussion of the black literary tradition, since he finally expresses the wish that black writers will see themselves as American authors who happen to be black rather than as authors who define themselves primarily in terms of their race. Were he to have looked at the accurate first edition, perhaps his conclusions about the beginnings of the African American novel would be somewhat modified.

4. I am grateful to Professor Marc Conner and Professor Vernon Miles for these specific examples of Johnson's use of anachronism. Conner's "The Wanderer and the Householder" is especially useful.

5. The etymology of the tribe's name is Johnson's own. S. X. Goudie also notes the similarity between Allmuseri and "All/*erimus,* meaning 'We shall be all'" (119 n.8).

Chapter 4: Lumber for the Platform

1. Jonathan Little makes much of this particular distinction, arguing that Johnson reimagines Bigger's Lebenswelt in Faith's experiences. See *Charles Johnson's Spiritual Imagination,* 58–61.

2. Gary Storhoff posits something similar in his assessment of *The Sorcerer's Apprentice:* "the controlling motif of the volume is a competition of alternative metaphysics, pitting the artist who creates reality against the skeptical materialist who would segment and divide it" (539).

3. Frederick T. Griffiths notes the parallels between these stories and the writer's actions. He says of Moses, for instance, that his creation of Mingo is comparable to a writer who "plants his 'spitting image' on the page" ("'Sorcery'" 536). He further notes that "Mingo" functions in a sense as "a tragicomic prologue not only to the tales in *Apprentice* but arguably to the whole project of Johnson's novels" (537).

4. Johnson's signifying incorporation of *Frankenstein* into his story is so extensive as to bear separate examination. Of particular interest is what Shelley has to say regarding the importance of reading and writing. I am grateful to A. A. Markley IV for his insights regarding Johnson's indebtedness to Shelley.

5. The Mason-Hughes and Mason-Hurston relationships are well documented. See Rampersad, *The Life of Langston Hughes,* 1:156–210, and Hemenway, 104–87.

6. See Ashraf H. A. Rushdy, "The Phenomenology of the Allmuseri: Charles Johnson and the Subject of the Narrative of Slavery" (380–83), for a discussion of the healing power in this relationship. Griffiths and Little also comment on the importance of Allan healing Richard (Griffiths, "'Sorcery'" 529; Little, *Charles Johnson's* 132).

7. Similarly, in *Oxherding Tale* Andrew must break free from just such a mentality to escape his father's fate. These two men are part of a larger pattern in Johnson's work where black children (usually sons, with the notable exception of Faith Cross) must move beyond the boundaries of their father's limited views of racial identity. The healing Johnson's artists accomplish in transforming their fathers might reasonably be extended to Johnson's relationship with his own father. I find the dedication of *The Sorcerer's Apprentice*—"For my father"—compelling in this regard. Furthermore, recall the story of Benny Lee Johnson's initial resistance to Johnson's desire to be an artist; one sees reflected in it the images of these fictional fathers whose worldviews hold their children back from creativity and a unified worldview until the younger generation can break free from the elder's limitations.

8. Storhoff notes Rudolph's "feeling of oneness with other people" and also emphasizes his "transformation of vision" (547).

9. Little suggests, by contrast, that "The Sorcerer's Apprentice" might be part of Johnson's efforts to come to terms with his teacher (see *Charles Johnson's* 127–31).

Chapter 5: "There Is a Foundation for the House I'm Building"

1. A partial list of works in the genre includes Margaret Walker's *Jubilee* (1966), Ernest J. Gaines's *Autobiography of Miss Jane Pittman* (1971), Sherley Anne Williams's *Dessa Rose*

(1987), and Barbara Chase-Riboud's *The President's Daughter* (1994). In each case, the author adopts the conventions of the slave-narrative form and uses them as the structure for his or her fiction. For an excellent discussion of these narratives and their classification into a four-part system of neo–slave narrative types, see Rushdy, "The Phenomenology of the Allmuseri." See also Coleman, "Charles Johnson's Quest for Black Freedom in *Oxherding Tale.*"

2. Given her insatiable appetites and her penchant for destruction, Flo most closely resembles the Hindu goddess Kali. As Rudolph Byrd notes, Flo also resembles Kamala, a character in Herman Hesse's *Siddhartha* who is based on Kama, the Hindu God of Love. The latter reference is compelling, as Johnson has explained his intention of responding to that novel with *Oxherding Tale.* For an extended analysis of the relationship between the texts, see Rudolph P. Byrd, "*Oxherding Tale* and *Siddhartha.*" For further discussion of Flo's "feeding" on Andrew, see Rushdy, "The Phenomenology of the Allmuseri," 389.

3. Henry Louis Gates Jr. notes: "Reed's concerns, as exemplified in his narrative forms, seem to be twofold: (1) the relation his own art bears to his black literary precursors . . . and (2) the process of willing into being a . . . literary language . . . that allows the black writer to . . . simultaneously critique both the metaphysical presuppositions inherent in Western ideas and forms of writing and the metaphorical system in which the blackness of the writer and his experience have been valorized" (218). See "On 'The Blackness of Blackness': Ishmael Reed and a Critique of the Sign," in *The Signifying Monkey,* 217–38. For a discussion of postmodern principles that Reed uses, see Hutcheon, *A Poetics of Postmodernism.*

4. Robert Elliot Fox notes that the pun "Massa Swille" prefigures this in its veiled reference to the "master's will" (68). Uncle Robin, who is clearly identified as a parody of Josiah Henson, "does" his master's will to his own advantage, thereby undermining and signifying on the entire traditional notion of subservience that distinguishes Stowe's character. Furthermore, the image of the slave subverting his master's will also invokes Hegel's master-slave paradigm in that Uncle Robin ultimately has more power than Massa Swille. By being in the position of subservience as steward of Swille's estate, he can control his master in a manner that clearly indicates who has "real" freedom in this setting. This, of course, marks an interesting intersection of Reed's and Johnson's ideas on the nature of freedom and allows us to see the numerous levels on which the two authors connect.

5. References to Melville's novels and stories appear throughout Johnson's corpus. Most recently, he borrows the form of Melville's "Bartleby the Scrivener" in "Executive Decision" (1998), a story about affirmative action. As I have noted in discussing *Being and Race,* the idea of honoring the forms of previous writers is critically important to Johnson. This choice indicates the high esteem in which he holds Melville as a predecessor.

6. For a discussion of *Pierre,* see William B. Dillingham, *Melville's Later Novels.*

Chapter 6: "Dualism Is a Bloody Structure of the Mind"

1. Johnson does not stop with the national designation of "American" literature, although I have in order to make my point about his impact on American letters. *Middle Passage,* like all of Johnson's novels, integrates elements from a much broader range of literary traditions. One sees, for example, references to Conrad's sea stories, Homer's

Odyssey, and Jonathan Swift's *Gulliver's Travels* throughout the novel. In fact, the acknowledgments at the beginning of *Middle Passage* note that at one point Johnson had intended to call this novel *Rutherford's Travels*. In an earlier version, Rutherford and his shipmates make several stops during the journey, disembarking at each port and encountering a new tribe of people. As he revised, Johnson realized that the story broke down every time the ship anchored. Nevertheless, he retains elements of the Swift-influenced version in the published novel. When Rutherford fears the other passengers aboard the *Juno* and keeps to himself, associating only with Squibb and Baleka, he resembles Gulliver after he returns home, fearing the touch of the Yahoos and consorting most comfortably with his horses, who remind him of the Houyhnhnms.

2. I use the terms "bad nigger" and "good nigger" as they function in the African American folk tradition to indicate blacks whose actions would be deemed "bad" or "good" by the whites; a "bad nigger" is rebellious, a "good nigger" submissive. See Levine, *Black Culture and Black Consciousness*, 407–20.

3. One finds the rhetoric of abolishing the master's house and substituting black models for white throughout *The Black Aesthetic* (1971). See especially Karenga, "Black Cultural Nationalism"; Gayle, "Cultural Strangulation: Black Literature and the White Aesthetic"; and Fuller, "The New Black Literature: Protest of Affirmation."

4. Celestin Walby notes specific antecedents for this passage in Egyptian and Dogon mythology (663–64). These references to other traditions further confirm the international bent of Johnson's aesthetic vision.

Chapter 7: "Just Possibly I Was Composing a Gospel"

1. Two early photos of Johnson prove the point. In a promotional shot for his drawing show, *Charley's Pad*, he sits smiling at his drawing table in cardigan and tie. By contrast, the author photo for *Half-Past Nation Time* shows him smiling at his drawing table wearing a dashiki and a large Afro. Although the latter pose might well be ironic, given that volume's ambivalence about the politics of black cultural nationalism, I am inclined to read it as another indicator of tensions in Johnson's early positions. Whichever is the case, in *Dreamer* one sees him resolve the conflict firmly in favor of traditionalism.

2. Johnson's use of the father/son model as a means of exploring black male identity places him in the middle of an ongoing conflicted discussion. In the past two decades, scholars have offered a multiplicity of answers to the question of what it means to be a black man and a black father in America. Robert Staples examines the living conditions for slaves that broke down the patriarchal nature of many of the West African cultures from which the slaves came; John L. McAdoo demonstrates that black and white fathers respond to their children similarly; and Clyde W. Franklin II expounds on the various constructions of black masculinity that black studies programs need to address as they explore the identity-formation process. The richness and variety of these studies affirms Johnson's sense of black manhood and fatherhood as multifaceted.

3. For a comprehensive discussion of King's Chicago experience, see James R. Ralph Jr., *Northern Protest*.

4. For a discussion of Du Bois's essentialist ideas, see Sundquist, *To Wake the Nations*, 485–86.

WORKS CITED

Abrahams, Roger D. *Deep Down in the Jungle: Negro Narrative Folklore from the Streets of Philadelphia.* New York: Aldine, 1970.

Adell, Sandra. *Double Consciousness/Double Bind: Theoretical Issues in Twentieth-Century Black Literature.* Urbana: University of Illinois Press, 1994.

Adler, Joyce Sparer. "*Benito Cereno:* Slavery and Violence in the Americas." In *Critical Essays on Herman Melville's "Benito Cereno."* Ed. Robert E. Burkholder. Boston: G. K. Hall, 1992. 76–93.

Andrews, William L. Introduction to *The Oxford Frederick Douglass Reader,* ed. William L. Andrews. New York: Oxford University Press, 1996. 3–19.

———. *To Tell a Free Story: The First Century of Afro-American Autobiography, 1760–1865.* Urbana: University of Illinois Press, 1986.

Baker, Houston A., Jr. "The Black Man of Culture: W. E. B. Du Bois and *The Souls of Black Folk.*" In *Long Black Song: Essays in Black American Literature and Culture.* Charlottesville: University Press of Virginia, 1972. 96–108.

Baldwin, James. *Go Tell It on the Mountain.* 1952. New York: Dell, 1985.

Beaver, Harold. Introduction to *The Narrative of Arthur Gordon Pym of Nantucket,* by Edgar Allan Poe. New York: Penguin, 1975. 7–30.

Bell, Bernard. *The Afro-American Novel and Its Tradition.* Amherst: University of Massachusetts Press, 1987.

———. "W. E. B. Du Bois's Struggle to Reconcile Folk and High Art." In *Critical Essays on W. E. B. Du Bois.* Ed. William L. Andrews. Boston: G. K. Hall, 1985. 106–22.

Bellis, Peter J. *No Mysteries Out of Ourselves: Identity and Textual Form in the Novels of Herman Melville.* Philadelphia: University of Pennsylvania Press, 1990.

Bellow, Saul. *Henderson the Rain King.* New York: Viking, 1959.

Bernstein, Richard. "Imagining a Cain to Shadow Dr. King." Review of *Dreamer,* by Charles Johnson. *New York Times,* 8 Apr. 1998, p. C8+.

Boccia, Michael. "An Interview with Charles Johnson." *African American Review* 30 (1996): 611–18.

Bolster, W. Jeffrey. *Black Jacks: African American Seamen in the Age of Sail.* Cambridge, Mass.: Harvard University Press, 1997.

Brodhead, Richard. *Hawthorne, Melville, and the Novel.* Chicago: University of Chicago Press, 1976.

Brown, William Wells. *Clotel; or, The President's Daughter: A Narrative of Slave Life in the United States.* 1853. Salem, Mass.: Ayer, 1988.

Buell, Lawrence. "Reading Emerson for the Structures: The Coherence of the Essays." In *Critical Essays on Ralph Waldo Emerson.* Ed. Robert E. Burkholder and Joel Myerson. Boston: G. K. Hall, 1983. 399–413.

Byrd, Rudolph P. "*Oxherding Tale* and *Siddhartha:* Philosophy, Fiction, and the Emergence of a Hidden Tradition." *African American Review* 30 (1996): 549–58.

Chase-Riboud, Barbara. *The President's Daughter.* New York: Crown Publishing, 1994.

Chesnutt, Charles W. "The Goophered Grapevine." 1887. In *Collected Stories of Charles W. Chesnutt.* Ed. William L. Andrews. New York: Penguin, 1992. 1–13.

———. *The House behind the Cedars.* 1900. New York: Penguin, 1993.

———. *The Marrow of Tradition.* 1901. Ann Arbor: University of Michigan Press, 1969.

———. "Po' Sandy." 1899. In *Collected Stories of Charles W. Chesnutt.* Ed. William L. Andrews. New York: Penguin, 1992. 14–24.

Chopin, Kate. *The Awakening.* 1899. Ed. Margaret Culley. New York: W. W. Norton, 1976.

Cleaver, Eldridge. "The Death of Martin Luther King: Requiem for Nonviolence." In *Post-Prison Writings and Speeches.* Ed. Robert Scheer. New York: Random House, 1969. 73–79.

———. *Soul on Ice.* New York: McGraw-Hill, 1968.

Coleman, James W. "Charles Johnson's Quest for Black Freedom in *Oxherding Tale.*" *African American Review* 29 (1995): 631–44.

Conner, Marc. "The Wanderer and the Householder: The Two Poles of Charles Johnson's Vision." Paper presented at the Twentieth-Century Literature Conference, Louisville, Kentucky, February 1999.

Crouch, Stanley. "Aunt Jemima Don't Like Uncle Ben." 1979. In *Notes of a Hanging Judge: Essays and Reviews, 1979–1989.* New York: Oxford University Press, 1990. 29–34.

———. "Charles Johnson: Free at Last!" 1983. In *Notes of a Hanging Judge: Essays and Reviews, 1979–1989.* New York: Oxford University Press, 1990. 136–43.

Detweiler, Robert. *Story, Sign, and Self: Phenomenology and Structuralism as Literary-Critical Methods.* Philadelphia: Fortress, 1978.

Dillingham, William B. *Melville's Later Novels.* Athens: University of Georgia Press, 1986.

Doherty, Joseph F. "Emerson and the Loneliness of the Gods." In *Critical Essays on Ralph Waldo Emerson.* Ed. Robert E. Burkholder and Joel Myerson. Boston: G. K. Hall, 1983. 424–33.

Dorsey, James. *Up South: Blacks in Chicago's Suburbs, 1719–1983.* Bristol: Wyndham Hall, 1986.

Douglass, Frederick. *Narrative of the Life of Frederick Douglass, an American Slave, Written by Himself.* 1845. In *The Oxford Frederick Douglass Reader.* Ed. William L. Andrews. New York: Oxford University Press, 1996. 21–97.

Dreiser, Theodore. *Sister Carrie.* 1900. Ed. Donald Pizer. New York: W. W. Norton, 1991.

Du Bois, W. E. B. *The Quest of the Silver Fleece.* 1911. New York: Negro Universities Press, 1969.

———. *The Souls of Black Folk.* 1903. New York: Signet, 1982.

Ellis, Trey. "The New Black Aesthetic." *Callaloo: A Journal of African-American and African Arts and Letters* 12 (1989): 233–51.

Ellison, Ralph. "Change the Joke and Slip the Yoke." In *Shadow and Act.* New York: Random House, 1995. 45–59.

———. *Invisible Man.* 1952. New York: Random House, 1980.

———. "What America Would Be Like without Blacks." 1970. In *Going to the Territory.* New York: Random House, 1986. 104–12.

Emerson, Ralph Waldo. "Circles." In *The Portable Emerson.* Ed. Carl Bode and Malcolm Cowley. New York: Penguin, 1981. 228–40.

———. "Experience." 1844. In *Selections from Ralph Waldo Emerson: An Organic Anthology.* Ed. Stephen E. Whicher. Boston: Houghton Mifflin, 1957. 254–74.

———. "Fate." 1860. In *Selections from Ralph Waldo Emerson: An Organic Anthology.* Ed. Stephen E. Whicher. Boston: Houghton Mifflin, 1957. 330–52.

———. *Nature.* 1836. In *Selections from Ralph Waldo Emerson: An Organic Anthology.* Ed. Stephen E. Whicher. Boston: Houghton Mifflin, 1957. 21–56.

———. "Self-Reliance." 1839. In *Selections from Ralph Waldo Emerson: An Organic Anthology.* Ed. Stephen E. Whicher. Boston: Houghton Mifflin, 1957. 147–68.

———. "The Over-Soul." In *The Portable Emerson.* Ed. Carl Bode and Malcolm Cowley. New York: Penguin, 1981. 209–27.

Equiano, Olaudah. *Equiano's Travels.* 1789. Ed. Paul Edwards. Oxford: Heinemann, 1967.

Foster, Elizabeth S. "Emerson in *The Confidence Man.*" In *The Confidence-Man: His Masquerade.* Ed. Hershel Parker. New York: W. W. Norton, 1971. 333–39.

Fox, Robert Elliot. *Conscientious Sorcerers: The Black Postmodernist Fiction of LeRoi Jones/Amiri Baraka, Ishmael Reed, and Samuel R. Delany.* Contributions in Afro-American and African Studies No. 106. New York: Greenwood Press, 1987.

Franklin, Clyde W., II. "'Ain't I a Man?': The Efficacy of Black Masculinities for Men's Studies in the 1990s." In *The American Black Male: His Present Status and His Future.* Ed. Richard G. Majors and Jacob U. Gordon. Chicago: Nelson-Hall, 1994. 271–84.

Frye, Northrop. *The Educated Imagination.* Bloomington: Indiana University Press, 1964.

Fuller, Hoyt. "The New Black Literature: Protest of Affirmation." In *The Black Aesthetic.* Ed. Addison Gayle. New York: Doubleday, 1971. 327–48.

Gaines, Ernest J. *The Autobiography of Miss Jane Pittman.* New York: Dial, 1971.

Gardner, John. *On Moral Fiction.* New York: Basic Books, 1978.

Gates, Henry Louis, Jr. *The Signifying Monkey: A Theory of African-American Literary Criticism.* New York: Oxford University Press, 1988.

Gayle, Addison, "Cultural Strangulation: Black Literature and the White Aesthetic." In *The Black Aesthetic.* Ed. Addison Gayle. New York: Doubleday, 1971. 38–45.

———. "The Function of Black Literature at the Present Time." In *The Black Aesthetic.* Ed. Addison Gayle. New York: Doubleday, 1971. 407–19.

———. Introduction to *The Black Aesthetic.* Ed. Addison Gayle. New York: Doubleday, 1971. xv–xxiv.

Gelven, Michael. *A Commentary on Heidegger's "Being and Time."* DeKalb: Northern Illinois University Press, 1989.

Gleason, William. "'Go There': The Critical Pragmatism of Charles Johnson." Paper presented at the Twentieth-Century Literature Conference, Louisville, Kent., 25 Feb. 1999.

———. "The Liberation of Perception: Charles Johnson's *Oxherding Tale.*" *Black American Literature Forum* 25 (1991): 704–28.

Goudie, S. X. "'Leavin' a Mark on the Wor(l)d': Marksmen and Marked Men in *Middle Passage.*" *African American Review* 29 (1995): 109–22.

Griffiths, Frederick T. Letter to the author. 22 Jan. 1995.

———. "'Sorcery Is Dialectical': Plato and Jean Toomer in Charles Johnson's *The Sorcerer's Apprentice*." *African American Review* 30 (1996): 527–38.

Grossman, James R. *Land of Hope: Chicago, Black Southerners, and the Great Migration.* Chicago: University of Chicago Press, 1989.

Harper, Frances E. W. *Iola Leroy; or, Shadows Uplifted.* 1892. In *Three Classic African-American Novels.* Ed. Henry Louis Gates Jr. New York: Random House, 1990. 225–464.

———. "The Two Offers." 1859. In *The Norton Anthology of African American Literature.* Ed. Henry Louis Gates Jr. and Nellie Y. McKay. New York: W. W. Norton, 1997. 423–30.

Harper, Robert A. *The University That Shouldn't Have Happened, but Did.* Carbondale, Ill.: Devil's Kitchen, 1998.

Harris, William J. "Black Aesthetic." In *The Oxford Companion to African American Literature.* Ed. William L. Andrews, Frances Smith Foster, and Trudier Harris. New York: Oxford University Press, 1997. 68–70.

Hawthorne, Nathaniel. "The Artist of the Beautiful." 1844. In *Tales and Sketches.* Ed. Roy Harvey Pearce. New York: Library of America, 1982. 907–31.

Hayward, Jennifer. "Something to Serve: Constructs of the Feminine in Charles Johnson's *Oxherding Tale*." *Black American Literature Forum* 25 (1991): 689–703.

Heidegger, Martin. *Being and Time.* Trans. John Macquarrie and Edward Robinson. New York: Harper and Row, 1962.

Hegel, Georg Wilhelm Friedrich. *The Philosophy of Hegel.* Ed. Carl J. Friedrich. New York: Modern Library, 1954.

Hemenway, Robert E. *Zora Neale Hurston: A Literary Biography.* Urbana: University of Illinois Press, 1977.

Holy Bible. Revised Standard Version. New York: Thomas Nelson, 1972.

hooks, bell. "An Aesthetic of Blackness: Strange and Oppositional." In *Yearning: Race, Gender, and Cultural Politics.* Boston: South End, 1990. 103–14.

Hopkins, Pauline E. *Contending Forces: A Romance Illustrative of Negro Life North and South.* 1900. New York: Oxford University Press, 1988.

Hughes, Langston. "The Negro Artist and the Racial Mountain." 1926. In *The Portable Harlem Renaissance Reader.* Ed. David Levering Lewis. New York: Penguin, 1994. 91–95.

Hurston, Zora Neale. "High John de Conqueror." In *The Book of Negro Folklore.* Ed. Langston Hughes and Arna Bontemps. New York: Dodd, Mead, 1958. 93–101.

———. *Their Eyes Were Watching God.* New York: J. B. Lippincott, 1937.

Husserl, Edmund. *Ideas Pertaining to a Pure Phenomenology and to a Phenomenological Philosophy.* Book 1: *General Introduction to a Pure Phenomenology.* Trans. F. Kersten. London: Martinus Nijhoff, 1982.

Hutcheon, Linda. *A Poetics of Postmodernism: History, Theory, Fiction.* New York: Routledge, 1988.

Johnson, Charles R. "Accepting the Invitation." *Tricycle: The Buddhist Review* 10.1 (Fall 2000): 63–64.

———. "Alethia." 1979. In *The Sorcerer's Apprentice: Tales and Conjurations.* New York: Penguin Books, 1986. 97–112.

———. *Being and Race: Black Writing since 1970.* Bloomington: Indiana University Press, 1988.

———. *Black Humor.* Chicago: Johnson, 1970.

———. "Charles Johnson." In *Contemporary Authors Autobiography Series.* Vol. 18. Ed. Joyce Nakamura. Detroit: Gale, 1994. 223–43.

———. "China." 1983. In *The Sorcerer's Apprentice: Tales and Conujurations.* New York: Penguin Books, 1986. 61–95.

———. *Dreamer.* New York: Scribner, 1998.

———. "The Education of Mingo." 1977. In *The Sorcerer's Apprentice: Tales and Conjurations.* New York: Penguin Books, 1986. 1–23.

———. E-mail to the author. 3 Nov. 1996.

———. E-mail to the author. 7 Nov. 1996.

———. "An Ever-Lifting Song of Black America." *New York Times,* 14 Feb. 1999, sec. 2, pp. 1+.

———. "Exchange Value." 1981. In *The Sorcerer's Apprentice: Tales and Conjurations.* New York: Penguin Books, 1986. 25–40.

———. "Executive Decision." In *Outside the Law: Narratives on Justice in America.* Ed. Susan Richards Shreve and Porter Shreve. Boston: Beacon Press, 1998. 93–105.

———. *Faith and the Good Thing.* New York: Viking, 1974.

———. "The Green Belt: A Play for Television." *African American Review* 30 (1996): 559–78.

———. *Half-Past Nation Time.* Chicago: Aware, 1972.

———. Interview with the author. 23 Mar. 1991.

———. Introduction to *Oxherding Tale.* New York: Penguin, 1995. ix–xix.

———. "John Gardner as Mentor." *African American Review* 30 (1996): 619–24.

———. "The King We Left Behind." *CommonQuest,* Fall 1996, pp. 7–10.

———. "Kwoon." In *Playboy Stories: The Best of Forty Years of Short Fiction.* Ed. Alice K. Turner. New York: Dutton, 1994. 575–86.

———. "A Lion at Pendleton." In *Soulcatcher and Other Stories.* New York: Harcourt, 2001. 83–92.

———. "The Mayor's Tale." In *Soulcatcher and Other Stories.* New York: Harcourt, 2001. 93–101.

———. "Menagerie." 1984. In *The Sorcerer's Apprentice: Tales and Conjurations.* New York: Penguin Books, 1986. 41–60.

———. *Middle Passage.* New York: Atheneum, 1990.

———. "Murderous Thoughts." In *Soulcatcher and Other Stories.* New York: Harcourt, 2001. 103–10.

———. "On the Nature of Tales." Introduction to *QPB Treasury of North American Folktales,* ed. Catherine Peck. New York: QPB, 1998. xiii–xvii.

———. *Oxherding Tale.* New York: Grove, 1982.

———. "The People Speak." In *Soulcatcher and Other Stories.* New York: Harcourt, 2001. 67–73.

———. "A Phenomenology of *On Moral Fiction.*" In *Thor's Hammer: Essays on John Gardner.* Ed. Jeff Henderson. Conway: University of Central Arkansas Press, 1985. 147–56.

———. "A Phenomenology of the Black Body." 1993. In *I Call Myself an Artist: Writings by and about Charles Johnson.* Ed. Rudolph P. Byrd. Bloomington: Indiana University Press, 1999. 109–22.

———. "The Philosopher and the American Novel." In *In Search of a Voice,* by Charles Johnson and Ron Chernow. Washington, D.C.: Library of Congress, 1991. 1–18.

———. "Philosophy and Black Fiction." *Obsidian* 6.1 (1980): 55–61.

———. "Poetry and Politics." In *Soulcatcher and Other Stories.* New York: Harcourt, 2001. 25–32.

———. "Popper's Disease." 1982. In *The Sorcerer's Apprentice: Tales and Conjurations.* New York: Penguin Books, 1986. 125–46.

———. "*The Primevil Mitosis:* A Phenomenology of the Black Body." *Ju-ju* 15 (1976): 48–59.

———. "A Sangha by Another Name." *Tricycle: The Buddhist Review* 9.2 (Winter 1999): 43–47, 110–13.

———. "Searching for the Hidden Martin Luther King, Jr." *Seattle Times,* 14 Jan. 1996, B5.

———. "The Second Front: A Reflection on Milk Bottles, Male Elders, the Enemy Within, Bar Mitzvahs, and Martin Luther King, Jr." In *Black Men Speaking.* Ed. Charles Johnson and John McCluskey Jr. Bloomington: Indiana University Press, 1997. 177–88.

———. "The Sorcerer's Apprentice." 1983. In *The Sorcerer's Apprentice: Tales and Conjurations.* New York: Penguin Books, 1986. 147–69.

———. *The Sorcerer's Apprentice: Tales and Conjurations.* New York: Penguin Books, 1986.

———. "The Soulcatcher." In *Soulcatcher and Other Stories.* New York: Harcourt, 2001. 75–82.

———. "The Transmission." In *Soulcatcher and Other Stories.* New York: Harcourt, 2001. 1–11.

———. "Where Philosophy and Fiction Meet." *American Visions* 3 (1988): 36, 47–48.

———. "Whole Sight: Notes on New Black Fiction." *Callaloo: A Journal of African-American and African Arts and Letters* 7 (1984): 1–6.

Johnson, Charles, Bob Adelman, Robert Phelan, and Richard Woodley. *King: The Photobiography of Martin Luther King, Jr.* New York: Viking Press, 2000.

Johnson, Charles, and John McCluskey Jr., eds. *Black Men Speaking.* Bloomington: Indiana University Press, 1997.

Johnson, Charles, Patricia Smith, et al. *Africans in America: America's Journey through Slavery.* New York: Harcourt Brace, 1998.

Johnson, James Weldon. *The Autobiography of an Ex-Coloured Man.* 1912. New York: Random House, 1989.

Karcher, Carolyn L. *Shadow over the Promised Land: Slavery, Race, and Violence in Melville's America.* Baton Rouge: Louisiana State University Press, 1980.

Karenga, Ron. "Black Cultural Nationalism." In *The Black Aesthetic.* Ed. Addison Gayle. New York: Doubleday, 1971. 31–37.

Kiernan, Robert F. *Saul Bellow.* New York: Continuum, 1989.

Killens, John Oliver. Review of *Invisible Man,* by Ralph Ellison. *Freedom,* June 1952, p. 7.

Koplowitz, H. B. *Carbondale after Dark and Other Stories.* Carbondale, Ill.: Dome, 1982.

Kostelanetz, Richard. "Fictions for a Negro Politics: The Neglected Novels of W. E. B. Du Bois." In *Critical Essays on W. E. B. Du Bois.* Ed. William L. Andrews. Boston: G. K. Hall, 1985. 173–94.

Kutzinski, Vera. "Johnson Revises Johnson: *Oxherding Tale* and *The Autobiography of an Ex-Coloured Man.*" In *I Call Myself an Artist: Writings by and about Charles Johnson.* Ed. Rudolph P. Byrd. Bloomington: Indiana University Press, 1999. 279–88.

"Kwanzaa." In *Crossing the Danger Water: Three Hundred Years of African-American Writing.* Ed. Deirdre Mullane. New York: Doubleday, 1993. 657–58.

Larsen, Nella. *Quicksand.* New York: Alfred A. Knopf, 1928.

Lee, Maurice. "Du Bois the Novelist: White Influence, Black Spirit and *The Quest of the Silver Fleece.*" *African American Review* 33.3 (Fall 1999): 389–400.

Levine, Lawrence W. *Black Culture and Black Consciousness: Afro-American Folk Thought from Slavery to Freedom.* New York: Oxford University Press, 1977.

Lewis, David Levering. *King: A Critical Biography.* New York: Praeger, 1970.

Leyda, Jay. *The Melville Log.* New York: Harcourt, Brace, 1951.

Little, Jonathan. *Charles Johnson's Spiritual Imagination.* Columbia: University of Missouri Press, 1997.

———. "From the Comic Book to the Comic: Charles Johnson's Variations on Creative Expression." *African American Review* 30.4 (Winter 1996): 579–601.

Major, Clarence. *All-Night Visitors.* 1969. Boston: Northeastern University Press, 1998.

Marx, Karl. *Economic and Philosophic Manuscripts of 1844.* Moscow, Russia: Foreign Languages, 1961.

McAdoo, John L. "Black Father and Child Interactions." In *Black Men.* Ed. Lawrence E. Gary. Beverly Hills, Calif.: Sage, 1981. 115–30.

McSweeney, Kerry. *Moby-Dick: Ishmael's Mighty Book.* New York: Twayne, 1986.

Mellinkoff, Ruth. *The Mark of Cain.* Berkeley: University of California Press, 1981.

Melville, Herman. "Benito Cereno." 1856. In *The Piazza Tales and Other Prose Pieces.* Ed. Harrison Hayford, Alma A. MacDougall, and G. Thomas Tanselle. Chicago: Northwestern University Press and the Newberry Library, 1987. 47–117.

———. *The Confidence-Man: His Masquerade.* 1857. Ed. Hershel Parker. New York: W. W. Norton, 1971.

———. *Correspondence: The Writings of Herman Melville.* Vol. 14. Ed. Lynn Horth. Chicago: Northwestern University Press and the Newberry Library, 1993.

———. "The Encantadas, or Enchanted Isles." 1856. In *The Piazza Tales and Other Prose Pieces.* Ed. Harrison Hayford, Alma A. MacDougall, and G. Thomas Tanselle. Chicago: Northwestern University Press and the Newberry Library, 1987. 125–73.

———. "Hawthorne and His Mosses." 1850. In *Moby-Dick.* Ed. Harrison Hayford and Hershel Parker. New York: W. W. Norton, 1967. 535–51.

———. *Moby-Dick; or, The Whale.* 1851. Ed. Harrison Hayford, Hershel Parker, and G. Thomas Tanselle. Chicago: Northwestern University Press and the Newberry Library, 1988.

———. *Pierre; or, The Ambiguities.* 1852. Ed. Harrison Hayford, Hershel Parker, and G. Thomas Tanselle. Chicago: Northwestern University Press and the Newberry Library, 1971.

Merleau-Ponty, Maurice. "Faith and Good Faith." In *Sense and Non-sense.* Trans. Hubert L. Dreyfus and Patricia Allen Dreyfus. Evanston, Ill.: Northwestern University Press, 1964. 172–81.

———. "Metaphysics and the Novel." In *Sense and Non-sense.* Trans. Hubert L. Dreyfus and Patricia Allen Dreyfus. Evanston, Ill.: Northwestern University Press, 1964. 9–24.

———. *The Primacy of Perception.* Ed. James M. Edie. Evanston, Ill.: Northwestern University Press, 1964.

———. *Sense and Non-sense.* Trans. Hubert L. Dreyfus and Patricia Allen Dreyfus. Evanston, Ill.: Northwestern University Press, 1964.

Mitchell, Betty. *Delyte Morris of SIU.* Carbondale: Southern Illinois University Press, 1988.

Moyers, Bill. *Genesis: A Living Conversation.* New York: Doubleday, 1996.

Muther, Elizabeth. "Isadora at Sea: Misogyny as Comic Capital in Charles Johnson's *Middle Passage.*" *African American Review* 30 (1996): 649–58.

Nash, William R. "A Conversation with Charles Johnson." *New England Review* 19.2 (1998): 49–61.

Naylor, Gloria. *The Women of Brewster Place.* New York: Penguin, 1982.

Neal, Larry. "The Black Arts Movement." 1965. In *Cavalcade: Negro American Writing from 1760 to the Present.* Ed. Arthur P. Davis and Saunders Redding. Boston: Houghton Mifflin, 1971. 797–810.

Newman, Judie. *Saul Bellow and History.* New York: St. Martin's Press, 1984.

Pedersen, Carl. "Middle Passages: Representation of the Slave Trade in Caribbean and African American Literature." *Massachusetts Review* 34 (1992): 225–39.

Petry, Ann. *The Street.* Boston: Houghton Mifflin, 1946.

Pifer, Ellen. *Saul Bellow against the Grain.* Philadelphia: University of Pennsylvania Press, 1990.

Poe, Edgar Allan. *The Narrative of Arthur Gordon Pym of Nantucket.* 1837. Ed. Harold Beaver. New York: Penguin, 1975.

———. "William Wilson." 1839. In *Great Short Works of Edgar Allan Poe.* Ed. G. R. Thompson. New York: Harper, 1970. 245–60.

Porter, M. Gilbert. *Whence the Power? The Artistry and Humanity of Saul Bellow.* Columbia: University of Missouri Press, 1974.

Posnock, Ross. *Color and Culture: Black Writers and the Making of the Modern Intellectual.* Cambridge, Mass.: Harvard University Press, 1998.

Quinn, Michael. Telephone interview with the author. 15 Oct. 1998.

Ralph, James R., Jr. *Northern Protest: Martin Luther King Jr., Chicago, and the Civil Rights Movement.* Cambridge, Mass.: Harvard University Press, 1993.

Rampersad, Arnold. *The Art and Imagination of W. E. B. Du Bois.* Cambridge, Mass.: Harvard University Press, 1976.

———. *The Life of Langston Hughes.* 2 vols. New York: Oxford University Press, 1988.

Reed, Ishmael. *Flight to Canada.* New York: Random House, 1976.

Richards, I. A. *Principles of Literary Criticism.* New York: Harcourt Brace, 1926.

Richardson, Robert D., Jr. *Emerson: The Mind on Fire.* Berkeley: University of California Press, 1995.

Royster, Philip M. E-mail to the author. 10 Feb. 1999.

Rushdy, Ashraf H. A. "The Phenomenology of the Allmuseri: Charles Johnson and the Subject of the Narrative of Slavery." *African American Review* 26 (1992): 373–94.

Salaam, Kalamu ya. "Black Arts Movement." In *The Oxford Companion to African American Literature.* Ed. William L. Andrews, Frances Smith Foster, and Trudier Harris. New York: Oxford University Press, 1997. 70–74.

Scott, Daniel M. "Interrogating Identity: Appropriation and Transformation in *Middle Passage.*" *African American Review* 29 (1995): 645–55.

Sekora, John. "Comprehending Slavery: Language and Personal History in the *Narrative.*" In *Modern Critical Interpretations of "The Narrative of the Life of Frederick Douglass."* Ed. Harold Bloom. New York: Chelsea House, 1988. 153–63.

Sheehy, John. "The Mirror and the Veil: The Passing Novel and the Quest for American Racial Identity." *African American Review* 33.3 (Fall 1999): 401–15.

Staples, Robert. "The Myth of the Black Matriarchy." In *The Black Male in America.* Ed. Doris Y. Wilkinson and Ronald L. Taylor. Chicago: Nelson-Hall, 1977. 174–87.

———. "The Myth of the Impotent Black Male." In *The Black Male in America.* Ed. Doris Y. Wilkinson and Ronald L. Taylor. Chicago: Nelson-Hall, 1977. 133–44.

Storhoff, Gary. "The Artist as Universal Mind: Berkeley's Influence on Charles Johnson." *African American Review* 30 (1996): 539–48.

Sundquist, Eric J. *To Wake the Nations: Race in the Making of American Literature.* Cambridge, Mass.: Belknap Press of Harvard University Press, 1993.

Tate, Claudia. *Psychoanalysis and Black Novels: Desire and the Protocols of Race.* New York: Oxford University Press, 1998.

Toomer, Jean. *Cane.* New York: Boni and Liveright, 1923.

Twain, Mark. *Adventures of Huckleberry Finn.* 1885. Ed. Walter Blair and Victor Fischer. Berkeley: University of California Press, 1985.

Walby, Celestin. "The African Sacrificial Kingship Ritual and Johnson's *Middle Passage.*" *African American Review* 29 (1995): 657–69.

Walker, Alice. *The Color Purple.* San Diego: Harcourt Brace Jovanovich, 1982.

Walker, Margaret. *Jubilee.* Boston: Houghton Mifflin, 1966.

Watts, Alan W. *The Way of Zen.* New York: Random House, 1957.

Williams, John A. *The King God Didn't Save: Reflections on the Life and Death of Martin Luther King Jr.* New York: Coward-McCann, 1970.

Williams, Sherley Anne. *Dessa Rose.* New York: Berkeley, 1987.

Wilson, Harriet E. Adams. *Our Nig; or, Sketches from the Life of a Free Black.* 1859. Ed. Henry Louis Gates Jr. New York: Random House, 1983.

Wright, Richard. *Native Son.* New York: Harper and Brothers, 1940.

INDEX

WILLIAM R. NASH is an associate professor of American literature and civilization at Middlebury College. His articles have appeared in the *New England Review,* the *African American Review,* the *Southern Literary Journal,* and *Callaloo.* He has also contributed chapters to several edited collections.

The University of Illinois Press
is a founding member of the
Association of American University Presses.

Composed in 9/13 ITC Stone Serif
with ITC Stone Sans display
by Celia Shapland
for the University of Illinois Press
Designed by Paula Newcomb
Manufactured by Thomson-Shore, Inc.

University of Illinois Press
1325 South Oak Street
Champaign, IL 61820-6903
www.press.uillinois.edu